The COMPLETE IDIOT'S GUIDE TO

Hiking, Camping, and the Great Outdoors

by Michael Mouland

alpha books

A Division of Macmillan General Reference
A Simon & Schuster Macmillan Company
1633 Broadway, New York, NY 10019

Dedicated to Eric Morin, who would have liked the trees.

©1996 Michael Mouland

International Standard Book Number: 0-02-861100-4
Library of Congress Catalog Card Number: 95-83361

98 97 96   10 9 8 7 6 5 4 3 2 1

Interpretation of the printing code: the rightmost number of the first series of numbers is the year of the book's printing; the rightmost number of the second series of numbers is the number of the book's printing. For example, a printing code of 96-1 shows that the first printing of the book occurred in 1996.

Screen reproductions in this book were created by means of the program Collage Plus from Inner Media, Inc., Hollis, NH.

Printed in the United States of America

Publisher
Theresa Murtha

Editor
Lisa Bucki

Cover Designer
Michael J. Freeland

Designer
Kim Scott

Illustrator
Judd Winnick

Manufacturing Coordinator
Steve Pool

Production Team Supervisor
Laurie Casey

Indexer
Tim Tate

Production Team
*Heather Butler, Angela Calvert, Tricia Flodder,
Aleata Howard, Joe Millay, Erich J. Richter,
Pamela Volk, Megan Wade, Christy Wagner*

Contents at a Glance

Contents

16 Comfort Gear for Your Home Away from Home 181

Part 4: Getting There 191

17 Trailblazing Made Easy 193

18 Planning an Outdoor Vacation on the Water 207

Foreword

One day last week I sent four messages via electronic mail to associates throughout the United States, opened three "overnight" packages sent to my office, read five fax transmissions, surfed the World Wide Web for new sites, made and received about a dozen telephone calls, went home and watched a "live" news program on television (which had a segment about artificially-produced powder snow being sprayed on ski slopes in the Rockies), viewed half of a movie I had taped on my videocassette recorder, ate a frozen pizza with a salad of hydroponically grown lettuce, and went to bed.

It was time, I thought to myself as I tried to sleep. Time to get away from these machines and services and satellite hookups that supposedly make my life easier, and go up on a mountaintop somewhere and stick my face in the dirt.

Well, maybe not literally. Maybe. But the point is that as a member in relatively good standing of the species *homo sapiens sapiens*, I needed to spend some time somewhere away from civilization, at a place where I could witness the strength and beauty and mystery of nature as it has been for millions of years—and before my fellow *sapiens* did such a damned good job of insulating us from it. (I once met a New York City resident who told me about a weekend he had spent in the "country," as he put it. Visiting a friend who had moved to the suburbs, he couldn't rest at night because it was too…quiet—no blaring horns, wailing sirens, and blood-curdling shrieks to lull him to sleep.)

The need to forego modern—and, perhaps more appropriately, artificial—comfort and convenience and reconnect with nature is quite, well, natural. According to Dr. Richard Sherwood of the anthropology department at Pennsylvania State University, humans have been enjoying the so-called good life for only a comparatively short time. Although there is evidence of Neanderthals first living in shelters (read: *caves*) anywhere from 50,000 to 100,000 years ago, humans did not begin to form rudimentary versions of cities—and begin the practices of agriculture and animal domestication—until just 10,000 to 12,000 years ago. This is not to disparage or dismiss the myriad medical, social, technological, and cultural advances we have made since that time; it's just that we all have an understandable biological reason to feel the urge to roast a freshly caught trout over a campfire somewhere in the wilderness, especially after experiencing some supposed improvement in life such as a "moving sidewalk."

Unfortunately, the zeitgeist of the modern "outdoor experience"—going "back to nature" is another cliched term for the movement—is often misinterpreted in various media. Witness a recent television ad depicting a young man eating a bowl of breakfast cereal atop a misty peak at sunrise before, it is implied, he charges off deeper into the wildlands.

The beauty and solitude of this compelling image belies the difficulty of experiencing such a dramatic moment—not to mention the impracticality of backpacking fresh milk up the side of a mountain.

Which is what brings us to the book in your hands. *The Complete Idiot's Guide to Hiking, Camping, and the Great Outdoors* is somewhat of a misnomer because, simply by bothering to read it, you are admitting your inexperience in this form of recreation and have therefore elevated your level of competency in the outdoors—you're smart enough to want to learn something about it before jumping in. For instance, I've seen more than a few people who evidently thought they knew enough about camping to spend a night in the woods—only to spend two hours fumbling around at a dark campsite trying to erect a tent before finally retreating to the back seat of their car with a sleeping bag in one hand and a dim flashlight in the other. (Imagine this type trying to duplicate the feat of the breakfast-cereal guy.) True, there is no substitute for experience, but there's also no excuse for ignorance.

Michael Mouland, the author of this book, is fortunate enough to have years of experience with a pack on his back, hiking far into the wilds, spending the night on the ground and under the stars. He has learned quite a bit about the proper and improper ways to go about it. Mouland is also gifted enough to share such lessons and experiences with you in a straightforward, easy-to-read writing style. And, as an editor by vocation, I especially appreciate Mouland's innate love of both the sport and the natural world. Such a voice cannot be added to a manuscript with a blue pencil; one can only search for an author who possesses it. Megan Newman, the editor-in-chief for this book, conducted her search well. What this all means is that you will learn much more than you think.

So read and go forth and have fun by doing it right. And respect the wilderness while you are there, because it's really all that's left to define who we really are. You'll find that out once you're there.

Mike Toth

Senior Editor, *Sports Afield*

Introduction

Most of us are exposed to the outdoors when we are young. My first flirtations with outdoors began when my day camp climbed into a big yellow school bus and headed off into the country north of my hometown. On arrival at the camp, we unloaded our stuff, which at that time wasn't much: some toiletries, a pair of pajamas, and some potatoes wrapped in aluminum foil. Camping in those days meant holing up in a wooden bunk house with ten or twelve other kids and going on day-long hikes and canoe trips in the country when the sun rose. At night, our counselor made a campfire; we roasted marsh-mallows and cooked our foil-encased potatoes directly in the fire's embers. A lot of the time, we dined on camp food in the log dining hall, which included a free-flowing supply of "bug juice" that tasted remarkably like Kool-Aid. Life was simple, and "camping" this way was fun.

Today, life is more complicated. Most days revolve around solving problems and meeting tight deadlines. The desire to get away from it all is much stronger, but there is less time to escape from the duties and other obligations of modern life. This means that trips into the wilderness are less frequent and need to be planned more carefully. There is no yellow school bus to take us there, and basic needs like shelter and food are our own responsibil-ity. Most unfortunately, however, there is no camp counselor to lead the way and light a campfire for us at night.

When my friends and I first set out to experience the outdoors, we went to others who regaled us with stories about it. They told us of the simple pleasures of sitting around a campfire in the evening, of hikes in woods filled with the music of birds chirping in the trees, and of pleasant canoe rides along the shores of still lakes, accompanied only by the sound of water lapping against the sides of the boat. They told us that we needed a tent, a sleeping bag, some food—and to plan where we wanted to go.

With the call of the outdoors beckoning, a destination in mind, and some basic supplies, we headed off in a rented car—with a plan, but with little experience or knowledge of what camping was really about. We arrived at our campsite late, in the rain, and used a flashlight with dying batteries to read the tent set-up instructions that came with the lump of fabric and metal poles that we had spread over the ground. We discovered that it was hard to light a fire with wet wood collected from the surrounding forest, and that we had no other means of heating up our baked beans.

We eventually figured out how to pitch the tent and climbed into bed a bit hungry, but content that we had at least conquered a small bit of nature in accomplishing this one feat. By morning, the weather had cleared, and miraculously we awoke dry and unscathed to the sound of trees swaying in a gentle breeze. We managed to light a fire and boil some water for coffee. But the simple mistakes we made—not pitching our new tent for practice before heading off, and not having a camp stove—revealed that we needed to do more research in the future. Luckily, the weekend turned out to be lovely, and we learned some valuable lessons in the process.

In camping, experience is the best teacher. With a little foreknowledge and advice at the beginning, most of your trips will turn out as pleasant as our first trip did. This book is not a manifesto on how to survive in the wilderness in the event of a nuclear holocaust, nor is it a guide to hiking and climbing Mt. Everest. It is intended to impart some basic information on planning a fun-filled trip—and to help you, the reader, evaluate what equipment you'll need for your adventures. As you gain more experience, you'll develop your own methods for planning your outdoor vacations, but in the meantime, *The Complete Idiot's Guide to Hiking, Camping, and the Great Outdoors* will be there to provide insight into many aspects of the outdoors. By reading this book, you'll see what you need, and what type of trip you can plan. With every new endeavor, there is new terminology to be learned. Camping and hiking are pretty simple activities, but require some knowledge of what's out there. This book is designed to provide much of this information.

I wish a book like this had existed when my friends and I started out. If it had, we wouldn't have considered camping without a stove, and we would have *practiced* pitching our tent. We would have done some other things differently, too. We would have brought along better clothes and created checklists for our trip. Basic things like these can mean the difference between a successful adventure and a failed one. There are still some times when the weather turns bad and we forget to take something along, but this has never stopped us from thinking about our next camping trip. And that's what happens when the camping bug bites!

How to Use This Book

Whether your pleasure is a weekend of car camping or a week of backpacking or canoeing, this book is designed to get you where you want to go. You can dip into the introductory chapters at the beginning of the book, or delve into the techniques sections that come later. Or you can read up on the different methods of camping to get an idea *how* you want to spend your time outdoors. And you can, like any other book, read it from cover-to-cover if you're the conventional kind of person that likes to start at point A, finish at point Z, and go to points in between. The book is divided into six parts, each with its own take on camping. Dip in and dip out. Or read from cover-to-cover. The choice is yours.

Extras

In addition to clear and interesting explanations and advice, this book offers other types of information to point you in the right direction, help you sharpen your hiking and camping skills, provide hints and tips for planing a better outdoor vacation, define confusing jargon, or provide sidenotes that may simply be of interest. Look for these easy-to-recognize signposts in boxes:

Here's How

Tested and tried ways of doing things outdoors. Think of these as skill-building lessons that reveal ways of getting things done.

Conventional Wisdom

Hints and tips that promote outdoor fun. These boxes will make you sound like a veteran outdoor explorer.

Safe Camping

Cautions that will help you avoid potential hazards in the outdoors.

Rules

Outlines some of the rules that go along with the outdoor camping and hiking game that are of benefit to you and fellow hikers alike.

Acknowledgments

This book could not have been written without the involvement of several key people who provided creative energy, support, and encouragement along the way. Megan Newman at Macmillan came up with the idea for the book, and pushed me to produce and revise till I had an outline that hung together and made sense. Lisa Bucki was instrumental in transforming this book from binary code into a sensibly organized book. The people at Mountain Equipment Co-op in Toronto were patient with a most inquisitive member when I was doing research for the book, and I heartily thank them for spending time with me. Sean McSweeney was particularly forthcoming in providing information on equipment and the techniques that he uses on his frequent hiking and paddling trips. He imparted information as he does day-in and day-out to the customers who visit the co-op. Thanks! Gerry Wagschal helped write several chapters and provided a sounding board for many of the techniques and ideas described in the book. The accounts of hiking in Gros Morne National Park and on Baffin Island are from his pen. My friend Peter Kuitenbrouwer had the brilliant idea to go camping one summer weekend while we were sitting in his office high up in the Empire State Building, and showed us that we didn't need much more than a tent, sleeping bag, and mat to get started.

Thanks also goes to Ann Bramson at Hearst Books, Charles Smith, and Ken Winchester, who have encouraged me to do some great work over the years. Special thanks goes to Eileen, who helped me test out tents, sleeping bags, and canoes—and who at times allowed herself to be eaten alive by mosquitoes—all in the name of what can loosely be called "research."

Trademarks

All terms mentioned in this book that are known to be or are suspected of being trademarks or service marks have been appropriately capitalized. Alpha Books and Macmillan General Reference cannot attest to the accuracy of this information. Use of a term in this book should not be regarded as affecting the validity of any trademark or service mark.

Part 1
The First Time Around

It's another long, hot, humid weekend in the city. You look out the window and see your neighbors loading all sorts of outdoor gear into their cars. There are sleeping bags, stuff sacks, backpacks, pots and pans, and fishing rods. You suddenly feel left out. What kind of fun are you missing out on?

The idea of pitching a tent next to a lake is romantic. Time and again you've imagined hiking along trails, taking in the sights and sounds of the outdoors replete with the rush of wind in the trees. You'd like to try it, too, but the idea of an outdoor vacation seems formidable. You've never set foot in an outdoor store, and kind of think these places are for hunters, fishermen, and hard-core survivalists. There's so much to know, and you want to know it, especially when everyone at work seems to return from their outdoor vacations relaxed, tanned, and happy.

And now you are ready to take the plunge—after all, you've picked up this book.

But you need to know a few things before voyaging into nature. Much of it has to do with equipment, but some of it has to do with the normal planning that goes along with any vacation. Unfortunately, there are no travel agents for would-be outdoor adventurers. You'll have to do most of the planning, reservation-making, and so on yourself. Take heart in knowing that none of this is too hard! Most seasoned outdoor adventurers started out just like you.

Chapter 1

Preparation and Planning

In This Chapter

➤ Setting out a plan of action—on a limited budget and with limited time

➤ Where to get information on the places you want to visit

➤ How to coexist with animals and bugs

➤ Anticipating problems and solving them

Your decision to embark on your first extended encounter with nature—whether "extended" means a weekend getaway with some friends or a week-long hiking adventure with a companion—is usually surrounded by some uncertainties. Irrational (in retrospect) questions pop into your head: Where will we camp? What will we eat? How do we find our campsite? And what if we don't? What if we forget something? Do we have the right equipment?

Much of our mission here is to lessen the fear, anticipation, and bewilderment that goes with planning *any* vacation. Just because the wilderness (or some reasonable facsimile thereof) beckons *this* time doesn't mean that the right amount of planning can't help you ride out some of the inevitable bumps in the road—or should we say *trail*. Nothing goes completely right. But isn't that why we like to travel anywhere in the first place? To travel means to set our minds on a destination, get to it using our brains, and set our wits to conquer what stands in our way. And usually we have the chance to relax and renew our lives in the process.

Teaming Up and Setting Out

Your decision on where to go hinges primarily on the amount of time you have and your proximity to "campable" wilderness areas. If you're just starting out, ask friends and associates about places where they've gone, and how far, and how long it takes to get there. If you can team up with someone who's done it before, all the better. You can team up and benefit from another's experience—and you can use their equipment. Seldom will you need two portable stoves, and you may be able to share a tent at night if it's big enough. You'll need some stuff, but if you're going on a short weekender to a destination a couple of hours away you can minimize expenditures on items that the other person or people have.

When starting out, you're not going to need the best of everything, and you can scrounge around for the items that can be called into duty: Old pots and pans work just as well as the specialized nested ones that seasoned campers and backpackers use, though they may not be as light and compact. Borrow equipment that you can't put your hands on from other hikers. They'll be more willing to part with some of their stuff if you explain that you're going on a short trip—they're thinking about potential wear and tear on their equipment, and a light weekend jaunt is less foreboding in this respect than a trek in Nepal. Assure your lenders that you'll make good on any damage done.

If you can't find people to lend you equipment you'll need to get your hands on several, basic pieces of equipment, namely a tent, a sleeping bag, a sleeping mat, and, depending on whether you're car camping or hiking to a destination, a backpack. All told, the combination of these items can add up to $800 or more. Luckily, outfitters specializing in equipment rental are numerous and cater to those who only go camping once in a blue moon or are newcomers to the activity. Ask at your local camping store for the names and numbers of these outfitters, or when you're phoning around to check out destinations. For a nominal fee, outfitters can rent all manner of equipment—from backpacks, tents, and sleeping bags to canoes, flashlights, and stoves. For a group, this may be the way to go, since outfitters can put together all the necessary equipment for a weekend or week-long excursion. They can throw together a menu and food for a trip of almost any length. The only drawback to this approach is that it costs money, but it may be money well spent if you're getting to test different kinds of equipment before committing to a purchase. The other advantage of course, is that it cuts down on the planning needed for a trip, which is fun for some, but a drag for others.

Outfitters are also good sources for information on the area where you're camping, and sell maps and other publications.

And that brings up where to go.

The Plan of Action

➤ Pick a departure date and time; decide on the length of the trip.

➤ Someone should be in charge of transportation, whether it's renting a minivan or getting the group to the campsite or trailhead.

➤ Decide who is going to be the "group leader." This person should have some outdoor experience, or be the person who decided on the destination. Often different group members can be in charge of different things. For example, someone who has camped before can give advice on choosing campsites. If part of your trip will be undertaken in a canoe, someone in the group should have paddling skills and be able to show others what to do.

National Parks and Public Wilderness Areas

If you're lucky enough to live near a national park, state park, or provincial park, you can get in your car, fly along a highway, and be there pretty quickly. "Being there" (for most people) involves a fair amount of planning—especially if this is your first time out and you can escape most of civilization by car. You'll need basically the same equipment for a week*end* trip as you would for a week-*long* trip. The only variable here is food—the longer you're out, the more you'll need.

But let's begin with the basics.

The Bureau of Land Management is the United States largest landowner, with approximately 266 million acres in its control. The National Forest Service looks after some 74 million acres, and the National Park Service controls some 84 million acres divided over more than 350 "units." With this amount of public land available, it's likely that the outdoor vacationer will end up selecting a public campground over a private one.

In most cases, you'll have to purchase a permit for using any public land offering, whether it is for hiking, camping, or canoeing within a public wilderness area. It's also best to phone ahead and make a reservation for a campsite, especially if you want to camp during a busy holiday like the Fourth of July. (If you've got just the weekend, it's better to stick close to home.)

Campgrounds do have closing hours; you could be inviting unneeded stress if you get started after work on a Friday in summer (the peak season) with a three-hour-plus drive ahead of you. Not to mention the looming unpleasantry of having to pitch a tent in the dark. Don't despair; closing hours at campgrounds aren't that strict. If you arrive at the gate late, you can usually pitch your tent somewhere just for the night and relocate in the morning. (For that matter, you can almost always get to hiking trails the next morning as well.) But why make camp twice? There's an alternative to a rushed itinerary: Pack up the car the night before and leave early the next morning. You'll have one less night sleeping under the stars, but you'll be a happier camper for the experience.

Most likely you've been thinking about your outdoor vacation for some time. Daydreams aside, you'll need some idea of where you're going. Brochures, articles in outdoor magazines, or materials from your nearest state park, national park, or provincial park should put you in mind of some good first-time destinations. Most parks have visitor centers chock-full of maps and brochures that describe prominent features in the region and the activities offered by the park. Phone the park and order their brochures in advance.

Choosing a destination means choosing the right kind of campsite too. Some campgrounds offer only primitive campsites with cleared ground for you to set up a tent and a box privy. Other campgrounds offer running water and electrical hookups. And some even offer venues for adventure: Canoes and rowboats may be rented, groomed beaches may be used, and hot showers taken at comfort stations sprinkled throughout the campground. Campground brochures will reveal what's available—just be sure to call ahead to see what's offered as far as amenities are concerned. They may be key determinants in your choice of a destination.

The really nice thing about camping is that it doesn't cost that much. Campgrounds charge a nominal fee—ranging from $7 to $15 for using a campsite. Sometimes there will be an additional charge for a parking permit if you'll be leaving your vehicle in a lot while you're hiking in more remote locations, as well as the price for a backcountry permit. Undoubtedly, you'll find any price you pay modest, especially when you consider the beauty of the outdoors to be explored.

The National Park Service has gone high-tech; it even has a World Wide Web site on the Internet. If you have the right kind of computer, you can get to Service's home page at http://www.nps.gov/, where you can find information on most of the 54 national parks in the United States and Virgin Islands. An electronic "visitor center" describes each park, lists its camping and hiking rules, and offers up a virtual slide show of park highlights you may want to visit.

You can also use Alexander Graham Bell's invention to call the National Park Service's main headquarters in Washington, D.C. at (202) 208-4621. For some of the most-visited parks, book a site well in advance through MISTIX at (800) 365-2267. Parks that are heavily visited include Acadia, Grand Canyon, Great Smoky Mountains, Mammoth Cave, Rocky Mountain, Sequoia and Kings Canyon, Shenandoah, Yellowstone, and Yosemite.

The state of Maine and others attracting camping visitors offer World Wide Web sites for those considering outdoor vacations, and Parks Canada has also established a World Wide Web page at http://parkscanada.pch.gc.ca/. The tear-out card at the front of this book also gives you ideas on where to look for online information if you need it. You'll find links to other virtual departure points.

Rules

Dogs are welcome at most campsites and on hiking trails. In general, they must be kept on a leash at all times and their droppings picked up or buried. Always prevent dogs from harassing native wildlife—a run-in with a skunk or porcupine isn't fun for you or the dog.

Camping in the Lap of Luxury

Conventional wisdom holds that vacationing with a tent means an automatic rise in the discomfort quotient.

Not true!

The object of any camping and hiking trip is to explore the wilderness and natural world. Modern materials and equipment have been designed to make life on the trail quite a bit more comfortable than what it's imagined to be. Lightweight tents, cooking equipment, and bedding have evolved a long way since the days of cumbersome, heavy camping gear. Selecting the right backpack to carry all this lighter stuff into the woods helps ensure that your adventures will be memorable, but not as backbreakers.

Because every day will end with the need to sleep, put some thought into what you'll be sleeping *on*. For the weekend getaway, where you won't be venturing too far into the wilderness, consider selecting a one-inch-thick piece of foam rubber as a bed. Most big cities have stores that specialize in foam bedding; they'll cut a piece to size. If your plans include bringing a partner, have the foam cut to double size. Some specialty outdoor stores such as L.L. Bean carry pre-cut pieces of open-cell foam that are covered with fabric along with closed-cell foam mats. Other more pricey options include self-inflaters that feature slabs of open-cell foam sheathed in waterproof nylon. They have a value, and while not exactly the most compact of sleeping-mat choices, an open-cell foam mattress for your tent is one of the most decadent options available to the outdoor vacationer. Slumbering on foam may make you feel like the very image of a fat sheik comfortably nestled in an opulently decorated tent in the middle of the Sahara.

Here's How
In some of the more popular outdoor locations, it may be difficult to get a campsite reservation. If you can't go in the off-season, be sure to book your campsite as far in advance as possible. Some national parks have four-month waiting lists for camping sites. On long weekends, you may need to reserve a site six or seven months ahead of time. Some campsites even have lotteries for much-in-demand campsites. Plan as far ahead as possible!

Roughing It Is Out, Enjoying It Is In

There are many other alternative sleeping options outlined in Chapter 4, but a simple open-cell foam mat is just one way you can trim the roughing-it factor from a shorter trip. Other ideas include bringing along premade gourmet delights. If you have a portable gas stove, you can precook, package, and bring some favorite foods to spice up your short excursion.

When eating alfresco, you might want to take along some good liquid refreshment besides water. In many wilderness areas, of course, glass containers are prohibited; you may be morally barred from bringing anything breakable into camping and hiking areas.

I'LL TELL YA!...

Conventional Wisdom
Many hikers and campers use a stainless-steel Thermos to keep drinks, soup, and other liquids warm. Unlike glass-lined Thermos bottles, these are practically indestructible. On a backpacking trip, thermoses may be heavy and warm drinks may be better made on a lightweight camp stove.

To avoid breakage, consider carrying liquids in reusable plastic water bottles. If you'd rather not have one more container to throw away (and you don't mind adding another item to your checklist), fill several wineskins before the trip.

Weighty accoutrements are sometimes only practical for the weekend outdoorsperson who doesn't plan to hike for more than two or three hours at a time. Hardier adventurers can choose from a variety of specialty foods designed to provide energy, but not weight. For example, adding a little water can bring to life quite a few freeze-dried foods, powdered beverages, and other magic potions that transform themselves into food.

Making Lists and Checking Them Twice

Don't get stressed if you're packing and it's your first time out. As with any other vacation, the key to remembering the items you need to take along is to make lists. Tailor your list to your trip; you can carry more in the back of a car or in a canoe than you can in a backpack.

I'LL TELL YA!...

Conventional Wisdom
Add and subtract from the items needed for your trip according to how much room you have, or how much weight you're willing to carry. Camping from a car trunk is different from camping from a backpack.

However long your list, resist the temptation to bring useless gear; you won't need a portable iron, steam machine, hangers, shoe polish, or other citified accoutrements for your encounter with the outdoors. Of course, an outdoor vacation does require some specialized equipment and supplies; get to know what's needed by browsing through some of the later chapters in this book. Then you can make informed choices as you decide which of the items described next you're going to need.

Nearly everyone has a friend, or at least an acquaintance, who's familiar with some of the items needed for a basic camping trip. Call on these people to help you begin your list. Who knows—maybe your friend can lend you some equipment. The other option is to visit specialized camping stores and talk to those in the know. Explain what you're doing, what you think you need, and how long you expect to be outdoors. Good outlets hire salespeople who actually *go* hiking, camp, and vacation outdoors on the side. Consult these people for "insider's" advice on equipment and planning—they may even offer tips on good hiking and camping locations in your neck of the woods.

Conventional Wisdom

I'LL TELL YA!...

Seek advice from those working in specialized camping and outdoor gear stores. More than likely, they are committed outdoors people themselves and can give "inside" advice on what to take and where to go. They may give you the lay of the land and ease any tribulations about venturing off for the first time.

Checklists, Checklists, and More Checklists

In the fullness of time, you'll develop your own way of organizing an outdoor vacation yourself. In the meantime, here are some lists that you can add to and build on. As you consider bringing any of these items, always remember weight (especially if you expect to hike to a destination). Many of the items listed are nice to have, but in no way necessary for the success of a trip. (Some seasoned backpackers would consider a few of them downright superfluous; when in doubt, ask.)

Wilderness guides, nature guides, and novels are some of the extras that campers may want to take along. Expect that something will be forgotten, and try to improvise.

The Basic Equipment Checklist (for a weekend outing):

- ✓ Sleeping bag
- ✓ Sleeping mattress (Chapter 4)
- ✓ Tent (Chapter 4)
- ✓ Food (Chapter 6)
- ✓ Water (Chapter 6)
- ✓ Pocketknife (Chapter 6)
- ✓ First aid kit (Chapter 23)
- ✓ Flashlight (Chapter 16)

Conventional Wisdom

I'LL TELL YA!...

Choose quick-drying synthetic materials when purchasing camping and hiking clothes. Not only are they lighter, they tend to be more durable for outdoor use. Laminates such as Gore-Tex are designed to keep you dry in a rainstorm while still being "breathable"—allowing perspiration to pass through the fabric to the outside.

✓ 50-foot lengths of rope or nylon parachute cord (in bear country)

✓ Waterproof matches and a butane cigarette lighter

✓ Camp stove (Chapter 6)

✓ Appropriate clothes (Chapter 15)

✓ Insect repellent (Chapter 21)

✓ Sunscreen

✓ Topographical map of area (Chapter 9)

✓ Compass (Chapter 10)

✓ Whistle

✓ Toilet paper

General Clothing Checklist

✓ Chamois shirt (Chapter 15)

✓ Hat, bandana, or duck-billed cap (Chapter 15)

✓ Head netting (can be included as part of cap, above) (Chapter 15)

✓ Hiking boots (Chapter 13)

✓ Synthetic, wool, or silk long underwear (Chapter 15)

✓ Quick-drying synthetic pants (Chapter 15)

✓ Rainwear (Chapter 15)

✓ Running shoes or sandals (Chapter 13)

✓ Shorts (lightweight synthetics can double as bathing suit) (Chapter 15)

✓ T-shirts

✓ Waterproof utility bag for clothes

✓ Windproof jacket

✓ Hiking socks (Chapter 15)

Personal Effects Checklist

✓ Backpack

✓ Compass (Chapter 10)

✓ Extra flashlight batteries (Chapter 16)

✓ Extra pair of glasses or contact lenses (with solutions)

✓ Full-size knife (Chapter 6)

✓ Garbage bags (Chapter 6)

✓ Matches (Chapter 6)

✓ Self-sealing sandwich bags

✓ Sunglasses

✓ Water container (canteen) (Chapter 6)

✓ Water purifier (Chapter 6)

Kitchen Checklist

✓ Biodegradable dishwashing detergent (optional) (Chapter 6)

✓ Extra stove fuel (Chapter 6)

✓ Fireplace grill (Chapter 6)

✓ Food (Chapter 6)

✓ Pots and pans (Chapter 6)

✓ Spatula

✓ Water carrier

Personal Hygiene Checklist

✓ Comb or hairbrush

✓ Dental floss

✓ Gardening trowel (for burying waste if privies are not available)

✓ Towelettes

✓ Nail clipper

✓ Shaving supplies

✓ Soap

✓ Toilet paper

✓ Towel

✓ Washcloth

Don't Be Bothered by the Bears and Bugs

First, since you've decided to ferret out a natural setting in a national park, campsite, or other wilderness area, encounters with nature and wildlife are possible. (Isn't that why we're doing this thing outdoors?) Unfortunately, man's encroachment on nature is increasing and you may notice such signs in the form of high-tension electrical wires, a water-runoff viaduct, or a swath of land once cleared for the laying of a pipeline.

I'm not telling you not to bother to seek out nature, for it is in nature that we can still take time to reflect and get away from the noise of the cities, the pollution, and hustle and bustle that goes along with the urban experience. Seeking out nature affords us with the chance to see a clear blue sky filled with stars, swim in unchlorinated pools of water, and hear the howls and hoots of nature's creatures. Follow the rules for observing animals given in Chapter 22, and try not to disturb them in their natural environment.

While we're on the subject of animals, it's pretty much a given—but important to remember—that you're likely to encounter wildlife in the woods. The chances of coming face-to-face with an animal, is pretty remote, but you'll probably *hear* plenty of animals doing their thing. As you become more and more acquainted with the outdoors, you may be able to identify the animals making those noises behind the trees. In some wilderness areas, organized wolf howlings are an exciting part of the outdoor experience. Rangers take groups of nature-seekers into the woods for a communal howl in an attempt to raise the haunting bay of wolves in the distance. In moose country, keep an eye out for moose in the woods. If you encounter one of these majestic creatures, *stop and stand still* so you don't scare it away or alarm it. Most moose will go about their business rooting for food, and it is quite a sight to see. Slow down when driving to a trailhead or to a campsite in areas where moose are present. A collision with a moose can be deadly for both of you.

If a moose does appear in the road, stop and honk your horn. At night, stop, turn off the headlights, and honk. Any moose with an ounce of sense will hightail it for the trees. Remember, all animals encountered in the wilderness can be unpredictable. Avoid getting too close, and if an animal appears agitated move slowly away to avoid startling it.

In bear country, you want to avoid attracting these animals by suspending foodstuffs from trees. Most parks and public wilderness areas will alert you to the likelihood of encountering "dangerous" wildlife and tell you what steps to take in discouraging these animals from visiting your campsite.

There are animals that you only want to see or encounter from a distance. One of the most feared is the bear, which has become "civilized" by humans who have tempted and fed these potentially dangerous animals with food. Feeding animals in the woods is very poor form: Not only do animals begin to crave human offerings, they actually begin to depend on them for sustenance. Bears that return to campsites time-and-time-again for handouts usually end up being destroyed by authorities.

Because the smell of food may summon unwelcome company in the form of bears, all food and garbage should be suspended out of the reach of bears. Find a tree at 300 feet from camp and suspend all food in a sturdy bag 10 feet off the ground from a tree branch. The bag with food should be hung 10 feet out from the tree trunk so it can't be reached by bears that have climbed the tree trunk. Food should also never be stored in a vehicle in areas where bears are prevalent. Recent reports of bears smashing car windows to get a snack are increasing. Likewise, never store food inside a tent, or for that matter anything that smells good (including toothpaste). You may be in for a rude awakening.

Admittedly, the most irritating "wildlife" in the wilderness areas are the mosquitos, black flies, and horseflies. They can be a real pain in the . . . well, you know. Mosquitos are most prevalent in the early part of the summer and taper off toward the end of July. The height of black-fly season overlaps with the mosquito season in July, and depending on what part of the country you're in, horseflies will arrive on the scene at different times as well. What does this mean for the outdoor vacationer? Simple: Arm yourself against these little devils with insect repellent, and wear appropriate protective clothing.

Select an insect repellent that contains the chemical DEET. (Be sure to follow all manufacturer instructions when using pesticides.) Keep in mind, however, that DEET has a "meltdown" effect on some plastics, and many outdoor photographers simply detest the stuff because it can damage their expensive cameras. An alternative to this potentially offensive chemical is to look for repellents that contain citronella. Take along a variety of repellents; try them all to see which one is most effective.

Another strategy for repelling insects is to avoid wearing dark clothing, particularly dark blue and black (two of the bugs' favorite shades). Stick to lighter colors like pale yellow and light tans. Clothing should also be loose fitting and have tight cuffs. A hat is essential to keep bugs out of your hair; heavy socks can help prevent bugs from leaving those oh-so-annoying ankle bites.

In addition to these home-brewed methods of fending off irritating insects, there are bug nets that are pulled over the face and neck, and bug jackets (which include this feature) that create a virtually impenetrable barrier between you and the bloodthirsty pests.

Ticks

In grassy eastern woodlands deer ticks may be a hazard because they carry Lyme disease. To avoid being bitten by ticks, which are usually no bigger than the head of a pin, make sure your lower extremities are covered adequately. Frequent inspections of your lower extremities by a member of your camping party can stave off tick bites. Also make sure to apply insect repellent on your lower body.

Safe Camping
Insect repellents are almost always necessary in the woods. Always follow label directions, and avoid applying DEET-based repellents around mucous membranes—the eyes and mouth.

Signs of Lyme disease include a reddish spot on the skin that has a pale center. Muscular pain, headaches, and fever are other symptoms to watch for. If these symptoms crop up after you've been in the woods, consult a doctor and advise him or her of your camping activities.

Some Ground Rules

There is no garbage pickup in the wilderness; you'll have to "pack out" most of whatever garbage you bring in. Bring plastic garbage bags for the purpose. Small sealable sandwich bags are useful for storing small amounts of garbage. In other words, expect to be a pack horse for your trash.

Rules

Check with area authorities about building campfires. Most wilderness areas don't permit the use of scavenged ground cover as firewood. If you want hot meals, a camp stove is essential in many areas.

Gauging Your Abilities

If you're new to camping, or are bringing the family, make sure you don't plan an activity that is out of your league. Rock climbing may sound like fun, but it's an activity that has

Safe Camping
In bear country, you'll have to suspend food, garbage, and pots and pans from a rope in the trees. Do this religiously; an assault from a hungry bear can be dangerous. Suspending food will also deter other animals seeking a free meal.

its dangers. Seek instruction from local clubs that offer lessons and expert guidance in activities you'd like to try. Even novice hikers might want to go along with a group the first few times, and there are typically trips planned for your level ability leaving every weekend in camping season. Don't take unnecessary chances, and keep an eye on others in your group—make sure that everyone is comfortable with the activity being undertaken, whether it is hiking, canoeing, or swimming against a gentle current in a river. Try and plan your adventures with a partner, but if you're traveling by yourself, watch out for the human safety hazards too.

Safety

Safety on the trail has much to do with whether adventurers are traveling solo. If traveling solo, women need to take the same precautions as men, but maybe a few more too. As mentioned earlier, traces of man's encroachment on nature will certainly be found in all but the most out-of-the-way places. With the number of established hiking trails opening up, the floodgates have also opened for plenty of crazies and kooks as well.

The best advice is to stay away from people encountered on the trail who make you feel uncomfortable in any way. This goes for solo campers and hikers, and everyone else who ventures into America's forests. It's a good idea to avoid divulging your route or plans to anyone who isn't an official. (Be sure to leave an itinerary with friends and family.) Camp off the beaten path when possible; if anyone stops and seems overly inquisitive about your trip, fib about your plans. If all this sounds suspicious and antisocial, aren't you trying to get away from it all anyway? Why introduce urban ills into your Midsummer Night's Dream?

> **Conventional Wisdom**
> *Backpacking*—as opposed to camping from the trunk of a car—means driving to a trailhead, putting on a backpack containing all of your supplies for a specified period of time, and trekking off along a trail to camp.
>
> I'LL TELL YA!...

Expecting the Unexpected

Now that you're high on venturing into the great outdoors, there is the chance that nature won't cooperate. Your weekend may be ruined by showers and temperatures may plummet to ungodly lows. The best thing you can do about it is to be prepared; the next best thing is not to get mad if these things happen. Anticipate the worst by including foul-weather gear in your backpack or trunk. There are worse ways to relax than spending a day snuggled inside a tent reading a book as the rain pitter-patters against the rain fly. Cold weather is more of a problem, but follow the advice in Part 3 and carry warm clothing when there is a chance of cool weather.

If you do venture out, dressing for the weather ensures that you'll manage any potential discomfort. A rain poncho is a must-have, as is a good tent. Check out weather advisories before heading off. A weekend postponed is a weekend gained some other time. With any kind of outdoor event, plan for contingencies; get hiking and camping partners to agree on a rain date for another trip.

When the weather agrees, sometimes the people in your group won't. While a course on diplomacy isn't appropriate here, experience teaches that a group leader, self-appointed or otherwise, who acts in good faith by making decisions for others is always welcome.

Empowering the unhappy person in a group can also help smooth things over. Be prepared to forgive bad decisions and remain unfazed in the face of other people's mood swings.

Hiking and camping isn't for everyone. The naked outdoors can be overwhelming for some people until they learn to chill out and accept the pleasures of the experience.

The Least You Need to Know

➤ You don't need every piece of specialized camping gear now. Borrow or rent equipment the first time around until you're convinced that vacationing outdoors is for you!

➤ Plan short weekend trips with friends if you're new to camping and hiking. Of the many shared experiences, nature always offers indelible memories.

➤ Browse through state and federal brochures when planning an outdoor vacation. There are literally millions of acres of prime camping and hiking land under the control of the Bureau of Land Management, the National Park Service, and the National Forest Service.

➤ Understand that the wilderness can be overwhelming for some. If you're traveling with a group, have someone act as a group leader.

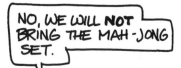

Chapter 2

Different Strokes for Different Folks

> **In This Chapter**
>
> ➤ Whom to go with
>
> ➤ Learning how to camp with kids
>
> ➤ Choosing a guided trip

In the previous chapter, I touched on how to deal with the people you've teamed up with to go along on your outdoor vacation. Chances are that you know the person (or people) you're traveling with, and know they can improvise and contribute something to your trip, whether it's a sense of humor or some camping skills.

This chapter discusses various camping situations and reveals that, in most cases, traveling with others, whether family members or good friends, is the most fun and rewarding part of a trip.

Two's Company, Seven's a Crowd

A group can consist of two or more people, but camping with more than six people can be *problematic*.

Most campsites are set up for two or three tents. Two is probably more realistic; ask anyone who's tried to find two spots in the same campsite that offer even, fairly level ground free of rocks and roots. You'll also have to determine whether you're going to sleep alone inside your own tent, or share a tent with someone else. Space is rather tight in most tents; you won't have the same privacy as you would sleeping alone.

But before discussing who you're going to get into bed with, consider the bigger picture.

Deciding where to go will be equally difficult (if not more so) among four or five other people. It takes time to gather maps, brochures, and assorted publications; study them; decide on a group plan; and then bring your plan to the group for approval. You might benefit from someone else's experience, especially if somebody in the group knows of a destination and can steer the group toward that plan of action.

You should consider some other things too:

➤ Put together a group of compatible people who are energetic and willing to embrace the "gestalt" of the outdoor adventure.

➤ If you're renting equipment, someone should research and price what's available, and then make the arrangements. Someone should also be in charge of making campsite reservations and securing permits and fishing licenses (if necessary).

➤ Check out the status of campfires at your destination. If they are prohibited, you'll have to use a portable stove for cooking.

➤ One person in the group should be in charge of food—buying it and packing it included. This person could also be in charge of designating the cooking rotation (if there is one).

➤ Another person should be in charge of cutlery, cooking pots, pans, and assorted "hardware" needed.

➤ Check water availability. Make sure there's water at each campsite and decide how you will treat it: iodine, filtering, or boiling.

Rules

Wilderness is disappearing at an alarming rate, according to the Sierra Club and other world-watchers. Practice minimum-impact camping by respecting the fragility of nature. Leave no camping area any different from how you found it.

Family Camping

Family camping usually means gearing up for a camping or hiking trip with one or more relatives, and typically means at least camping with a spouse. More often than not, it involves children—and this is where the fun begins.

Unlike adults, children can't be counted on to assemble their own stuff for a trip. That part of the event will be left to you. But there are some things that kids can be involved in before taking off, and that includes having them participate (if they're old enough) in looking over the route maps and brochures with you to get them prepared for the outdoors.

If they're lucky, they've been exposed to the concept of the wilderness through scouting and may already be looking forward to putting some of their book-learning, knot-tying skills, or campfire craft to work. Maybe they've been to camp for a week or more in the summer; if so, they might be more familiar than you are with canoeing, backcountry hiking, and outdoor cooking.

The point is that kids should be acclimated in some way beforehand. Set the scene for them or get them involved in an organized outdoor excursion to whet their appetite. (In most cities, for example, the YMCA offers day camp and outdoor camping opportunities for kids of all ages.) Before venturing off as a family, consider sending Junior on one of these outings. Better yet, have a night in the backyard—tent, stove, and all. Kids will see what it's like to sleep outdoors in a tent.

Use your discretion to decide what age is appropriate for a child to come along. Some say even one- and two-year olds are old enough for a trip. Whatever the age, many insist that kids be launched on an outdoor career before they hit their teens (and develop a liking for malls instead of trees).

Certainly, extra gear is a consideration when it comes to kids. The amount of stuff needed in civilization, never mind the woods, is often overwhelming, and may preclude any extensive hikes. Car camping may be the only way to bring all the necessary stuff along and still keep it near you.

If children are old enough, hike to a destination and set up a base camp. Take day hikes away from the base camp. And don't push the envelope by leading the entire family, kids and all, on a furious "death march" through the bush. Take your time, wake up when you want—treat an outdoor vacation as *vacation*, not a triathlon.

Special Considerations for Kids

Clothing is another matter. With the recent explosion in outdoor fashion, one can get every conceivable type of gear and clothing in kid-size versions. Remember, *children should be dressed as warmly as you are* in the fall; in summer, make sure your kids are adequately protected from bugs (who may consider these tender little humans as something akin to suckling pigs if they are aren't wearing some kind of repellent).

The sun is another consideration—for yourself, and especially for children. Use extra caution around water; rays reflected from the water are potentially as strong as those coming from the sky.

In any case, plan on entertaining kids the same way you would at home. Here are some ideas for amusing children on an outdoor outing, using some of the natural amenities around you:

➤ Collect frogs and tree toads. In a container of some sort, smaller frogs and toads will sit on the backs of bigger ones. Dead insects can be dangled in the container, and kids (and adults) can watch amphibian tongues unfurl and lash out to catch the insect.

➤ Go on nature walks and try to spot wildlife. Use a small notebook to make a log of the wildlife you discover.

Here's How
A homemade remedy for insect bites and stings is to mix the common household cleaner ammonium hydroxide with several drops of baby oil in a small bottle. Swab the solution directly onto insect bites for instant relief from stinging and itching on the trail. Commercial preparations, including hemorrhoid creams, are also effective for treating insect bites.

➤ Show kids how to use binoculars and teach them how to study the landscape, birds, and animals.

➤ Look for animal tracks and draw them in a notepad. Try and guess which animals left the tracks.

➤ Make a swing from a piece of rope looped and tied around a thick tree limb.

➤ Collect firewood for the evening's campfire. Also look for perfect sticks on which marshmallows can be speared.

➤ Try to light a fire without matches using a magnifying glass or the lens from a pair of glasses.

➤ Have someone sit with their eyes closed and try to touch them without them hearing your approach.

Guided Trips

For first-time adventurers (or those not especially confident about taking off by themselves the first time), going with a guide may be the best way. A guided excursion may be ideal for the single adventurer who is uncomfortable with the idea of the outdoors or doesn't have a partner to go with.

Guided trips are outdoor vacations organized and put together by companies specializing in extended "package" trips. Wilderness trips are often conducted by experienced guides who offer tips along the way. Guided trips like these are great for those who don't have equipment and the skills needed for more involved camping trips because everything is often provided—from hiking boots and packs to tents and sleeping bags. Often, the only thing you have to worry about is getting to the departure point for the trip at hand, whether it is by airplane, car, or bus. So, in considering the cost, these trips may be bargains when you consider that you won't have to buy specialized equipment for the trip.

Guided trips come in all shapes and colors, from weekend canoe camping excursions to two-week long adventures to different parts of the world. And they cost anywhere from several hundred dollars to three or four thousand depending on the nature and duration of the trip. You can find companies offering a variety of trips in outdoor magazines and from brochures available at your local camping supply store.

Guided trips also offer the opportunity to explore a range of camping locations and "mix" different activities in one trip. Such excursions may include a canoe trip to a campsite one day, a day-long hike the next, and then a hike or canoe trip to another location. The great thing about guided tours is that you can show up with minimal gear— often nothing more than a pair of hiking boots and some warm clothes.

While this can take some of the thrill out of the planning that accompanies a do-it-yourself trip, it may be the answer for those who are short on time, or for those short on ideas about where to go.

Finding the Guided Trip to Fit the Bill

As with the do-it-yourself trip, you'll have to scour local camping stores, chambers of commerce, and other sources for the names and phone numbers of guided trips. Typically, guided trips are offered on a package basis; you purchase a weekend-long trip or longer. Most have some theme attached to them—bird watching, kayaking, canoeing, or cycling. Others may offer a nature-appreciation theme; still others may offer instruction that builds your hiking and camping skills.

Whatever the theme, the more adventurous can parachute into a situation and enjoy a range of locales with like-minded adventurers. How about sea kayaking the coasts of Baja and dining by night on seafood at a beach camp? Or hiking through the rainforests of Costa Rica?

The world is your oyster with this kind of trip.

Getting There

With a guided trip there isn't much to getting there. Just hook up with the group at a pre-arranged time and date and get going. In most cases, this means getting to a bus or train stop and getting aboard. Guided trips to exotic locations will mean plane reservations and more transportation planning. Proprietors offering guided trips can often help with arrangements.

Traveling Solo

Guided treks can be a great getaway—that said, there are times when traveling solo is preferable to visiting the wilderness with someone else. Just be prepared to consider the gravity of this decision. Not only will you *not* be able to discuss the pros and cons of taking this trail or that one, you'll have no one else to talk to for long stretches of time. This is okay for some people, but a little unsettling for many others (myself included).

Also consider that you won't have a partner to share in some of the chores and minor hardships that go along with living life on the trail. You'll have to carry all the gear yourself; you won't have an extra pair of hands to collect firewood. And no one will have "interesting" theories of tent-pitching to expound to you in the dark (or at least hold the flashlight) as you run the flexible poles through the small hoops and clips protruding from the collapsed mound of fabric on the ground. Never mind those other niceties that are much more difficult (if not impossible) when you go it alone—for example, looking to borrow a can opener when you've discovered yours has disappeared.

Still, some more experienced hikers and campers insist that the thrill is in the utter independence of pursuing an adventure solo.

Safety First

This *modus operandi* isn't recommended for beginners—and may even be hazardous in situations where novice campers depart from the reach of others for even short periods of time. Consider that an injury from routine encounters with rocks and twigs will mean that you'll have to cope alone. If others discover you injured along the way, they'll have to deal with the situation. The likelihood of *their* trip being ruined is close to 100 percent. If you've left word about when you expect to return, and then don't, someone will have to be sent to look for you at considerable expense and inconvenience. Depending on your particular mode of travel—especially if it involves canoes or kayaks and a large body of water like a lake—traveling solo can be downright dangerous.

When traveling alone make sure to

➤ Leave an itinerary with friends and family.

➤ Let friends and family know how you're progressing by phoning from trailheads and ranger stations along the way.

➤ Take care of medical problems before you leave—you won't have someone else to rely on to go get help if a problem crops up.

➤ Carry a credit card. It is waterproof and is useful if you need money for medical treatment or need to arrange an emergency departure by plane, or simply, if you lose all your cash.

➤ Arrange for someone to alert authorities on a certain date if your contact person back home doesn't hear from you.

Still, the pros of going solo are that you'll be able to reflect on the wonders of nature uninterrupted, and that you can take pride in knowing you have accomplished the trip on your own. Solo adventures aren't for everyone, and sitting next to a raging campfire by one's lonesome may not be as much fun as if others were at your side, but many swear by it. Just take care, and camp or hike with someone a few times before embarking on a trip by yourself.

Vehicles

The family car is usually called into service as a camping caravan. Depending on the size of the vehicle, and number of campers going along for the ride, you may need to add car racks for such items as bicycles, canoes and kayaks, packs, and so on. Several manufacturers offer racking systems exactly for this reason, and they can be adapted to carry everything from skis to rowboats.

Backpacks are another matter, and they can take up a full seat by themselves when fully packed. You might want to consider renting a bigger vehicle if your car doesn't look like it's going to fit everyone and everything. Minivans are ideal for camping excursions simply because they're so roomy—but be sure to reserve as far in advance as possible. In peak vacation periods, minivans for rent may be hard to come by on short notice. Of course, if camping is your thing and you get more bold, a four-wheel drive may be in the cards. These vehicles can plow through mud and uneven terrain with ease, and you can feel like you're on safari.

Planes, Trains, and Automobiles

In most cases you'll have to figure out how to get to your camping destination yourself. The weekend camper or hiker probably has a car, or is able to rent one fairly easily. Those without the luxury of automobiles will have to rely on buses and railroads to get them to their location—or at least close enough to it that a taxi or shuttle of some sort can be arranged.

Safe Camping

Parking at popular trailheads can be risky. An alarming number of automobile break-ins are reported every year. If you plan to park near a trailhead, you should leave your car at a local gas station, motel, or other business instead. For a nominal fee, most will accommodate.

In most cases, you can hire a taxi (whether official or not) at a rural terminus with some degree of ease. If no taxi is readily available there, ask at a local store or gas station to see whether anyone can offer such a service. As long as you display a modicum of politeness (and don't resemble Charles Manson), someone is bound to oblige.

Stop and Smell the Roses

The whole idea behind getting into the outdoors is to relax. If you're a Type-A personality, try and take this into consideration, especially when traveling with others. Getting from Point A to Point B may be important to some people and not to others. Take time to enjoy the fresh air, stop and sit down for a few minutes every once in a while, and take your time if possible. The unpredictability of an adventure in the outdoors should be counted on. The weather may change, the terrain you travel over may be more difficult than you thought, or you may just feel plain tired one day. Adjust your itinerary accordingly, and be prepared for delays and unexpected disruptions. Remember, you're on vacation even if you're moving from place to place yourself.

The Least You Need to Know

➤ Choose a guided trip if you can't rustle up others to go with you. Outdoor clubs can provide lists of outfits specializing in weekend and week-long adventure holidays.

➤ Make lists of provisions needed for an outdoor vacation. Add to and subtract from the items needed according to how much weight you're willing to carry in your backpack, or how much you're going to pack into a car trunk.

➤ Children can fit into an outdoor vacation. Just remember to take along some amusements for them, and to introduce them in advance to the idea of the outdoors.

➤ Refuse the urge to "get on with" an itinerary. The idea of an outdoor vacation should be to progress at a leisurely pace, and to take time to stop and smell the flowers.

Chapter 3

More about When and Where to Camp

In This Chapter
➤ How to gear up for your trip
➤ Evaluating the quality of a campground
➤ Staking out quiet turf in a sometimes-crowded place
➤ The benefits and challenges of an off-season trip

Not everyone lives a stone's throw from a slice of wilderness—and not everyone can afford more than three days just to *get* to a place resembling wilderness. Most, however, can get somewhere in three to four hours with a little planning.

While some self-styled outdoor snoots turn their noses up at camping from the trunk of a car, so-called "car camping" may be the best way to enjoy a short visit to the outdoors. And whether they are willing to admit it or not, a good many "advanced" outdoorspeople began appreciating wilderness this way, and got more adventurous later on.

Besides, camping from the trunk of a car doesn't mean being car-bound. You can partake of the many other recreational activities that surround a car-camping experience. You may depart on an early morning canoe trip, touch down on a secluded island, and return to your car campground later. Likewise, you can strap on a backpack and head off along a trail for a day's hike. Or take a tent, and spend the night deeper in the woods and return the next day to your campsite.

For now, car camping may be an ideal way for those short on time and skills to get to the edge of the wilderness and take in some of the joys of an outdoor vacation.

Camping from Your Trunk versus Backpacking

Car camping can be more than just pulling into a wooded lot, pitching a tent, and then watching others do the same. In fact, car camping can deliver many of the same pleasures as venturing into the backwoods with a backpack. And, this style of camping is as close as you can get to having all the amenities you're used to at home, without staying home.

Choosing a destination from the many available will be one of the first challenges. You might start by phoning the tourism bureau for the state you want to visit to request a list of campgrounds. Tourism officials may be able to recommend a location during the call. Otherwise, wait for the brochures to arrive and select a destination based on the following criteria:

➤ Does the campground have extensive day hiking trails?

➤ Is there a lake to swim in?

➤ How booked does the campground get?

When you've chosen a campground, be prepared to jump—make sure you phone ahead to make reservations well in advance. Long weekends in the summer get booked quickly; you may have to go farther afield than originally planned. Or (more likely), the campground does not accept reservations, and it's first come, first served.

Most campgrounds require permits, and you might want to secure these in advance as well. If you camp from your car for one night, hike to a more remote campsite the next, and trek to another the following night, park officials may require you to file an entire trip itinerary. Park authorities don't want to have to scour an entire wilderness area if you go missing.

CAUTION

Safe Camping
Country roads are often unpaved, can be soft in places, and sometimes muddy after a heavy rain. Carry traction aids in the trunk. The metal variety are commercially available from auto supply stores. These metal grates are placed in front or behind the drive wheels of the car to provide traction. For a do-it-yourself alternative, roll up two 10-foot-long-by-20-inch-wide strips of carpeting and pack them in with the camping gear. When mud, sand, or ice hamper driving, unroll the strips and place them under the car's wheels to provide traction.

I'LL TELL YA!...

Conventional Wisdom
Car camping may be the way to go for those new to camping. You'll feel more comfortable knowing that your trunk contains what you need, and it's nice to know that anything you forgot is usually a short drive away into town or to the campground commissary.

If you're intent on showing up at a campground, pitching a tent, and staying put for a few days, look for a campsite away from any intersections of roads. Scope out the area thoroughly before settling on a particular site; try to choose a location that isn't sandwiched between two other sites.

Most car campgrounds offer all the amenities of a Motel 6. Not only will such campgrounds have toilet and shower facilities, most will also have a fireplace equipped with a cooking grate. Many have a store where provisions can be purchased in cases where something was forgotten.

> **Conventional Wisdom**
> I'LL TELL YA!...
> When car campgrounds are up for grabs, choosing one where your neighbors look as though they are there to relax rather than party all night may be better than setting up and waiting for others to pull in beside you. At least you'll know what you're getting into.

You may be asking yourself what point there is of camping in such "civilized" conditions?

The answer is fairly simple: When time is short or you're uncomfortable with your untried camping skills, car camping offers a taste of the outdoors with very little danger of too much going amiss. All the amenities will be there, and you won't have to worry about going without a shower for days on end.

What you won't get is a true taste of the wilderness because the groomed conditions of such campsites often mitigate many of the natural things that go along with backpacking into the woods.

The following chart illustrates the difference between car camping and backpacking, if only by listing the amount of stuff you can take with you on these two styles of outdoor vacations.

Car camping and backpacking checklist—what you should pack for each style of trip

Equipment	Car	Backpack
Tent	X	X
Ground sheet	X	X
Stove	X	X
Fuel	X	X
Cutlery	X	X
Mug	X	X

continues

27

Car camping and backpacking checklist—what you should pack for each style of trip—Continued

Equipment	Car	Backpack
Backpack	*	X
Hip pack	X	*
Umbrella	X	
Sleeping bag	X	X
Sleeping mat	X	X
Water bottles		X
Filled gallon container for water	X	
Pocket knife	X	X
First-aid kit	X	X
Waterproof matches	*	X
Wood saw	X	*
Hatchet	X	
Toilet paper rolls	X	*
Toilet paper packets		X
Water purifier		X
Hairbrush	*	X
Insect repellent	X	
Insect headnet		X
Pencil for marking maps		X
Biodegradable soap	X	X
Camera and film	X	*
Cash	X	X
Extra car keys	X	X
Waterproof wallet	*	X
Flashlight	X	X
Candle lantern	*	X

Equipment	Car	Backpack
Extra candles for lantern	*	X
Hats	X	X
Hiking boots	*	X
Sneakers	X	*
Rain outfit	X	*
Sunglasses	X	X
Binoculars	X	X
Hiking socks		X
Gloves	*	*
Laundry bag	X	
Sealing sandwich bags		X
Cooler	X	
Toothbrush	X	X
Toothpaste	X	X
Razor	X	*
Shaving cream	X	*
Signal mirror		X
Highway maps	X	*
Topographic hiking maps		X
Rope	X	X
Compass		X
Watch	X	X
Alarm clock	X	
Sunscreen	X	X
Freeze-dried food		X
Snacks/energy food		X
Salt and pepper	X	X

* Depends on length and type of trip

Choosing a Quiet Location in a Crowded Campground

Unfortunately, not all campers regard camping as a chance to a have a quiet commune with nature. Too often, after too much beer, neighboring campers can get noisier than is tolerable. Campground rules often stipulate quiet time between the hours of 8:00 p.m. and 8:00 a.m., but there is no guarantee that campers will stick to this rule (or any other rules, for that matter).

Other inconveniences include the arrival of other campers after official gate-closing hours. The flash of a car's headlight beams in the night just as you're touching down in dreamland is not only annoying, but can also be angering. In consideration of others, you might want to plan your arrival at a campsite before others start heading off for bed.

This section provides suggestions for finding a campsite that enables you to have the relaxing experience you're seeking, and gives you more guidance about being a polite neighbor.

Hiking for 20 Minutes Gives You an Advantage

One good thing about camping is that it's not that hard to get away from the crowds. A recent survey of visitors to U.S. National Parks discovered that a majority of car campers (including those arriving in RVs) never ventured far from their vehicles. This means that if you're prepared to hike a little—say, about 20 minutes away from the main parking and camping area—you can probably find a campsite where you'd avoid most of the other people who've migrated to the same campground. (Assuming, of course, that the campground offers more remote campsites.)

Conventional Wisdom
Respect your neighbors. If you like meeting people in adjacent campsites don't assume that others feel the same way. Always be sure to respect others' privacy.

Some campgrounds also offer sites even farther away— spots you can only reach by taking a short canoe ride. Such steps help minimize the chances of being stuck next to a camping party that invades your space with noise, or by the very presence of others in an adjacent lot.

Strategies for Minimizing Disruption

Most car campers carry a reasonable amount of equipment with them. There are others who carry too much. Try not to disrupt your campground neighbors with your activities.

Plug-in air mattress pumps, extremely bright lights, and a full compliment of camping "toys" seem almost a nuisance in the outdoors and often diminish the reason for being close to nature—getting away from it all.

In one of my early camping excursions in the Catskills outside New York City, neighboring campers on the right had invaded a rather small camping plot and filled it with two minivans, two family-size tents, and a giant gazebo. The gazebo was used as a form of shelter, but was erected primarily for late-night and early morning prayer sessions. To the left, a large family busied themselves for close to three hours unpacking and setting up folding tables and chairs, a portable dishwashing and sink setup, and what could have been an apartment-size stove and oven. Besides the obvious theater it afforded us, the family had plugged a noisy air compressor into a power source somewhere in one of the vans. They spent several hours blowing up air mattresses.

Undoubtedly everyone slept comfortably next door, but the noise from the compressor polluted our space the whole time before we settled to sleep ourselves.

Later we were awakened by the zealots in the lot on the *other* side.

Such are the downsides of car camping. But there is a lesson to be learned from this story: Seek out the most secluded spot you can, and try to select a site that doesn't put you between two other campsites.

Here's How
If you arrive at the campground after dark, you can use your headlights to help you see what you're doing as you set up. But make sure you're not blasting campers in adjacent lots with strong beams from your lights.

Conventional Wisdom
I'LL TELL YA!...
Hiding an extra car key under a bumper or in some other place near the car reduces the chances of a costly tow job or the inconvenience of waiting for an extra to be sent from home. Keys can easily go missing if dropped in dense foliage or down cracks between rocks. Use waterproof tape to attach the key, or a magnetic container designed for the job.

Look for Lakes, Trails, and Other Diversions

The best campgrounds have the most to offer.

Not only will they have typical car-camping facilities—which are, when you get right down to it, parking lots in the woods—but they will also offer hiking trails, biking trails, and opportunities for swimming and enjoying the simpler pleasures of exercise. The best way to discern between the good, the bad, and the ugly is to get your hands on a map of the campgrounds you're planning to visit.

Campground layouts are provided at visitor centers and in brochures provided by land managers. Most campsites also offer a close-up, numbered layout of the campsites, which normally means you can reserve one you particularly like.

Example of a
campsite map

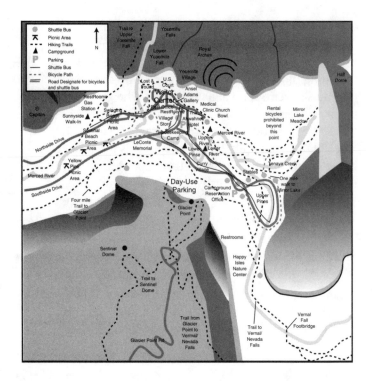

If you see the term *interior camping* or *backcountry camping*, it's a clue that your prospective destination has a certain amount of wilderness that can be explored beyond the camping spots designed for cars. In the beginning, start out by camping from the trunk of a car on the first night, then scout around and pick a campsite not too far into the interior of the park. Move camp and set up there on the second night.

If you move from an established campground to an "interior" campground off the beaten path, you may need to get another permit for the secluded site. You will probably need to move your car to a lot set up to accommodate campers who have departed for an interior trip. Depending on the time of year and usage level, you may be expected to stay there. Before embarking on foot to the site, make sure to reserve a campground site for your return. You can drive back and park there when you return.

This approach lets less experienced campers get a taste of camping in the "real" country, truly away from it all.

Getting Away from It All—Or Most of It, Anyway

No matter what kind of camping you have in mind, the likelihood of experiencing its downside hinges on the time of year you head to the country. This much I can reasonably guarantee: If you plan a trip over a long weekend in the summer (provided you can get reservations), you *will* experience some kind of gridlock—either on the highway or at the campsite itself.

The Early-in-the-Season and Off-Season Advantage

Like all travel, planning camping trips early and late in the season offers you several advantages to going at peak times. If swimming isn't a high priority, try camping in the spring—when long, hot summer days haven't heated the lakes to optimum temperatures, attracting legions of bathing campers. Be forewarned, though: Spring coincides with the hatching of mosquito larvae in many parts of the country, and these pesky insects can put a real damper on any camping excursion. Take along plenty of insect repellent and consider bug netting for the head.

In fall, visitors to campgrounds can enjoy crisp, cool nights, no insects, few people, and the splendor of colorful foliage (in those parts of the country where it changes). You may be disappointed, however, when you try to make reservations; many campgrounds in the East close down for the season at the end of October.

Staying Warm Off-Season

Spring and fall ushers in all kinds of weather. Be prepared to handle rain and colder weather, particularly at night. In the summer, almost any sleeping bag will do, but in spring and fall, you'll need a sleeping bag designed to keep you extra toasty and warm. Such super-duper sleeping bags cost upwards of $150, but will be well worth the extra bucks in the face of night frosts.

Select a sleeping bag filled with down or with one of the tried-and-true synthetic fills such as Hollofil II, Polarguard HV, or Lite Loft (Chapter 5). Sleeping bags for spring and fall use should be rated as a *three-season bag*, or designed for use in temperatures as low as 20° F. Summer-weight sleeping bags are rated for use in temperatures above the freezing point.

Safe Camping

CAUTION

Don't wear cotton in cold weather. Cotton gets wet easily and stays that way while causing your body temperature to drop. It has no insulating value and when it gets wet it can be dangerous in cold conditions. Blue jeans, which are made of cotton, are terrible camping clothes when it's chilly. Choose wool or one of the popular synthetics instead.

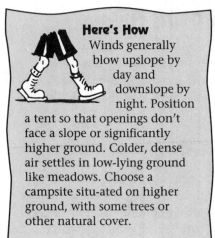

Here's How
Winds generally blow upslope by day and downslope by night. Position a tent so that openings don't face a slope or significantly higher ground. Colder, dense air settles in low-lying ground like meadows. Choose a campsite situ-ated on higher ground, with some trees or other natural cover.

A Layering Primer

In addition to bringing a good sleeping bag, dress in layers. As the day gets progressively colder, don more outerwear to combat chilly temperatures. The proverbial happy campers are those who dress in three layers of clothing:

➤ An inner layer (the underwear) should be made of polypropylene and polyester in different weights. This keeps moisture (sweat) away from your skin to keep you dry.

➤ A mid-layer of wool (or synthetic) should fit comfortably—not too tight, not too loose. This insulates or traps air between you and the outer layer.

➤ A third, synthetic outer layer is needed as a wind shell. It blocks the wind and keeps you dry as well.

If your camping takes place in wet conditions, choose a shell made from Gore-Tex—a breathable, waterproof fabric that offers protection from wind and rain.

Talk to Those in the Know

At the risk of sounding like a broken record, remember to consult others about possible camping spots. Someone in your office, a close friend, or a friend-of-a-friend may be able to recommend a good campground. The farther away from major metropolitan areas you travel, the less likely your chosen campground will be congested; acquaintances may know of campgrounds well off the beaten path, out of common circulation, and relatively undiscovered by others.

The Least You Need to Know

➤ Pick campsites carefully; when car camping study the layout and tour the campsites before you settle on one for the night. Order some maps of the campground along with travel brochures. Picture where you'd like to camp in advance, then reserve a particular site (likewise in advance) if you can.

➤ Avoid selecting a site situated between two others. You may end up being "the monkey in the middle."

➤ Reserve campsites well in advance. On long-summer-weekend holidays, popular campsites get booked early. If a particular park is already crammed on its peak dates, don't despair; why escape to a place overrun with visitors anyway? Try going in the off-season instead.

➤ Pay attention to climate and season; plan for the weather accordingly. Be sure to bring along rainwear or warm clothing for comfort in cooler temperatures.

➤ Hiking, even just 20 minutes from the main campground, may give you more privacy than just pulling up at a typical car-camping spot.

Nighttime under the Stars

Nothing is quite like the peacefulness of sleeping in a tent beneath a sky profusely speckled with twinkling stars. Fresh, unpolluted air wafts around you, and you fall into a deep sleep listening to the sound of leaves rustling in the wind.

This scenario is idyllic. But what if a torrential downpour were to ruin your dreams? Instead of drifting off to sleep, the scene changes to one where the wind howls in the darkness and rain pelts down on the thin nylon that separates you from the cold, cruel realities of conditions outside. And then you *are* wet, as wind picks up and water falls in large drops into your cocoon.

But let's not imagine the worst. A good tent, properly pitched, will provide protection from the worst weather conditions. I like to think of a tent as a portable cottage—something you can erect in minutes, into which you can throw yourself and your equipment after a long day of hiking, driving, or fooling around in the woods. An added bonus of a tent is that you'll never have to pay property taxes on it after you buy it.

In this chapter, you'll learn about tents and their contribution to the overall pleasure of the outdoor experience. They're a necessity for enjoying the outdoors, and there are a wide range to choose from—for every use and every budget.

Tents and Tarps

Tents can be your most important piece of equipment when you're faced with heavy weather. Although a tent can be more of an encumbrance than a necessity in parts of the country where rain seldom falls (such as the desert), it still affords some measure of privacy—and in some cases, protection against critters—as a payoff for lugging it around.

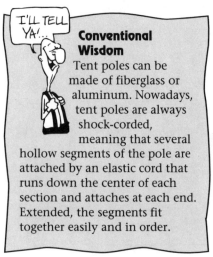

I'LL TELL YA!...

Conventional Wisdom

Tent poles can be made of fiberglass or aluminum. Nowadays, tent poles are always shock-corded, meaning that several hollow segments of the pole are attached by an elastic cord that runs down the center of each section and attaches at each end. Extended, the segments fit together easily and in order.

Here's the good news: Thanks to synthetics, tents aren't heavy like they once were; modern lightweight fabrics can make "lugging" a misnomer.

Tarps, in contrast to tents, are heavy pieces of coated nylon that you can make into a sort of tent-without-a-floor; all you need are some ropes and a bit of ingenuity. Store-bought tarps are 10 or 12 feet square and have grommets (eyes) at the corners and edges. These are where you attach ropes leading from anchor points such as trees, branches, and stakes in the ground. You may want to carry both a tent *and* a tarp, but this (of course) is a weight question that depends on whether you're car camping, backpacking, or canoe camping. On some trails, you may not need a tent or a tarp. Land managers in many places provide lean-tos for campers.

Since tarps require some thinking about how to set them up—and where to find those natural anchor points to suspend them from—they are favored by more advanced campers and hikers. A tent, on the other hand, is for every kind of camper—weekender, wilderness wanderer, or canoe camper.

Beg, Borrow, or Steal the First Time Around

Before pulling out the plastic, lay your hands on the fabric. As with all equipment (except hiking boots and clothing), you should try to rent or borrow a tent to gauge performance and features.

A tent may very well be the biggest equipment purchase you'll make; it is certainly one of the most important. Tents come in all shapes and sizes, designed for many different—sometimes specialized—purposes. Some are easy to pitch, some are near impossible.

And then there is size.

Take capacity ratings with a grain of salt and make sure to crawl inside with your partner(s). Backpackers would never lug along a four-person tent, because it would take up an entire backpack. But if you're car camping, anything goes as far as weight.

With all this in mind, try out several sizes and styles before settling on one particular type. Renting or borrowing several types should help you with the decision.

Take a Crack at Setting It Up

Always pitch any unfamiliar tent before heading off on a trip. Chances are that if you leave in the evening, you'll end up setting the tent up in the dark. You'll want to have some idea of the tent's operating principles in advance—especially if it has more poles and attachments than you know what to do with.

A quality outdoor-equipment store will have a number of tents set up, and will allow customers to crawl inside to try them out. This is a good time to ask if you can take the tent down and pitch it again. Every salesperson should oblige, and this is a great way to gauge how fast it will take in the real outdoors, imagining that it is night and you are tired and hungry.

Instructions that come with tents can be bewildering. There's nothing like hands-on experience to make up for those mystifying diagrams and tangled directions that fall far short of clarity.

Don't Fly Off the Handle

Most tents are double-walled. The inner canopy is made of breathable nylon, while the outer fly is coated for waterproofness: The *rainfly* and the tent itself. The purpose of the rainfly is to protect the tent and its contents (you included) from the elements. Typically, you'll have to set up the tent by running interlocking aluminum tubes that are shock-corded together through sleeps or hooks along the outside of the tent (this sounds more

Here's How
Always air out a tent before putting it away to prevent rotting and staining from mildew. When taking a tent down, make sure you shake out any debris from the inside; twigs and stones can rip and puncture the fabric. Always *stuff* a tent back into its stuff-sack; don't fold it. Creases from folds can weaken fabric fibers.

complicated than it is). When done correctly, the mass of tent fabric will magically take shape and become what you'd expect to see: a portable cottage with an entrance.

You place the fly over the top the tent and stake it down at several points along the ground. Crisscrossing poles support the fly and hold it about 2 to 4 inches off the tent. This arrangement effectively creates a region of airspace that offers a little insulation, allows condensation from inside the tent to escape, and prevents rainwater from migrating through the tent's fabric into the tent.

The fly is really the waterproofing system in nearly all tent designs. The tent itself is the undershell that contains everything else.

Choosing the Portable Cottage

When it comes time to buy, you'll be able to select from several shapes and sizes. Modern-day tents feature a system of crisscrossing poles that act as the "ribs" for the tent, a waterproof fly, and several anchoring pegs that hold everything together when the wind rises.

Evaluating tent designs can be a little daunting; many will have similar features but look completely different when erected. Most tent designs, however, are variations on the following five configurations.

The A-Frame

This tent is becoming outmoded as newer, sexier-looking dome tents take over the market. Experienced campers, however, swear by their reliability in the face of bad weather—in spite of their old-fashioned design, which features two sloping sides falling away from a rigid center pole, a design that catches the wind but sheds water quickly. This design offers less interior space for the size than more contemporary designs but offers more interior height. A-frames are often lighter in weight than domes because there are often fewer poles. A-frames tend to cost less than their dome-shaped cousins, and this may be only one of the reasons to choose this tried-and-true design.

A-frames are a tried-and-true design that are appealing because they cost less than fancier designs.

The Dome Tent

This style of tent is by far the most popular recreational tent around. It offers plenty of floor space and is designed to ride out heavy winds. Domes tend to be a little harder to pitch than A-frames, because three or more flexible poles have to be threaded *in just the right way* through a number of sleeves or clips. The whole operation only becomes obvious after the tent has been erected. Some manufacturers color-code the sleeves, and this helps. In bad weather, having practiced pitching your tent beforehand will be a dress rehearsal if you have to do it quickly.

Dome tents offer plenty of floor space and are designed to ride out heavy winds.

41

Domes are here to stay, however, for several reasons. They offer maximum room for their size and weight, and their crisscrossing poles make them extremely rigid—therefore good in windy conditions.

Domes are classified as *freestanding*, meaning you can pitch them without using guylines and stakes, attaching these after the tent is up. Freestanding tents also offer the added convenience of portability; you can set them up in one location and move them—in one piece—to another (within a reasonable distance) if your first site is too rocky or uneven.

"Freestanding" does *not* mean leaving your tent unstaked. At the very least, staking is required to help pull the rainfly taut (and therefore rainproof) at midpoints on each side of the tent. Bear in mind that an unstaked freestanding tent *can become airborne* when hit with a good gust of wind.

The Hoop Tent

This tent design may have been the precursor to the more adaptable and improved dome tent. Designed for use by serious backpackers (and others who opt to shed the weight of heavier tents), the hoop tent is a usually cylindrical design with curved sidewalls. Hoop tents are lightweight because they only use two poles but are a bit less spacious than domes or A-frames.

Hoop tents are for weight-conscious backpackers.

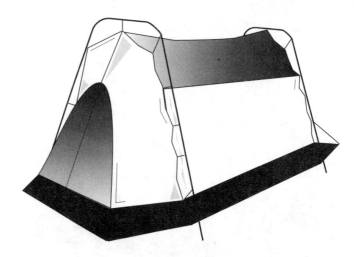

Some of these tents feature a fold-back covering that permits occupants (in pleasant weather) to see the sky through extra-big panels of mosquito netting. Although this design can withstand high winds, some models with sloped entrances encourage rain to migrate inside.

The Bivvy (Tent and Sack)

Bivouac (or *bivvy*) sacks are one-man "tents" that typically exist in the domain of the serious hiker. These "tents" resemble narrow tubes that have the unfortunate reputation of sealing in body moisture because the walls of the tent aren't allowed to "breathe" as they do in other tent designs. Bivvies often have a large hoop that supports the front end, keeping the fabric off your head.

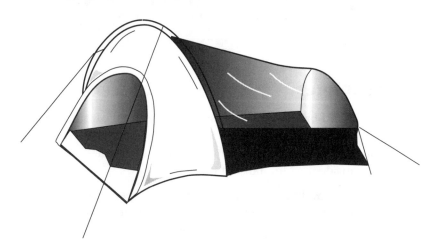

Bivouacs come in two styles: A tent version, which is essentially a hoop tent, and a bivvy sack, which encloses a single person like a cocoon.

Besides the breathability problem, there is also no room for camping gear inside the tent; equipment left outside could be soaked in a downpour. In this case, you'll have to cover your equipment with some sort of rainproofing—in the form of plastic garbage bags or under a rain poncho, or tarpaulin.

"Bivvy" sacs have no supporting ribs. In effect, the bivvy sac is a form of sleeping bag cover that offers some waterproofing and wind protection (not insulation). There is even less room inside these types of "tents," which have the unfortunate nickname—and rightly so—of "body bags."

Family-Sized Tents

Last, but not least, are family-sized tents designed to accommodate up to six people. These are made more for car campers; they're less practical for backpackers, cyclists, or those traveling by canoe. These weighty monsters are really more like the equivalent of a log cabin with apartment-size rooms and "windows;" they weigh between 20 and 30 pounds. Some models are made from a cotton/polyester blend, others from a nylon or polyester, and still others from canvas.

These tents are meant for campers who plan to stay at the same site for longer periods of time.

Family tents are multiroom tents designed for those who want to stay put for a while.

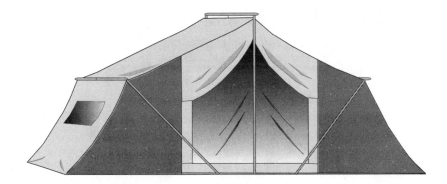

Vestibules and Other Features

Many tents come equipped with vestibules. A *vestibule* is essentially a tent's front porch. It is designed to protect gear from the elements and can offer a canopy under which to cook in foul weather. (*Never cook inside a tent.*) A vestibule also gives you somewhere to put your shoes—a place that is not inside the tent, but not outside either.

Most tents offer mesh storage pouches that are good for storing small personal items like watches, compasses, and small flashlights. Just don't forget to *remove* those things when you stuff the tent back into its sack. Many manufacturers include a small loop (not to be confused with tent poles) in the mid-center of the tent that you can use to suspend a flashlight.

> **I'LL TELL YA!...**
>
> **Conventional Wisdom**
> Look for tents with nylon-coil zippers. They're less prone to breaking than metal zippers, and are lighter. Examine a tent's zippers carefully: Sticky or recalcitrant zippers may be a sign of future trouble.

Even if weather isn't a problem, insects sometimes are. Well-built tents feature finely woven insect netting in their roof panels, entrances, and end panels. Depending on the time of year and location, a tent is valuable as a shelter from the elements and an impenetrable barrier to mosquitoes and black flies. Such netting lets you see your surroundings while holding off the invasion of biting insects.

Groundsheets

Although the bottom of your tent is made of reinforced material that is thicker than either its rainfly or tent walls, the forest floor is an abrasive place. To prevent accidental punctures from rocks and the like, lay a plastic ground cover under the tent's floor. This *groundsheet* should be cut to fit the shape of the tent floor—as big, but no bigger. A groundsheet that peeks out from the edges of the tent will channel water underneath, and no degree of waterproofing will stop water from seeping inside. You can buy material for groundsheet at both outdoor equipment and hardware stores. Plastic from hardware stores is perfectly fine and often cheaper.

Tent floors should be made of the same type of tough, waterproof material used in the first six inches of the tent walls (nearest the floor) to form a sort of plastic "bathtub" shape in the bottom of the tent. Lighter-weight tents have ground-level seams that are sealed with waterproof tape. The rest of the tent will be made of non-waterproof taffeta. Seams on the tent floor will be "sealed" with lengths of waterproof tape. But check: Some manufacturers don't seal the seams and you'll have to do it yourself. Remember to examine a tent's wall seams as well. Tents are manufactured with bound and lap-felled seams. *Bound seams* are created by stitching through a layer of material folded over two other pieces being joined; they are the weaker of the two types.

Lap-felled seams are created by placing the two pieces of the fabric being joined over one another, then folding and stitching them together. Better quality tents are made using as many lap-felled seams as possible, and have bound seams when more than two pieces of material are joined. Generally speaking, lighter, better tents employ lap-felled seams, which are flatter than bound seams.

Rules

Rainflies have to be seam-sealed every few seasons. Water tends to leak through needle holes in a tent's stitching; therefore manufacturers often include an applicator bottle of sealant designed to close these tiny holes. Spread the fly (and the tent if it is not seam-taped) out on the ground; run a thin coating of sealant along the seams. Allow the sealant to dry according to the instructions on the bottle, and then apply a second coat. Sealing seams every season helps ensure that your tent will perform the way it's supposed to.

A Tent for All Seasons

Tents are designed for use in specific seasons; ask yourself in which season(s) you plan to use your tent. *Three-season* tents are designed for use in spring, summer, and fall. So-called *four-season* tents are manufactured with the worst weather in mind, but ventilation will not be so good in warm weather. Such heavy-duty tents have more poles and extra waterproofing to withstand blistering winds and raging rainshowers and snowstorms. They are also quite a bit more expensive than the three-season variety; a four-season may be overkill for weekend or summer camping unless you plan to do your camping in snowy conditions.

Rules

Picking out an untouched site may be a nice idea, but where designated spots exist, set up there in respect for nature. Such "established" sites make it easy to put up a tent, but more importantly are designed to encourage low-impact camping by localizing usage.

Pitching Tents—Practice Makes Perfect

On one trip we failed to set the tent up before setting off. On arriving at our campsite we spent the good part of an afternoon trying to figure out how to pitch what was reputed to be one of the better-designed tents on the camping scene. The thing was—and still is—a nylon Rubik's Cube with a system of crisscrossing poles that defied comprehension in how they fitted together.

Although varied designs and configurations make it hard to describe every conceivable tent-pitching scenario in detail. Tents come with pitching instructions, and these are most often straightforward and to the point, complete with pictures and diagrams that attempt to make everything foolproof.

But always remember one Golden Rule: Practice pitching a tent before heading off on your vacation!

Pitching a tent in a backyard in perfect weather when no wind is interfering with the procedure is very different from pitching the same tent in field conditions—which can include billowing winds. And the flimsy little instruction manual that came with the tent won't seem straightforward when you're rushing to set the thing up against the threat of darkening skies and thunderclouds.

Even if you *have* practiced pitching the tent (do this at the beginning of every season), here is one good plan of action.

Lay the tent, rainfly, and other components on the ground to see what you're working with. The tent should be right-side-up, with the floor on the ground and the pole sleeves and hooks exposed and evident. The rainfly should be laid out similarly, so that any pole loops are also exposed.

Next, assemble all the poles and lay them out on the ground according to size (some clever designs employ poles that are all of the same length). The first order of business for most tents is to run the main poles through the nylon loops and hoops so that the poles crisscross.

The next item is to magically transform the tent from a heap of nylon on the ground into—egads!—a structure that you and your fellow travelers can sleep under. This will involve tensioning those crisscrossed poles so they fit into pegs or grommets at opposite corners of the tent. Some tents need to be staked at several key points before you can feed the poles through the nylon and plastic hooks. And older-style A-frames have rigid poles that support the tent and fit together without bending.

Rules

The most boring-looking campsite may be the best one. On well-traveled trails, use the designated campsites instead of trampling on virgin territory. Designated sites will also have an obvious place where heat-generating fires may be set, if permitted.

Once the main part of the tent is up, place the fly over the top of the tent and secure it to the tent structure itself. With this setup, you clip the tent to the underside of the fly or otherwise suspend it under the fly after setup. Because there are so many varied designs, you're on your own at this point to assemble according to package instructions.

The final step is to anchor the tent at key points with plastic or metal alloy stakes, and guylines if necessary. In fair weather you might be tempted to forego this final step if you're working with a freestanding tent. If a strong wind rises up, your tent may take on wind and take flight if the conditions are right, regardless of the fact that it is filled with gear.

Windy Days and Windy Nights

In high winds, you'll have to deviate somewhat from the general recommendations just given.

Gather together stones, small logs, or other heavy objects to hold down the tent and fly when they are laid out on the ground. If you can, involve others in pitching the tent when wind conditions get blustery. Stake the tent at one or more of its corners to help prevent it from taking off in a sudden gust. The next step is to get all the tent poles together and plan a strategy for getting them into place. Thread the poles through the tent's loops and tension the poles in place.

The Least You Need to Know

➤ You should decide how you'll be using the tent. If backpacking is the name of the game, concentrate on light weight. (There is a trade-off between weight and comfort in some cases.) The less you add to the weight of the backpack, the better.

➤ Estimate future camping requirements. Will the tent be used for one person? Two? Three or four? Select a tent with an eye to future needs.

➤ Choose a tent that's easy to set up. Its main purpose is to protect you from the elements; if the weather changes suddenly, you want to be able to take cover in a hurry.

➤ Always rehearse tent pitching before and after you buy a tent. In windy weather and in the dark you should have a pretty good idea of how the tent comes together.

AND WE CAN DO EACH OTHER'S HAIR, AND STAY UP ALL NIGHT AND TALK ABOUT BOYS—

Chapter 5

What You Need for the Slumber Party

In This Chapter

➤ Selecting the right sleeping bag for the trip

➤ Evaluating which fill is best

➤ Choosing a sleeping bag on the basis of temperature rating

➤ Picking the best sleeping mat for the job

Getting the right sleeping bag is important. Not only is it one of the big three investments you have to make (the others are a tent and—for hikers—a backpack), it is also one piece of equipment that will add to your enjoyment of the whole trip. And a satisfied outdoor vacationer is, well, a happy camper.

Believe it or not, choosing a sleeping bag may seem more complicated than selecting a tent. Sleeping bags come in a wide range of designs and shapes, filled with a variety of natural and synthetic materials (some with space-age names; others with wide-ranging claims to fame). Choosing a sleeping bag, however, is a relatively simple matter.

The main thing to remember when shopping for a sleeping bag is that its main function is to keep you warm on chilly nights. Ideally, it should also be as comfortable to sleep in as your bedding at home. Think of a sleeping bag as part of a whole comfort *system* that begins with the tent and ends with a soft sleeping mat underneath. In-between, there's you, tucked away and warm in your sleeping bag. A good sleeping bag costs $100 and up.

The Lowdown on Sleeping Bags

Sleeping bags work by trapping warm air created by the body to prevent it from cooling off. A sleeping bag should also be *breathable* (that is, allow perspiration vapor to escape). The larger the airspace inside the bag, the less efficient the insulating properties of the bag. There are three main styles of sleeping bags: the *mummy-shaped* bag (so named because its shape resembles an Egyptian mummy), the *tapered* bag, and the *rectangular* bag. Each design has different insulating properties because of its shape, and each, depending on the fill inside, will do a better job of keeping the person inside warm.

Sleeping bag styles

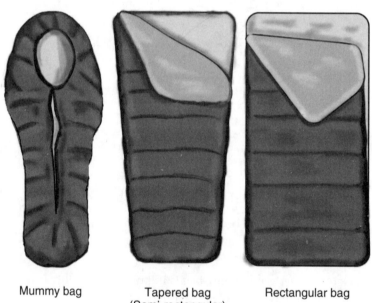

Mummy bag

Tapered bag
(Semi-rectangular)

Rectangular bag

Mummy Bags

Efficiency has almost everything to do with shape, or more specifically, with how little or how much airspace there is to heat in the bag. The more airspace, the more there is to heat. Tapered and mummy-shaped bags reduce the amount of airspace inside the bag; therefore, they are warmer than rectangular bags.

The mummy has become the high-performance, lightweight standard for sleeping bags. Because the amount of space inside a mummy bag is limited by its shape, it's the style most often chosen for trips of all kinds. It's practically *de rigueur* for those expedition-style trips that border on daredevil adventures into the frozen wilderness.

Mummy bags completely encapsulate the occupant and may seem constraining when compared to rectangular bags. Mummy bags should also feature closing hoods that tighten up around the head with the pull of a drawstring. All this in the name of limiting airspace? Is it worth the trouble?

Well, yes and no.

A tight-fitting bag will keep you warmer than a looser one will. But if you're doing most of your outdoor sleeping in spring and summer, you won't need extra-heavy-duty temperature protection. And don't forget region and topography. Temperatures at higher elevations will be cooler than in low-lying areas. If you're traveling in Alaska or Newfoundland, temperatures at night may also be cool in the summer.

As with all equipment, the acid test is finding the perfect fit for your body type—meaning your girth and length, to put it plainly. Climb into as many sleeping bags as you can before settling on the one you want to live with for years. Check out how it feels, and how your feet feel in the "foot box" at the end of the bag. Mummy bags designed for use in extremely cold weather will seem the most constraining, simply because they are designed to protect the person inside from the vagaries of hypothermia. Warmth will have a lot to do with what insulation the bag is filled with, too; in the quest for the perfect bag, shape is only one ingredient in the mix. Equally important for backpackers is weight. Sleeping bags can weigh anywhere between just over a pound and a half to six pounds, depending on the amount of insulation and season the bag is designed for. Bags designed for summer use will be lighter than those designed for winter. Down bags weigh less than synthetics when compared to each other's insulating capabilities.

If you toss and turn in your sleep, plan to venture into the outdoors only when it's warm, and entertain the possibility of sleeping in close proximity to others, then a rectangular bag may be for you. Many of these bags are zippered all around and can be joined together without much trouble. Some mummies offer this option too, but because they have hoods, they don't join together as conveniently.

Rectangular bags have no hoods at all, and in the face of colder weather don't offer the same insulating properties as mummy bags. Shape is also a factor: There is more dead airspace to warm inside the bag because it isn't tapered, which means less efficiency in keeping you warm. Some manufacturers offer a compromise between the mummy and the rectangular bag: A tapered bag with a fold-down hood that isn't as wide as a rectangular bag, but not as constraining as a mummy bag.

In addition to their reduced efficiency, rectangular bags are often heavier and bulkier. Thus they are a less-than-ideal choice for backpackers, who often encounter colder temperatures.

Conventional Wisdom
Sleeping bags should have an insulated panel running along the length of the zipper. This *draft tube* prevents heat from escaping through the zipper.

There is an obvious trade-off between the heat-efficient mummy and the inefficient, but roomier, rectangular bag. Recreational campers will not have much need (or appreciation) for the insulating advantages of the mummy bag. If you fall into this category, remember to try on your sleeping bag before purchasing it. Any sleeping bag should feel as though it would be warm and cozy in cool weather, but also allow you to loosen it up or fold it down when temperatures heat up.

Down Fills versus Synthetic Fills

The warmth and insulating properties of any sleeping bag are related to what material, and how much, it is filled with. You will have two basic choices of fill: synthetics or down.

Down

Down-filled models will be more expensive than synthetics, but last longer and are warmer. As any duck or goose could tell you, feathers are a terrific insulator. Add to this down's warmth-to-weight ratio and you have a winning combination. Backpackers and cyclists will especially appreciate the weight factor of down-filled bags.

Down bags are rated according to their *fill power:* 650 cubic inches per ounce means that one ounce will fill 650 cubic inches of space. A rating of 500 to 550 is pretty standard; a 750 to 850 fill rating is considered excellent. As fill power increases, so does price. When considering a particular bag, evaluate it carefully according to the season you'll be outdoors.

Conventional Wisdom
Those who are allergic to feathers and animals should consider purchasing a sleeping bag filled with one of the synthetics. If your eyes tear or you sneeze around down-filled pillows, you may be allergic to feathers. Check with your physician or an allergist.

Sleeping bags (and other garments) are filled with one of two kinds of down: goose or duck. Downs of equal fill power perform equally well, and there is nothing inherent in goose down to make it better than duck down. But the best goose down has a higher fill power than the best duck down, which tops out at about 550 cubic inches per ounce. Check the fiber content labels on the sleeping bags to make sure you're purchasing the right down fill.

Synthetics

Synthetic-filled bags are a cheaper alternative to the down-filled varieties. They appear on the market in an ever-expanding variety, but essentially all are packed with some kind of proprietary fibers (whether chopped or continuous filament).

Synthetic-fill bags are not as warm for their weight as down-filled equivalents, and they don't last as long. On the upside, they are less expensive and are more resistant to wetness. When wet, they also retain some insulating value; sodden down-filled bags do not. Down bags also hang on to moisture longer, which can add extra weight—and may contribute to night-time discomfort if the bag hasn't had a chance to dry.

All sleeping bags are rated according to seasonal temperatures:

40° = Warm weather (Summer) (1 1/2 pounds)

20° = Three season (Spring, summer, and fall) (3 to 4 pounds)

0° = Cold weather (Early spring and late fall) (3 to 4 pounds)

-15° = Cold weather (Winter) (6 pounds)

This guide is only representative because some people adapt to temperatures differently than others. Bags are rated for the average male, sleeping in a tent on a sleeping mat. As a generalization, women tend to sleep colder. Most people find bags rated for 20°F quite satisfactory for most conditions. If you're the type of person that gets colder than others at night and needs more covers, then go one step up in a bag's insulating capability.

Safe Camping
Avoid alcoholic beverages in cold weather. They may contribute to hypothermia in extreme cases, despite an initial feeling of warmth on the part of the drinker. The best cold-weather drinks are a cup of hot soup or tea.

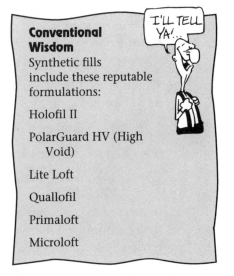

Conventional Wisdom
Synthetic fills include these reputable formulations:

Holofil II

PolarGuard HV (High Void)

Lite Loft

Quallofil

Primaloft

Microloft

Bag Construction

The way your bag is built has to do with the way the fill is held in place between its inner and outer surfaces. Any fill will move around inside the bag if it isn't held in place in some way, and this is accomplished by compartmentalizing the fill in a number of different ways.

Down bags need baffles or chambers to keep the loose feather insulation in place. Bags filled with synthetics are sewn together or shingled because the insulation is usually spun together as a whole and doesn't have to be contained the same way.

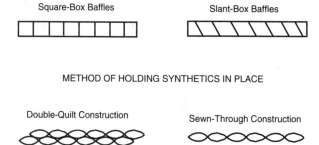

METHOD OF HOLDING DOWN IN PLACE

Square-Box Baffles

Slant-Box Baffles

METHOD OF HOLDING SYNTHETICS IN PLACE

Double-Quilt Construction

Sewn-Through Construction

Never mind about all the complicated double-speak about the merits of one type of construction over the other. Just pay attention to what season the bag is rated for and whether you want a synthetic-fill bag or one filled with down.

Whatever the fill pattern and method, a sleeping bag should be designed for three important functions:

➤ To hold insulation in place

➤ To protect against wind

➤ To permit perspiration vapor inside the bag to escape

In most cases, a sleeping bag's outer shell is made from taffeta nylon or ripstop because of their lightness and fine weave. They may also be made from poly taffeta, microfiber, or Dryloff.

The inner lining should be both soft and able to *wick* body moisture away. The inner lining may be made of nylon, but may not feel as nice against the skin as a blend of nylon and polyester. Sleeping bag liners may also be used, both as an extra layer for warmth and as a removable and washable add-on.

Care

Any time spent in the outdoors will cause you to get a little dirty. Clothes can be cleaned easily, but more care is required with sleeping bags.

Every attempt should be made to discourage sleeping bags from taking on moisture. This means airing sleeping bags out whenever possible, and preferably on a daily basis. All bags should be encouraged to loft, meaning that they should be removed from their carrying sacks and shaken out periodically. And sleeping bags are never meant to be stored for long periods in their traveling bags. Doing so compresses the fibers—especially in synthetic bags—and results in a loss of insulating properties. Store sleeping bags flat, or hang them up in a large bag. Many manufacturers provide storage bags for exactly this purpose.

Cleaning

Synthetic bags may be cleaned in a washing machine. For best results (and to avoid extra strain on the bag), use a commercial machine that spins clothes clean instead of a standard machine that uses an agitator blade.

Down sleeping bags shouldn't be dry cleaned either because most dry cleaners can't handle down bags, but washed in a commercial machine with no agitator, and with mild soap. Dry the bag on low, and tumble dry with a number of tennis balls to encourage the bag to loft.

Take extreme care when handling a wet down bag. Down absorbs a tremendous amount of water and can become extremely heavy—so heavy, in fact, that the inner walls holding the down in place can be damaged beyond repair. And remember: Each time you wash a down bag, it loses some of its capability to insulate against the cold. It's better to remove surface dirt without washing, or at least tolerate it, than to risk a cleaning mishap.

> **I'LL TELL YA!...**
>
> **Conventional Wisdom**
> Ask at the store where you purchased your sleeping bag about how it can be cleaned. They may have specific advice for your type of sleeping bag.

Blow-Up Bedding

Besides the cocoon, you'll require some kind of sleeping mat to soften out the bumps in the ground. My preference for trips where there isn't much carrying involved—like a canoe trip without portaging (carrying your canoe over land)—is a 2 1/2-inch-thick foam mattress covered in fabric. Although this type of mat is extremely comfortable, it's too heavy and bulky for backpacking, cycling, or other trips that require compactness and weight. Inflatable mattresses have all but disappeared from the outdoor bedding scene, and for good reason: They inevitably got punctured and needed patching. They were also cumbersome and heavy. That's why God created Therm-a-Rest mattresses.

Therm-a-Rest Mattresses

No matter what type of camping you end up doing, it won't be long before you encounter a seeming miracle of modern design and ingenuity in outdoor sleeping technology. The Therm-a-Rest mattress is a compact piece of outdoor bedding that becomes a lightweight roll you can conveniently attach to the bottom of a backpack. This self-inflating mat has a nylon outer shell covering (and bonded to) a foam-cushioned core. It comes to life when you unroll it and open a valve in one corner that allows air into the inner chamber. Blowing into the valve for a few seconds speeds up the inflating process.

Conventional Wisdom

A hammock strung between two trees can become a sort of wilderness couch. A hammock weighs almost nothing and can even be used as a bed on warm, clear nights when insects aren't a concern.

Nothing beats the Therm-a-Rest mattress for comfort, compactness, and portability. These mats are quite durable, though you should take care not to snag one on a branch or lay it over sharp stones on the ground. A repair kit for the mat is available; keep one in your backpack on longer trips so you're not left without a comfortable bed to look forward to in the evening.

Therm-a-Rest mats come in a number of configurations, including an ultra-light weight for trekkers with serious weight concerns. They are also available in two lengths: three-quarter and full. Try each out; determine which length and weight are right for you.

Closed-Cell Foam Mats

For a more rugged—and cheaper—night's sleep, consider one of the *closed-cell* foam mats for your night under the stars. These mats come in three-quarter and full-length versions and offer a reasonable comfort-to-weight-to-price ratio. Some manufacturers incorporate a ridged design that adds comfort and traps air in pockets for greater insulation against cold ground. Closed-cell mats are available in different thicknesses and weights from a range of manufacturers; you'll have to try out various mats in the purchasing process.

Pillows

A pillowcase stuffed with clothes works nicely as a pillow in the outdoors, but there are other options. Commercially available inflatable pillows offer a little more comfort for the weary traveler, as does the inflated bladder from an expired box of wine.

The Least You Need to Know

➤ There's no substitute for climbing into a sleeping bag to determine whether it's the one for you. Forget about being embarrassed; reputable outdoor equipment stores encourage this kind of behavior.

➤ Some people run warmer or colder than others; the makers of sleeping bags may not have your particular body-comfort levels in mind when they temperature-rate their products. If you seem to get colder than others, select a bag that's rated for colder weather.

➤ Down-fill sleeping bags are more expensive than synthetic-fill bags, but they last longer. Consider price versus longevity when buying a bag.

➤ Mummy-shaped bags are the *de facto* standard for serious sleeping bags. The mummy shape cuts down on dead airspace around the sleeper's body, making it more efficient (though more confining) than rectangular-shaped bags.

➤ A tapered bag is a good compromise if cold-weather camping is out of the picture. Purely recreational campers who camp in warm weather can stick to rectangular bags.

➤ Therm-a-Rest sleeping mats are the Cadillacs of outdoor bedding. They are quite durable and more comfortable than closed-cell foam bedding.

How to Be an Outdoor Gourmet

A big part of any camping trip—and vacation, for that matter—is food and mealtime. Much has been made of mealtimes outdoors, but two issues are the biggest:

➤ How much to bring. Carry enough for the length and type of trip you have in mind.

➤ How you plan to carry it. Lugging food in a backpack is a weighty concern; stuffing it into a canoe, car, or other "holding" tank limits wear and tear on your body.

The amount of food that the body needs each day is also a determinant—and that can vary with the type of activity you'll be involved in. Hiking burns more energy than canoeing; hikers will therefore feel hungrier at the end of the day than those who just loll around a campsite reading. Younger people with higher metabolisms will burn more calories and need to eat more food than an older person. Those involved in outdoor activities use the *two-pound rule*: A typical calorie requirement will hover around 3,500 to 4,500 calories per day. The rough equivalent in food weighs two pounds.

No-Muss, No-Fuss Culinary Skills

Success in the wilderness kitchen depends on planning—a lot of it. Square One is to make sure you bring enough food, but not too much. Make lists, check them twice, and tailor them to your trip. On a longer backpacking trip, each person in the party may be responsible for his or her own food selection—and for carrying it—provided everyone agrees. Another plan of action is to designate one person in the party to be responsible for all matters relating to food, including making sure that cutlery (Lexan or some other plastic that stands up to washing), plates, pots, and pans come along.

The Weekend and Week-Long Picnic

The general rule of thumb is that you can take whatever you want on trips lasting only two to four days. You'll have to be more selective on trips lasting five to seven days; combine lightweight (such as freeze-dried or dehydrated) foods with the heavier ones (such as canned foods). On trips lasting more than 10 days, you'll have to take along *only* lightweight foods.

Safe Camping
The smell of food may summon unwelcome company. Bears are a problem in many parts of the country. This means that all food must be suspended, out of the reach of bears, before turning in for the night. Find a tree at least 300 feet away from camp, and suspend all food in a sturdy bag 10 feet off the ground from a tree branch. The bag with food in it should be at least 10 feet away from the tree trunk.

Whatever your carrying method and trip length, menu planning should be kept plain and simple. I've been on too many trips where each person in the party brought along enough food for everyone else. This resulted in too much spoilage and meant that all the effort spent in transporting the food was also wasted. Planning is paramount to success in the wilderness kitchen.

The food you bring with you should match the type of trip you're undertaking. On a backpacking trip where weight is a big concern, freeze-dried, dehydrated, and dried foods will help limit weight. On backpacking trips take essential equipment along with as much food as possible. Try and select foods that provide a lot of energy for their size and weight. A jar of peanut butter, for instance, is a better choice than a jar of jam: peanut butter ounce for ounce will provide more calories than jam. On trips where food and equipment doesn't need to be lugged on your back, canned foods and pre-prepared meals packed in airtight plastic containers can come along. And be sure to look at the recommended preparation time on the product packaging. Some meals take only minutes, while others take a lot longer. You'll want to factor cooking times into the time it takes to set up camp, as well as the extra fuel you'll need for longer-to-prepare meals (see the section on camp stoves later in this chapter).

Most freeze-dried hiking "meals" aren't that appetizing under normal circumstances. But after a hard day's hike, they will seem wonderful after you bring them back to life with water. One word of advice here: A meal intended for two is *really* only meant for one, and usually needs to be supplemented with something else. Another word of advice: Freeze-dried meals are quite expensive.

Another matter is hot food and cold food. There's nothing like a hot meal at the end of the day. To accomplish this luxury, you'll need to heat food over a campfire or portable camping stove, which I'll cover later on in the chapter.

Rules

Washing dishes in the outdoors is more of a chore than at home. All handwashing and dishwashing should be done at least 100 feet from bodies of water; food particles should be buried. Do not rinse plates, pots, and pans in natural sources of water—it introduces food that shouldn't be there. Try to use only heated water to clean your dishes in the wilderness. Avoid using soap; sprinkle the dishwater over a large area when you're done.

Menu Madness

Putting together a decent menu in the outdoors is a bit of a challenge if you're carrying your food into the woods. Below you'll find some suggestions for assembling the basic elements for a reasonably varied menu. Note that the idea here is to mix and match items from other meals. Remember to pack more of the items that you're going to borrow from other meals; try to vary what you're serving from day to day.

Breakfast of Champions

Coffee and tea

Eggs (carried in special egg holders or padded box, also in powdered versions)

Bacon (for shorter trips)

Grapefruit/oranges

Honey (can be used as a sweetener)

Cereal (Cream of Wheat or instant oatmeal for a hot breakfast)

Powdered milk/condensed milk (depending on weight constraints)

Noodle soup (chicken or ramen)

Bagels (bread goes moldy faster)

Lunch

Cheese

Crackers

Bagels

Peanut butter

Sardines

Apples

Dinner

This meal takes more mixing and matching than others. Try to put together meals that consist of at least four kinds of foods: carbohydrates, protein, vegetables, and sugars (for dessert).

Pasta (vermicelli cooks fast)

Kraft dinners

Potatoes (instant flakes)

Rice (fast-cooking, such as Minute Rice)

Couscous

Soups (dehydrated packages and ramen)

Tuna (canned)

Chicken (canned)

Turkey (canned)

Tomato paste

Grated romano or parmesan cheese

Carrots

Onions

Cabbage

Snacks and Desserts

Chocolate bars

Gorp (a trail mixture of nuts, seeds, M&Ms, dried fruits, and dried oatmeal flakes)

Granola

Dried fruit

Fruitcake

Hot chocolate (instant, pre-sweetened variety)

Marshmallows

Understanding Nature's Waterworks

Humans and most animals can survive without eating for long periods of time. But without regular doses of water, dehydration can result in heatstroke and hypothermia. It is important to drink water regularly, especially in hot weather (in which the body requires at least *four quarts of water or more a day*).

Carry a filled canteen or water bottle at all times, and try to fill up at designated spots along a trail or campground. Natural water sources may *look* crystal-clear and clean, but don't assume they are. The recent emergence of *giardia lamblia*—an organism transmitted from the feces of animals and humans—has created the need for water purification in the backwoods. Giardia (which takes about two weeks to incubate) may cause cramps, diarrhea, and vomiting. Make sure you purchase water purification tablets or a filter where you buy camping gear. You're usually safe bathing with clean-looking water, but don't drink it or brush your teeth with it.

Rules
Always make sure that you are indeed allowed to build a fire from scrounged wood in a campground. Some state and federal parks require that you purchase pre-cut wood or bring your own.

You have three choices here: To run water taken from lakes and streams through a $30 to $200 water-filtration device, boil water before you drink it, or add commercially available water-purification chemicals—usually in the form of iodine—to water.

Those with thyroid conditions or anyone who is pregnant should avoid using iodine. Follow the package directions on the tincture, tablets, or crystals that come with the preparation you choose. In addition, chemically treated water may have to be flavored with Kool-Aid or some other powdered additive to mask an unpleasant taste. Choose water filters that can remove viruses, or use iodine in locations where viruses are a concern (overseas).

Water needs to boil for at least three minutes before all microorganisms are destroyed. This takes time and stove fuel. Still, it is an almost surefire way of making water potable. The downside is that if you want a cool glass of water on a hot day, you'll need to wait for the water to cool off.

Good water filters are expensive; they boast filter screens of between 0.2 and 1.0 microns. The lower the screen's number, the more pathogens and bacteria it removes. The screens inside these devices will need replacing as time goes by, and water filters, though compact, are *still another* piece of equipment that has to be packed and carried.

> **I'LL TELL YA!..**
>
> **Conventional Wisdom**
>
> Extended outdoor vacations of a week or more—especially those for which you establish a "base camp"—may benefit from organizing all kitchen equipment in one container or *wanigan*. Some kind of hard-edged box is best for such a purpose, although it's not practical for hikers.

Grills

Car campers may have the luxury of bringing along a vital piece of backyard gear: a gas or briquette grill. Propane grills are handy because you turn on the gas and ignite it with a match—no muss, no fuss. Briquettes are another matter. You have to saturate the pieces of charcoal in fuel and light the charcoal, causing it to flame up. The noxious fumes created are antithetical to your wooded surroundings. A gas grill can be turned off, briquettes are left until they turn to ashes and then you have the hassles of disposing of them. Some camping carnivores insist that meat tastes better if cooked over charcoal. But is it really worth the extra hassle?

Having a Gas—Choosing and Using Stoves

Without a reliable source of heat for cooking, outdoor mealtime can be a major disappointment. Many experienced campers rely solely on cooking their food over an open fire, but this method is unreliable for two opposing reasons: During dry spells, officials often initiate fire bans to minimize the risk of forest fires; in rainy weather, the average outdoor adventurer may find that a campfire is difficult—sometimes impossible—to start. Many wilderness areas don't allow fires at all. Cooking on a stove is your only option in this case. For these reasons alone (not to mention sheer convenience), it's absolutely vital that outdoor vacationers invest in a good camp stove.

Stoves are available in a range of configurations that burn a variety of fuels. There are many makes and models on the market, so making a choice can be perplexing. But once you compare the type of outdoor vacationing you'll be doing with various stove models and prices, you'll have fewer choices than you thought. Good stoves cost between $40 and $100.

Camp stoves are designed to burn at least one type of gas; some burn several varieties, just in case their owners can't find a particular type of fuel where they camp. Fuel systems for the stoves come in three basic configurations: refillable built-in fuel tanks, refillable detachable tanks, and cartridges.

White-gas stove with built-in tank. Multi-fuel versions are also available.

Multi-fuel stove with separate, detachable fuel tank

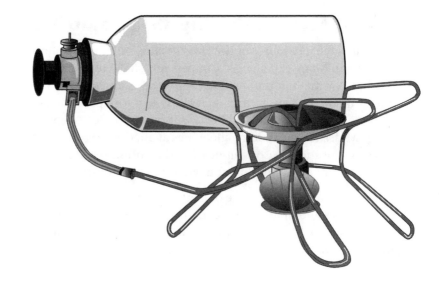

Butane/propane stove with screw-in cartridge

White Gas

White gas is essentially a highly refined version of the stuff you put into a car. This extremely clean-burning fuel produces a good deal more heat than other fuels. Widely available in North America, it is the fuel of choice for many campers and hikers because many stoves have been designed to burn it as their main fuel. White gas must be pressurized to burn, so you have to pump up the fuel tank before you light the stove. When you've got it going, the fuel line heats up; the gas inside the line vaporizes and expands.

Since the gas in this type of stove is under pressure, users should be aware that these stoves can flare up suddenly. Two designs are common; your white-gas stove may have a *ported burner* or be a *plate burner*. Plate burners burn noisily. Ported burners are quieter and operate similarly to home gas stoves.

White-gas stoves are the most popular type in use; manufacturers of *multi-fuel* stoves have adapted white-gas stoves to work with other fuels, such as kerosene and unleaded automotive gasoline. These alternative fuels are dirtier, which means more cleaning and stove maintenance than you'd have from burning white gas alone. Campers who find themselves without a ready supply of white gas will certainly appreciate having other options, especially overseas and in colder conditions. On the road, white gas is readily available from local merchants. If you'll be camping a lot, purchase a one-gallon container at the beginning of the season; they usually cost about $12.

Kerosene

Kerosene was the precursor to gasoline as fuel, and is still used in remote parts of the world where white gas is difficult to find. It is also the gas of choice for high altitude mountaineers. It is harder to light, and stoves that use it require priming. (Priming involves spreading a combustible paste on the burner to preheat it. This is also necessary when starting white-gas stoves in cold conditions.) Kerosene stoves operate in the same way as plate burner white-gas stoves: Vaporized fuel is forced out over a circular plate where it becomes the cooking flame. Kerosene tends to produce soot when it burns, and in most cases gives off a smell. As an alternative fuel in multi-fuel stoves, it is less desirable than white gas. In a pinch, however, it will do the job quite faithfully. Kerosene is widely available from camping stores and hardware stores alike, and is cheaper than white gas as a fuel.

Butane and Propane

Butane and propane cartridge stoves are handy, lightweight models designed for backpackers who *don't* plan to scale Mount Everest on their next free weekend. A pressurized cylinder of butane (sometimes containing a combination of propane and butane) screws onto a burner designed to accept it. Butane cartridges are available in North America and Europe, and are a good choice for warm-weather campers and hikers who don't demand the extreme heat created by white gas. Of course, lower heat means you may have to wait twice as long for water to boil, but ease of use (no pumping or priming) may outweigh the extra cooking time. A downside to these stoves is that as you use up the butane inside the cylinder, the pressure drops—and so does the burner's heat output. Winter campers often bypass these stoves. Butane and propane cartridges are available at camping stores and are also stocked by hardware stores in regions where camping is popular. A cartridge runs about $7 to $8.

Rules

When a butane or propane/butane tank is empty, remember that you have to *pack it out* with all other unburnable garbage. Sadly, the increased popularity of these convenient stoves has a side effect: many well-traveled campgrounds are now littered with expired blue canisters.

Setting Up

Setting up your stove may be the most important part of using it. Look for a flat, even place to perch the stove. Because a camp stove's burner area is small, use the smallest pots and pans possible when you cook as they can become easily unbalanced. Some stoves may flare up if dirty or improperly primed, and there is a chance of personal injury: ensure that shirt cuffs are not dangling and that long hair is pulled back.

Safe Camping
Never use a stove to cook inside a tent! Not only is there a fire hazard (even though tents are made of fire-retardant materials), but the oxygen supply inside the tent can be severely depleted. If bad weather leaves you tent-bound, lean out the tent entrance to cook outside or in the vestibule.

When you shop for a camp stove, have the salesperson demonstrate how the stove works, even if that means filling it up with fuel and taking it outside to light on the sidewalk. If a thorough demonstration isn't possible, be sure to try the stove out in the backyard before you pack it for your trip. The last thing you want is to find out that either you don't know how to use the stove, or that it doesn't work. Release the pressure on tanks that are pumped up before packing them away inside a backpack or car trunk. Loosen the fuel tank cap to release pressure.

When the camping season is over, empty the stove's tank if you use one of the Coleman Peak I models. Store fuel bottles and partially used tanks of fuel in a garage or tool shed. White gas is highly flammable.

Ovens and Other Cooking Gadgetry

When you go to buy your stove, you'll probably encounter a range of other cooking apparatus. There are Dutch ovens that work with charcoal briquettes (bulky items), reflector ovens that use the heat created by a campfire to disperse heat over open or closed pots and pans (good for making a store-bought cake mix), and convection ovens that circulate heat around a closed pan. These cooking luxuries may seem like extravagant (and weighty) extras to most backpackers, but they may be suited for car and canoe campers who have *plenty* of room for extra equipment and food. Campers should pre-prepare baked items before heading off on a journey.

Those who prefer to stick to their cooking with just a stove should consider a few practical items to go along with their stoves. A windscreen, for example, will boost the efficiency of any stove, even in the absence of gusty winds. Windscreens are often designed with particular stove models in mind; so be sure to ask for one that fits the stove you've chosen.

Although old pots and pans will do an adequate, even admirable job, consider a set of specially designed camping pots that nest together. These space-saving sets feature pot lids that double as frying pans, and pot handles you can transfer from one pot to the next. If you do bring pots from your collection at home, they should be able to do double- or triple-duty. You can use a saucepan, for example, to cook soup and boil water; a frying pan may be used as a mixing bowl, a shallow pot for frankfurters and beans, and as a *frying pan* for the morning meal of bacon and eggs. When you plan your menu, don't forget that you'll need very much the same cooking implements you'd want at home—including spatulas and soup ladles.

For most of us, coffee is fairly important in the morning. In most cases, instant freeze-dried crystals will suffice. But for the more picky coffee drinker, there are espresso makers designed for the outdoors which do an admirable job of both making coffee and frothing milk—proving that life on the trail and in the woods isn't devoid of luxury.

Here's How
Established campsites will have an obvious place where fires can be built. Usually the fireplace is ringed with logs or stones where campers sit around the campfire. By keeping the fire low—or using embers after the fire has died down—pots and pans can be set right on top. Better yet, pack a small grate and support it on small stones over the heat. The grate will help stabilize pots and pans placed on top of it.

Other Stuff for the Shopping List

Besides food and a means of cooking it, you'll also need a number of items from the supermarket. Remember to pack paper towels, a pot scrubber, sealable plastic sandwich bags for spices and leftovers, garbage bags for unburnable garbage, Tupperware containers for food storage, and matches.

The Least You Need to Know

➤ Outdoor menu planning depends largely on the type and length of the trip. Week-enders can take almost anything; those planning a longer venture into the woods will need to pack lightweight, freeze-dried pouches of food available from outdoor-supply stores.

➤ Take along some "comfort" food for variety. Some favorite cookies or a cake can liven up a meal and add variety to the outdoor menu.

➤ For shorter trips, prepare meals in advance by pre-cooking as much as possible (pasta sauces can be cooked up, then stored in airtight plastic containers).

➤ All outdoor adventurers will need a stove of some kind. The most popular of these stoves use white gas or butane as fuels. Stoves that use white gas have hotter flames and therefore cook more quickly than models that burn butane. Butane stoves, however, tend to be easier to operate and may be suited to the short-term camper and hiker, and they are often cheaper.

➤ Always read the instructions that come with the stove and practice using it before you start your trip.

➤ People require approximately four quarts of water per day to maintain themselves. In hotter weather (or on long hikes), make sure you carry enough water in a canteen or can get appropriate water to purify from natural sources.

➤ Before drinking water from a natural source such as a lake, pond, or stream, be sure to purify it; use a filtering device, boil the water, or treat it with chemicals.

Fishing for the Camper

Imagine hiking through the woods and stopping for a break at a beautiful body of water—a sparkling river or a crystal clear lake. You muse about whether there are fish in there. Your head fills up with dreams about a peppy school of perch—or robust rock bass cooling off in a deep pool. And as the sun sets and you begin to prepare dinner—an aluminum envelope of freeze-dried chicken stew—those dreams seem even more appetizing.

Many campers and backpackers would like to try their hand at fishing. Some know there is nothing better than sitting by a quiet lake on a sunny day, listening to chirping birds and the purr of your fishing reel pulling your line through the water. Those are days that make the office seem a million miles away. Suddenly you feel a slight tug on the line.

A few moments later, you reel in that pretty speckled trout and realize the other important reason for fishing: Tonight's dinner will be a heck of a lot tastier than that package in the pack.

Still, despite all the pleasure it offers, many backpackers and campers don't think about fishing at all. Maybe they're scared off by movie images of fly fishermen with 10-foot-long rods wading though raging rivers in big rubber boots. Or perhaps they're just worried about every backpacker's biggest nightmare: Extra weight.

Well, luckily, you don't have to be an expert in fly fishing to catch trout. Nor do you have to weigh yourself down with lots of extra gear just to go fishing on a backpacking holiday—whether for food, fun, or both. In this chapter I'll tell you what you need to know about fishing while backpacking and camping—ultralight fishing from the shores of lakes, rivers, and streams.

Choosing a Packable Rod-and-Reel Set

The first thing you'll need to buy is a good, lightweight rod and reel. There are many kinds available on the market, but only a few are geared to the backpacker or camper. Go to your sporting goods store and tell them you want an ultralight rod and reel. There are several good models that are easy to disassemble; once apart, they take up little space in your pack. It's best to buy your rod and reel together, so they fit right, the same way you would buy hiking boots. Many of these ultralight sets have their own carrying case and together weigh less than a pound.

Reels

The camper should know about three basic types of fishing reels; each is fitted to a certain type of rod. *Casting* reels have a button on the back that you press to release the line. The line is rolled up on a spool and housed inside a metal casing. *Spinning* reels are similar except no metal casing covers the spool. They are less bulky than casting reels and better suited to backpackers. Both types of reels use *monofilament* fishing line. When you want to release the line on a spinning reel, you pull back on the half ring until it clicks open. *Fly* reels are bigger, and do not have a lever or a button.

Line

Monofilament line is made out of nylon. It is translucent and comes in a variety of colors and strengths. The strength of the line is known as the line's *test*. This is an estimation of how much weight the line can handle. The bigger the test, the bigger the fish the line can take without breaking. Always remember to loosen the drag before you begin fishing. Even the biggest pound test can break if it is completely taut when pulled in by a fish.

Fly line, which is much thicker than monofilament, is made of braided nylon coated with silicone. It's designed to be controlled with both rod and hand. At the end of the fly line, you attach an artificial, tied fly made of colored thread and a hook.

Both fly line and nonattachment line come in various *pound tests*, which are simply a measure of their strength. Ultralight reels normally use line no heavier than four-pound test.

Rods

Be sure you buy the type of rod that fits the type of reel you've chosen; the most popular are made out of graphite. A normal spinning or casting rod-reel set is best for all-purpose fishing, not only fly fishing. Fly fishing requires more skill, and is best done in rivers. Even if you decide on something more sophisticated (like fly-fishing gear), make sure everything you buy is ultralight. Some fishing rods are ten feet long when extended; these are much too large for backpacking, even in pieces. The ultralight varieties are between five and six feet long when assembled. They come apart into smaller pieces that fit together, or open and close like a telescope. Both models are easy to store in your pack.

Bait, Lures, and Flies

The craft of fly fishing involves whipping your rod back and forth, moving the line onto the river or stream so the fake fly looks like the real thing. Some of these flies are beautifully hand-tied and look remarkably real. Flies are rarely used with spinning or casting gear. Instead, spinning and casting usually involves live bait (like worms and minnows) or *lures*—fake bait. Lures come in many different varieties and sizes. Some lures are shiny, others look like minnows or make movements attractive to fish. They are especially useful when live bait is not available. Find out what kind of fish will be in the area you will be fishing in—and then bring the lures that those fish love. Fishing stores will provide this information, and most national parks and public wilderness areas provide information in the brochures they send regarding what species are found and where to find them.

> **Conventional Wisdom**
> There are hundreds of fishing lures on the market, but only a few main types. *Jigs* are used by motioning the top of your rod up and down, which makes the lure bounce on the bottom. *Spinners* have shiny blades that rotate quickly through the water when you reel your line in. *Spoons* make wobbling motions which are attractive to fish.

I'LL TELL YA!...

One of the most popular lures is a red and white colored spoon, known as "the daredevil." The daredevil is especially effective for catching perch or pike. And there are the lures that are made to look like real minnows. You may also see combinations, such as a spoon with a few small spinners on top. It's also good to mix some lures with live bait. Try attracting fish by tying on a small spinner a few inches above your baited hook. It's like putting up a neon sign above a restaurant.

Tackling the Fish

Now that you've got your rod and reel, you're also going to need something to put on the end of your line to attract the fish. The materials you need to do this are called *tackle*. For the type of fishing you'll be doing on a backpacking trip (I'm assuming you will be using either casting or spinning gear), keep your tackle to a minimum:

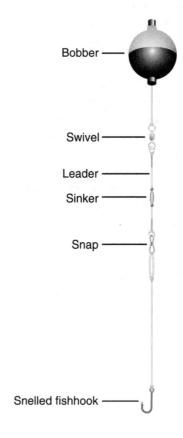

Bobber

Swivel

Leader

Sinker

Snap

Snelled fishhook

➤ A couple of light sinkers. These help you cast the line farther from shore; normally they're used with live bait.

➤ Some hooks (different sizes).

➤ Split shot—made of lead (like weights), but lighter.

➤ Lures (two or three, including the daredevil).

➤ Small bobber. Used with bait, it floats on the water and is pulled down when a fish takes the bait to tell you that you need to reel the fish in.

➤ Extra line.

➤ Knife or nail clipper for cutting line.

➤ Filet knife.

➤ Snap swivels. Once attached to line, these let you switch tackle without retying your line.

➤ Stringer to put your catch on.

I've found that the best place to keep your tackle (except the bobber and knife) is in one or two small 35mm film containers. Forget about the larger tackle boxes. You don't need them—they take up a lot of space and are just extra weight. The type of tackle you choose will depend mostly on the type of fish in the area you've chosen for your excursion. Don't be embarrassed to ask locals what's biting; try to use the bait and lures they're using.

Here's How
There is no need to get squeamish about putting a worm on a hook. Done right, it's fast and simple. Take the worm in your fingers. Starting with one end, slide the worm over the full length of the hook, past the jagged part known as the barb. Drape a little of the leftover worm over the end of the hook. When placed this way, the worm will not fall off the hook when you cast into the water.

Landing the Catch of the Day

Catching a fish is a lot like playing a good game of poker. You can't change the cards you're dealt, but you can change the way you play them. Luck is involved, but skill is just as important.

There are days when the fish just aren't biting. Or times when you're fishing in one place, but the fish are off somewhere else. But you can really increase your odds of catching a fish if you know what you're doing.

Some of the best times to fish from shore are early in the morning and at dusk. In the middle of the afternoon, on a hot sunny day, you'll have a better chance of finding fish in deeper water—it's where they go to cool off! If you are fishing in a stream, for example, this may be a good time for you to look for them in deeper pools. While on a five-day backpacking trip through Newfoundland's Gros Morne National Park, I was surprised to learn that animals would frequently use man-made trails to get to their favorite spots. (After all, why scratch your back on itchy brush if you don't have to?) Similarly, fish may go to deeper water when it's hot, coming up to the surface when they're hungry and insects are floating on top. (Why boil yourself if you don't have to?) Ask locals, wilderness officials, or rangers about when the fish usually have their meals.

Who Said There Was No Homework!

The first thing you need to know is what types of fish can be found in the wildlife area you will be exploring. Look through some of the brochures on the region; call or write to the wildlife department in the area (or the local outfitter). Ask about the best time of year to fish, where to find the hot spots in the area, and the best time of day to go. Especially important is to find out when the legal fishing season for a specific species of fish begins and ends, where you can buy your fishing license, and how much it will cost. If you're fishing in a national park, you can usually buy a national park fishing license that enables you to fish throughout the park for a limited period. Table 7.1 lists and illustrates some of the more common fish you may be trying to hook.

Table 7.1 Common, and tasty, species of fish

Appearance	Name	Description*
	Yellow perch	Weigh less than a pound
	Brook trout	Measure about six inches long
	Lake trout	Weigh in at two to five pounds
	Bass	Weigh an average of three pounds
	Pike	Weigh an average of two to seven pounds
	Walleye	Weigh an average of two to three pounds

All found in freshwater rivers, streams, and lakes.

There are fish you *won't* be able to catch with your ultralight gear, such as salmon or muskellunge—some weigh as much as a small child. On the other hand, perch, rock bass, trout, smallmouth bass, walleye, and even small pike are fair game. They weigh just a few pounds each, and all are worth their weight in dinner. These fish can all be snared with your ultralight rod and reel and your film-container's-worth of tackle.

Once you know what types of fish are in the area, you can narrow down the tackle you need to bring on your trip. Ask your local sporting goods store to help you select the right lures for the fish you'll be trying to catch. Not all fish respond to live bait; some respond to nothing else. Trout are one of the tastiest and most beautiful fish out there, but also the fussiest. They usually respond just to flies, but when they are hungry enough have been known to chase a worm or a light lure. Some fly-fishing purists may cringe at the thought, but I have caught many brown trout from shore using just a hook, a weight, and a small worm. Besides the fish pictured previously, you may encounter bluegill, sunfish, and crappie in many lakes. There are many varieties of bass, so the picture here may not match what you catch.

In some cases, no skill is involved in fishing at all. Auyuittug National Park (located above the Arctic Circle on Canada's Baffin Island), boasts some rivers where the fish are so hungry they will bite even a bare hook.

Rules

You need to get a fishing license before you can start fishing. These licenses can usually be purchased at local bait shops, grocery stores, or national park offices. The license limits the species you can fish for and the seasons you can fish for them. Sometimes there are limits on how many fish of a particular type you're allowed to take out of the water. If you happen to be visiting a national park, you can usually buy a license that permits you to fish throughout the park. In some cases, nonresidents have to pay more for their fishing licenses than do residents. People caught fishing without a license may find themselves stopped by the local warden and slapped with hefty fines!

Rivers, Streams, and Lakes

Different types of fish live in different habitats; most have their preferences. Some live in lakes, others prefer rivers and streams. Trout, one of the most desirable fish to catch, can be found in all three. River fishing can be difficult for the beginner. It usually involves wading in the river—and often the water is moving so rapidly that it's hard to tell whether the fish are biting. Beginners may find lake and stream fishing easier.

When fishing in streams, look for potentially deep pools where the fish may be resting. I've found that when fishing in a lake from the shore, it can be a good idea to put your hook near a shady spot—underneath some low hanging branches or near some big rocks. This can be especially effective on a hot sunny day. Just be careful not to snag your line on a rock or a tree—that's a great way to lose your tackle!

Here's How

One of the easiest ways of finding live bait consists of buying worms or minnows at the local tackle shop. But let's say you forget to do this, or you're in the backcountry and there is none. What then? To find earthworms try uncovering large rocks or logs, and gently probing the earth underneath with a stick. Another way to look for them is to catch them sliding through the grass, at night, using a flashlight.

Reeling in the Big One

It's the end of a long day of hiking. You're sitting by a lake on a rock, your fishing rod in your hands. It's beautiful enough just enjoying the scenery and the quiet sounds of wildlife. Then it happens. A slight tug on the line. Then another. What do you do? Is it time to pull in the line? Or do you wait for another bite?

Nibble or Bite?

First, you must be able to distinguish between a nibble and a bite. This is not always easy to do at first; it comes with time and practice. Imagine your line with your bait or lure at the end. If the fish just toys with it, without putting the whole thing in its mouth, that's a *nibble*. If you're using a bobber, it will dance up and down a bit, but it won't be pulled under the water. It usually takes one or two nibbles before the fish really tries to eat the bait or lure. Now, that's a *bite*—which feels like a more serious tug on the line. Usually, a bite pulls the bobber on your line all the way under the water. This is the time to pull the rod back and set the barb of the hook (the jagged part) into the fish's mouth. And timing is everything. If you don't set the hook at this time, it may fall out and the fish will get away. If you try to set the hook when the fish is merely nibbling, you'll just pull away the bait or lure, and possibly scare off the fish.

To Drag or Not to Drag

Just because you've got ultralight gear doesn't mean you have to catch ultralight fish. You can reel in lots of respectable-size fish if you know the secret: Setting your drag on the reel. The *drag* is like a brake that controls the tautness of the line. If you set the drag for maximum tension, no matter how hard the line is pulled, it will not slip off the line spool. If you set the drag for minimum tension, it will slip a little. This is especially important when you're using ultralight gear with line that is only two- or three-pound test. If you set your drag to maximum tension, you risk breaking the line if a fish pulls hard on it. If you set it on minimum, the line will slip a little when the fish pulls, lowering its chance of actually breaking. Set the drag on your line before you begin fishing. When you buy your reel, ask a knowledgeable person at the store how to set the drag on your reel. Learn the joys of giving up a little line—and in return, getting back a fish!

Playing the Fish

Even after you've set your drag, it's still not a great idea to reel in the fish right after you've set the hook. If the fish makes a mad dash for it and tries to escape, you still risk breaking your line. The best thing to do is to cut the fish a little slack. Reel in some line, let the line go, and then let it run a little, and then reel it in again. It may take a little longer to land it this way, but your patience will pay off. Learning this technique will permit you to catch fair-size game fish using just your ultralight gear.

Landing the Fish

Imagine that you are an airline pilot trying to land a plane. You have to land it properly in order for it to be a success. It's the same in fishing. Sadly, no matter how big or beautiful the fish is, unless you pull it to shore, it's still the one that got away. Here are some helpful hints that should help you get that fish to its dinner engagement (though they'll work whether you choose to fry it or release it).

➤ Reel in the fish as close as possible to the shore, but be sure to keep it in the water.

➤ Fish are coated with a protective slime. If you intend to throw the fish back, be sure you *don't* scrape the slime off; otherwise handling the fish—especially if your hands are dry—can kill it by causing infection.

Using your left thumb and forefinger, grab the fish by its lower jaw. This will temporarily immobilize the fish and stop it from flopping around. Don't worry

about teeth; most of the small game fish you'll be catching don't have them.

➤ Nets can be useful but are too bulky for backpackers.

➤ Remove the hook from the fish by pushing on the shank—the base of the hook near the eye—with small pliers or your hand. Be careful not to cut your fingers on the hook, or the sharp edges of the fish's gills. If a fish hook gets stuck in your finger and doesn't come out easily, seek medical attention.

➤ Never try to land the fish by reeling it up to the top of your rod. You could break the line and may hurt the fish.

➤ If you decide to keep the fish, put it on your *stringer* and keep it in the water until you go back to camp. The typical stringer is a piece of cord with a metal tip and a loop at the end that you push carefully under a fish's gills; another model employs a chain with big snaps.

➤ Be sure you attach your stringer to something solid, or you risk losing your catch.

Freeing Fishy

Sometimes you will land a fish and realize that it's just a baby—only a few ounces—and too tiny to cook. Or perhaps it's a species that is not in season. Or perhaps you just lost your appetite for the big kill. Whatever the reason, you may want to throw it back. Here are some useful tips:

➤ Try not to wear out the fish by playing with it too much before you land it.

➤ Leave your fish in the water and never touch it with dry hands.

➤ Gently remove the hook; squeezing the fish will crush its internal organs.

➤ If the hook is too hard to remove or the fish has swallowed it, cut the line.

➤ Release the fish in quiet water. Never actually throw it back, this may hurt it or kill it. If the fish needs help recovering from the shock of being caught, hold it length-wise and gently move it back and forth in the water to move its gills and help it breathe.

Cleaning the Fish

Here are a few simple steps to cleaning fish to prepare it for cooking:

➤ First kill the fish by whacking it on the head with a heavy knife or a rock.

➤ Wrap a piece of linen or paper around the tail of the fish to ensure a good grip.

➤ If the fish has scales, scratch the inverse side of the scales with a knife to remove them (stroke the blade of a knife from tail to head). After scaling the fish, rinse it with water to remove extraneous scales.

For scaling, use a knife and stroke the blade from the tail of the fish to the head.

➤ Take a very sharp knife (the best ones are narrow with a small point at the end) and, starting at the throat, slit the underside of the fish lengthwise; cut all the way along the belly.

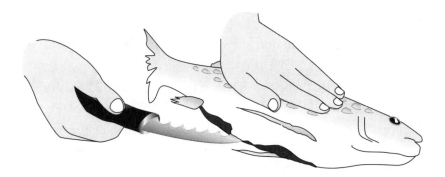

Place the fish on a flat surface, and slit it along the belly.

➤ Remove all the organs inside.

➤ Fillet the fish, or just pan-fry it whole.

➤ Dig a small hole in the ground and bury the fish entrails.

Having Fish for Dinner

It's easy to cook your fish. Put a little butter or oil in a frying pan. Fry it for just a few minutes on each side. Don't overcook, or your dinner may be ruined. Add salt, pepper, and lemon juice to taste. You might also try adding some garlic. Another way to cook fish is by wrapping it in thick aluminum foil and putting in the campfire for a few minutes with some spices. You can also use the foil as a plate.

Be sure you clean up properly after dinner to avoid attracting animals to your camp.

Don't Count on Your Fishing Skills Alone

No matter how good your fishing skills are, it's *not* a good idea to count your fish before they're caught. Don't plan on catching dinner on a backpacking trip. Instead, plan your meals before you leave—and *always bring along enough food with you*, including food for one extra day (just in case you get stranded). If you happen to catch a yellow perch, consider it a treat. You can always bring back the pouch of dehydrated goulash and use it on your next trip. If there is an emergency and you do get stranded in the backcountry, a fishing rod is valuable to have.

The Least You Need to Know

➤ For fishing on camping trips, all you need purchase is an ultralight rod and reel. Don't get bogged down with heavy-duty gear.

➤ Keep your tackle down to a bare minimum. A few essential lures, hooks, weights, bobbers, and knife are all you really need.

➤ Do your homework; research what type of fish live in the place you will be visiting. Find out what type of lures or bait they like. And don't forget to get your license!

➤ If you plan to throw some of your catch back, be sure not to manhandle them. Handling a fish excessively removes some of its protective slime, which makes the fish vulnerable to infection and may kill it.

Chapter 8

Practicing Low-Impact Camping

> ## In This Chapter
>
> ➤ How to get off the beaten trail and away from everybody
>
> ➤ How to practice environmentally friendly camping
>
> ➤ Dealing with garbage and refuse
>
> ➤ Building a low-impact fire

Low-impact camping means using the outdoors without deliberately changing it.

Each year, more and more of the planet's wilderness is felled for wood, burned, paved, and otherwise destroyed. People have reacted in many ways, and we are now striving to correct some of our sins of the past. Recycling, for instance, now exists in most cities in North America. It's a step toward conserving our environment. Many campgrounds offer recycling programs, too, and you should make every effort to use recycling receptacles.

Coinciding with environmental awareness, camping and hiking is becoming increasingly popular in North America and around the world. More and more people are taking to the wilderness for their vacations. The very fact that you're reading this book is living proof of this trend.

As more people are using the wilderness, we all have to be more careful about how we treat it. Otherwise, the following ravages of overuse will overtake areas of beauty:

➤ Garbage

➤ Barren, stripped land

➤ Exposed tree roots

➤ Downed plants, or absence of vegetation

➤ Numerous firepits on a single site

➤ Absence of available groundwood for campfires

➤ Scarred trees where branches have been torn away

➤ Bottles and cans in, or near, water sources like lakes, rivers, and streams

This chapter explains some basic techniques to help you avoid damaging the environment and to be kind to the campsites you choose.

Being Kind to Mother Nature

It's encouraging to see so many embracing nature, but also discouraging to see how nature is being treated by her many visitors. After a day's hike to a campsite, it's not uncommon to encounter signs that someone has been there before. Although rangers patrol many sites and try to tidy things up for the next visitor, often the previous visitors will have left garbage and other refuse behind as an ugly reminder that we are not alone, even though we'd like to pretend to be. Garbage is unsightly, and if it is edible, disrupts the natural environment in other ways. For example, it's an open invitation to animals who become reliant on mooching meals from the leavings of messy campers.

The first rule of campsite etiquette demands that all garbage be *packed out*. More and more this seems not to be the case, as I have witnessed on numerous occasions empty bottles and cans at campsites both north and south of the U.S.–Canada border. It is hard to believe that the campers who left this refuse weren't aware of their responsibility to remove it from their campsite.

To preserve the little bit of nature that we have left, it is important that you be aware of nature's fragility. You should be willing to respect nature in many ways. Instead of bemoaning the errors of others, use this list as a guide in practicing low-impact camping yourself:

➤ Pack out *all* garbage, including spent stove cartridges and other non-burnable trash.

➤ Leave no area any different from the way you found it (except to pick up others' garbage if it has been left behind).

➤ Stay on trails whenever possible, and don't create new paths by cutting down vegetation. If you hike off the trail, avoid sensitive ground such as meadows. If you must cross sensitive areas, try to walk along the borders instead of across the area itself.

➤ Avoid crushing plants underfoot; walk on rocks and compacted earth.

➤ Where campfires are allowed, don't cut down trees for firewood. Instead, gather fallen branches as far from the camps as possible. In public campgrounds, firewood can be purchased.

➤ Wash dishes away from lakes, rivers, streams, and ponds. Forego detergents, and use biodegradable soap—if you use soap at all.

➤ Do not harass or feed animals.

➤ Purchase and use biodegradable soaps and shampoos.

➤ Use designated firepits for campfires.

➤ Sound travels farther in the wilderness, especially at night, and over large bodies of water such as lakes. Out of consideration for others, keep voice levels down, especially at night when other campers may be trying to sleep. There are many that believe that the wilderness is no place for radios and tape recorders—especially if you're a fan of any group with a name resembling the Burstin' Tomatoes. If you must use a radio, wear headphones.

Rules
Pack in. Pack Out. Don't forget this cardinal rule; you can help preserve nature in its pristine beauty. All garbage should be brought back to civilization and disposed of properly.

Rules
Campers who choose coastal areas as their destinations should walk only on designated walkways, paths, and trails. The sandy environment is an especially fragile one, and walking over sand dunes can lead to severe erosion and environmental damage.

Selecting a Campsite

Choose an established campsite whenever possible. The damage to nature at these sites has already been done—and largely confined—to these areas. In campgrounds without designated sites, choose a location that is far enough off the trail that it won't ruin the view for other hikers. Try to camp 200 feet from any water supply to avoid contaminating water sources with possible run-off from camping activities. Look for a fairly level campsite scattered with ground cover from the forest, without too many rocks or tree roots in the ground. Pitching a tent in such a spot will help you avoid having to disturb your surroundings too much (*and* will help you get a good night's sleep). As part of the whole low-impact gestalt, choose a tent with muted colors that blend in with nature, and outdoor clothing to match (*except in hunting season*, when bright orange should be worn). Many tents come in a range of bright colors, but there are also tents that are made from khaki green fabrics, and others that blend into nature easily.

Rules
Most wilderness areas require that you buy a permit and register before setting off for remote camping sites. The purpose of this is twofold: to prevent overuse of natural areas and so that rangers and others will know where to go looking in case you get lost or hurt.

Conventional Wisdom
Try and stick to established trails when hiking. Have respect for untouched nature by trying not to cut through thick foliage or places where animals may be living.

Look for a place where your tent will sit on flat ground and where the circumference of the campsite is adequate enough to allow you to move around outside without having to squeeze between the tent and obstacles like trees and bushes. Of course, if you're camping in windy conditions, try and locate a windbreak behind which you can pitch the tent. A dense bank of bushes can act at a shield. If you need to, and there are no natural windbreaks, look for convenient places to attach guy lines from trees to the tent.

Generally speaking, try and locate a place for your tent mat which is level, and offers room to walk, cook, and string up a clothesline if you need to dry out clothes, air out sleeping bags or string up other items.

When you've found a suitable site, look around before setting up for the night. Analyze how the site can be returned to its original condition in the morning. And don't redecorate nature: Leave rocks and logs where they are. Moving them to more "convenient" locations may disrupt the natural order of things in the insect world. If possible, move on to another campsite after two or three days; it helps diminish the possibility of scarring the campground. When you do break camp, look around and see what you can do to make the area look untouched.

Wear soft camp shoes when walking around the campsite. Soft soles will do less damage than hard hiking-boot treads.

Leaving the Campground the Way You Found It

Can you cover up the areas where you've trodden over again and again on your way to the campfire? Have you left holes where the tent was pegged into the ground that need to be filled with earth?

One good way to cover up your presence is to gather pine needles and other light ground cover from the forest floor and sprinkle it generously over the campsite before you venture on to the another destination. As a last gesture to nature (and to those who follow in your footsteps), check and *make sure that all garbage has been picked up and packed out*. It's the most basic and oft-repeated rule of low-impact camping—and the most often ignored.

Dealing with Noisy Neighbors

As your outdoor experience increases and you venture farther afield, you will encounter situations that require a bit of diplomacy—especially in peak camping periods when the wilderness seems packed with others trying to escape the congestion and hassle of city life. Tent walls are much thinner than the plaster walls in most apartments, but some campers seem to forget this. When neighboring campers disrupt your peace and quiet, politely remind them that they are infringing on your outdoor vacation and attempts to relax. In most cases, this simple and reasonable request will be complied with. Sometimes, however, your request will be met with resentment and anger. You'll have two choices if this happens: To grin and bear it, or report the disruption to authorities. In most public campgrounds and hiking areas, there are straightforward rules that campers must abide by. Disturbing others is a Big No-No.

Shedding the Hordes

Summer is the height of the camping season, and it is probably when nature will beckon you into the wilderness—along with loads of others looking for a way to escape city heat and humidity. On shorter trips (where the wilderness area is near a large urban area), it's sometimes impossible to completely escape the large numbers of people who, like you, flock to the wilderness for a bit of peace and quiet. On pre-planned, longer trips, however, you can avoid the crowds by choosing more out-of-the way destinations.

The most popular destinations include many of the national parks, and popular hiking grounds such as the Appalachian Trail. If you've set your sights on an outdoor vacation in one of these places why not consider going *off season* (early in the summer or after Labor Day)? Generally, the days during these periods are still warm, and the nights are on the crisp side of cool—making for perfect hiking and adventuring days, and lovely sleeping conditions at night. As an added bonus, biting insects like mosquitoes, black flies, and deer flies won't be as bad at these times of the year.

Once you have more experience with the outdoors, you might want to try camping even more off season—in the winter. Be sure that you acquaint yourself, however, with the requirements for such a trip. You'll have to be adequately prepared to handle harsher (and mostly colder) weather conditions; equip yourself with suitable clothing and shelter. There are a number of seaside campgrounds and hiking trails in Florida that are part of the U.S. National Park System, so plans for a winter outdoor adventure need not be limited to the frigid Northeast Coast, Midwest, or rainy West Coast. If off-season camping doesn't appeal to you or just doesn't fit your schedule, then why not try camping and hiking on *weekdays* instead of weekends? Trails and campsites are generally less crowded during the working week, and will afford outdoor travelers the opportunity to experience nature without the usual deluge of weekend crowds. You'll encounter less litter, less noise, and fewer people when you camp during down times in the summer.

Another alternative is to choose a camping destination that is harder to get to. Some "interior" campsites, for instance, can only be reached by canoe. In one particularly popular provincial park in Ontario, a two-hour paddle almost ensures that you'll avoid almost all weekend crowds in the landlocked campgrounds. An island campground on a lake is ideal: You'll be able to experience the drama of both sunrise and sunset by changing sides on the island. Also, the increased breeze and wind on an island will help keep insects at bay.

If canoeing isn't in the cards, choose a hiking trail that leads uphill instead of over flat terrain, you're sure to shed more people than perspiration getting to your campsite.

Trail Etiquette: Traveling in Groups

Hiking and camping with a group of friends, or as a family, is half the fun of vacationing outdoors. But large groups may be disruptive to nature, as well as to other hikers and campers. If possible, disband into smaller groups, take different paths, and meet up later in the day. Remember to keep group revelry down—well below a dull roar—to avoid disturbing others. Your chances of encountering wildlife increase as the level of noise decreases.

Rules

Low-impact camping includes treating wildlife with respect. Hikers and campers should never molest or otherwise disrupt the natural flow of things in the woods. Stay relatively quiet and you're likely to see animals and birds at work and at play. Animals may never get very close, but they won't run away if you don't startle them.

Core Guidelines for Minimum-Impact Camping

➤ Pack it in, pack it out. All garbage should be disposed of properly, not in the woods.

➤ When hiking with others, hike in a single file to minimize the chance of widening a trail.

➤ Don't use soap to wash in water sources such lakes and streams; instead, jump into the water source, then get out taking a bucket of water with you at least 150 feet away from the water source. Lather up with biodegradable soap and rinse off there.

➤ Build only one *small* fire, if permitted, and use only existing fire pits. Better yet, make no fires at all and use camp stoves instead.

➤ Wash dishes away from water sources, and dispose of waste water in a shallow hole dug with a trowel.

How to "Go" in the Woods and Other Pressing Matters

The time has come to learn how to responsibly handle the ugly matter of disposing of human waste in the wilderness. Indelicate, yes. Important, absolutely.

Established campsites will offer toilets. These may be real flush toilets, chemical toilets, or outhouse-style toilets. This is the easy way out. At more backwoods or "interior" campsites, you might find primitive toilets placed some distance away from a campsite. On trails, such amenities may be few and far between though trailheads often offer outhouse-style toilets for use.

If you have to duck into a bush in the middle of a hike, try to position yourself as far from the trail as possible—and no less than 300 feet or more from any known streams, lakes, ponds, and other water sources. Heading up a hill is a good indication that you are traveling away from water sources. If there are no "facilities" at your campsite when you arrive, you'll have to make your own: Use a gardening trowel or flat stone to dig a 6-inch deep hole over which to squat. After the deed is done, place used toilet paper in a sealable plastic sandwich bag for disposal later on. Then cover your mess with earth. Try to make things look like they were before, and disguise the hole with leaves or material from the forest floor. Small disposal sites such as these are called *cat holes*, and are one of the most environmentally friendly ways to deal with human waste in the outdoors. If you need to make a number of cat holes, try to disperse them over a wide area. Don't bury toilet paper—bag it, as detailed above.

Daniel Boone Was a Man, but Women Like Camping Too

One recalls a TV ad for a certain brand of soap where a man, and then a woman, are seen showering in a makeshift shower stall in the woods. The camera cuts to the man's hand whittling away at the soap with a very "manly" knife. The woman in the shower praises the soap's fragrance: "Manly, yes. But I like it too."

The same could be said of camping and hiking: women like it too. The idea of the outdoors as only a man's domain is a fallacy. Women, in fact, may be better suited to the outdoors in many ways. With better endurance and a seeming ability to store larger amounts of energy, women are often more adept at conquering rugged and trying terrain. The women consulted in the writing of this book felt that when compared with their male counterparts, they performed just as well as campers and hikers in almost all cases. Period.

Which brings up the question of menstruation. The only problem with this aspect of camping is the special treatment of the trash created by menstruation. Since all hikers and campers *should* plan to pack out all trash, extra consideration for sanitary products needs to be made. Women should store used feminine hygiene products in a sealable bag and burn them in a campfire as soon as possible. Women hikers should carry towelettes for cleaning.

Of course, in campgrounds with showering and toilet facilities, none of this will be a problem. Touching down in one of these places before and after a trek will help out.

Large groups will need to dig a latrine and periodically add lye or some other chemical that promotes decomposition and kills odor (such as a biodegradable marine holding-tank chemical). Latrines need to be filled in completely with earth when the campsite is vacated. Larger groups should consult Kathleen Meyer's *How to Shit in the Woods* (Ten Speed Press) for the correct directions on the disposal of large amounts of waste.

The Bonfire of the Backwoods

Campfires are lovely things to relax around at the end of the day. They can be used for cooking, and they are sources of warmth on cool evenings. But they are also rife with controversy in this era of low-impact camping. Campers have stripped the woods of available fallen firewood, left unburned garbage in fireplaces, and scarred the wilderness with hordes of campfire sites.

As a general rule, established campgrounds along trails will have obvious places where fires are designed to be built—usually a "fire ring" made of stones. To stay true to the low-impact ethic, always keep your fires within these rings—and as small as possible. The less firewood used, the better. But even better, forego campfires all together: Most campers don't depend on their fires for cooking anymore; portable camping stoves are more reliable, easier to start, more efficient, and specifically built for cooking. Fire will heat up the entire pot or pan—handle and all. If you insist on building a campfire, keep tents far away to prevent errant embers from burning a hole in tent fabric.

Rules

Books of safety matches are unreliable in the outdoors, especially if they get wet from perspiration and rain. Carry a good supply of wooden matches that can be struck on any coarse surface in a waterproof container. Waterproof matches may also be purchased from stores specializing in outdoor gear. You can also make your own: Dip match tips in liquid wax to stave off damage from moisture, and carry them in a 35mm film canister. Or, better yet, carry and use a butane lighter.

Building a Low-Impact Campfire

One traditional "true test" of outdoor adeptness used to be the ability to build a campfire in almost any weather. This test was something of a necessity in bygone days, since any cooking demanded that a good fire be made. The challenge nowadays is to make a fire without adversely affecting the wilderness environment. This means that firewood should be scavenged from as far away from the campsite as possible to avoid stripping the surrounding land of all downed wood.

There are a number of recommended fire-building methods, but the following tried-and-true method is highly successful. It is based on the principle of building a fire in three stages, igniting increasingly larger pieces of wood.

The first stage is to gather *tinder*—small dead twigs, dry bark, or fallen evergreen needles—from around the bases of trees. The second stage is to add *kindling*, which is essentially larger dry sticks and fallen branches (about one-eighth to one-half an inch in diameter). These two materials are used to ignite the main, third part of the fire: the *fuel*, which is the larger pieces of wood (one inch in diameter and larger). After you gather the materials you need, follow these steps to start your fire:

1. Spread a good amount of tinder over the center of the area where the fire will be; lean some pieces of kindling against each other in a teepee formation over the tinder. Be sure that you've left sufficient space between the sticks to insert a match into the tinder.

2. Lay the bigger pieces of fuel over the kindling, also in a teepee formation. (You can add more fuel after the tinder and kindling have ignited.)

3. Ignite the tinder with a match, making sure the wind is blowing the flame *into* the tinder.

4. Once the kindling is good and hot, lay on bigger pieces of fuel for the fire.

Rules

Fire safety is of paramount importance in this time of diminishing woodlands. Before you depart from the campsite, *extinguish all fires with water*. Disperse the ashes. Don't build big fires; not only do they use up a lot of wood, they can burn out of control.

Don't burn your garbage in a fire. Better yet, try and limit your fires to only car campgrounds where established firepits exist. All garbage should be disposed of in receptacles provided at trailheads and campgrounds.

Not So Wild Animals

Pets are usually welcome at campgrounds and on trails as long as they are kept leashed or crated. But check with authorities to make sure that you can bring Fido along. Some areas don't allow you to bring pets into the area. If you do bring your dog, pick up their droppings or bury them. And always make sure that wildlife isn't harassed. A run-in with a skunk or porcupine is no fun.

The Least You Need to Know

➤ Low-impact camping means taking common-sense steps to lessen our impact on nature from camping and hiking in the backwoods. Clean up messes and restore.

➤ Plan to take your outdoor vacation during off-peak periods to avoid overcrowding the backwoods. In peak seasons, camp and hike during the week instead of weekends. Hike harder trails, or canoe to a destination.

➤ To dispose of waste without washrooms, use a small trowel to dig a six-inch deep hole and bury the dirty deed. Burn toilet paper in a fire—on the spot with a match, or later when you make a campfire.

➤ Travel in small groups to avoid disturbing nature. Larger groups may be disruptive to other campers and hikers by the noise created by many people. Where quiet times are not enforced, keep noise levels down at night as a courtesy to others who may be trying to sleep.

➤ Campfires are harmful to the environment. Build only small fires in designated spots and collect wood as far away from the campsite as possible. By doing this, you reduce the impact on the environment.

Part 2
Skills and Thrills

Heading out on a bigger or longer trip means learning how to read and use maps. Like a road map, trail- and park-maps are guides to established routes and identify camping areas and destinations inside wilderness areas. Maps also tell you how hard a trail will be, and whether you'll be hiking over flat terrain or climbing grueling hills.

In more remote areas, you'll have to use a compass with a map. Learn how to master this basic piece of navigational gear in the beginning, and you'll be well on your way to becoming an experienced hiker. When following the general instructions for using a map and compass in this part, do yourself a favor: Purchase a compass and practice using it. Compass concepts are not difficult to learn, but do require hands-on experience to fully understand them.

Rest assured that there's more to backpacking and hiking than maps and compasses. As you gain more experience in understanding nature's ways, you'll come to rely on your own intuition and interpretive skills. There's not much you can do about bad weather, but you can anticipate and prepare for it. Don't forget to stop and smell the flowers—look around and take in the outdoors while you're there. This part of the book teaches you to master some skills to realize the thrills. That's what it's all about.

Chapter 9

A Quick Lesson in Map Reading

In This Chapter

➤ How to read a map

➤ Why maps are so important

➤ How to know what maps won't tell you

Imagine you are visiting another city for the very first time. A city map would be a great help. It would tell you the distance between things, where essential services are (such as public transit, the post office, and hospitals), and even where to find some of the hotels and restaurants. The information might not be totally up to date—you'd probably still need to ask locals for help—but it would be a good start.

For planning a backpacking trip, a good map is even more essential. Unlike in the city, stopping to ask for directions will be a luxury on hiking trails. There won't even be people on some of them, and animals rarely give you an answer.

This chapter's designed to give you essential map-reading skills—from choosing the right map for your trip to understanding all the information presented on the map.

Types of Maps

You won't be using a city or highway map on the trail, the trail map's main purpose is the same: To give you as much information as possible about getting from one place to another.

The kind of map you'll need will depend on the type of trip you're planning to take. For a quick jaunt (lasting only a few hours) on a well-marked trail, a highly detailed map is not essential; a *national park map* will do. But if your trip involves a long, arduous hike—or even some bushwhacking (hiking through the brush without a trail)—a good *topographical map* could be the difference between a successful trip and a disaster. Remember, too, that maps are drawn to different scales: One inch on a national park map may represent 10 actual miles; an inch on a topographical map may be only one actual mile.

Let's take a look at the different kinds of maps you may use, and when to use each type.

Topographical Maps

These maps, also known as "topos," are a backpacker's best friend in the woods. The wilder the wilderness, the more important they become. Like other maps, they provide useful information about rivers, roads, and frontiers, but their most important feature is their system of *contour lines*. These lines, when read correctly, give you a detailed picture of the terrain: cliffs, passes, mountains, depressions, ridges, and ravines. Reading topos takes some practice, but soon you'll be able to tell the difference between a leisurely hike through the woods and a tiring trek over a monstrous mountain—just by looking at the map.

Here's How

The best way to get topos is simply to contact a map store. Look at the Yellow Pages in your area or call up your backpacking or sporting goods store and ask them where the best place to get maps is. These specialty stores carry a wide variety of topos and will usually order you the one you need if they don't have it. The topos cost between $4.50 and $6.50. Another way to get topos is to contact the USGS directly at 1-800-USA-MAPS. But the USGS will need to know the name of the map, known as the quadrangle name or the file number of the map. To get these, call the park office in the area you will be visiting and ask for this information.

The most common topographical map is produced by the U.S. Geological Survey (USGS), which provides maps covering every state. These maps cost between $4.50 and $6.50.

There are two basic types. Most backpackers prefer what is known as a *15-minute map* (one inch on the map equals one mile on the ground). These maps are more compact than the other type, called a *7 1/2-minute map* (one inch on the map equal abut 2/5 of a mile on the ground). A minute refers to a fraction of a degree. One minute is one sixtieth of a degree. The advantage of a 7 1/2-minute map is its more detailed picture of the land; the drawback is that the smaller scale means you'll need to carry more of them.

National Park Maps

National park maps provide the traveler with general information about major hiking trails, as well as where to find campsites, food, restrooms, good swimming and canoeing, and other outdoor joys. They are available free at park entrances. These maps are not detailed enough for the serious hiker and are usually of more interest to the motorist and car camper. However, if you are planning a very short hiking trip on a well-maintained, well-marked trail, a national park map may be all you need.

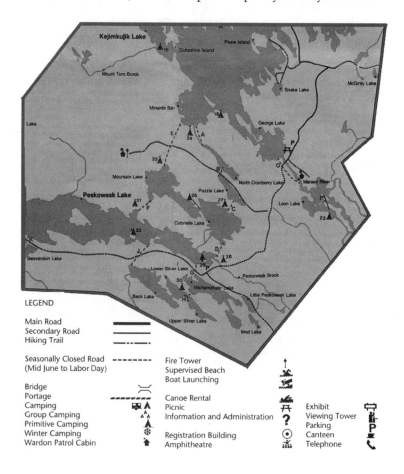

National park maps identify major land-marks, but don't provide enough detail for serious hiking.

LEGEND

Main Road	———
Secondary Road	———
Hiking Trail	—·—·—
Seasonally Closed Road (Mid June to Labor Day)	- - - - -
Bridge	⌣
Portage	- - - - -

Camping
Group Camping
Primitive Camping
Winter Camping
Wardon Patrol Cabin

Fire Tower
Supervised Beach
Boat Launching
Canoe Rental
Picnic
Information and Administration
Registration Building
Amphitheatre

Exhibit
Viewing Tower
Parking
Canteen
Telephone

Forest Service and BLM Maps

Bureau of Land Management maps contain some information useful to hikers (such as road numbers and hiking trails), but no detailed topographical information such as elevation levels. Forest Service maps use a scale of one inch on the map to every 5/8 mile on the trail. One half inch on a BLM map is equivalent to one mile on the trail. This smaller scale allows BLM maps to cover a lot of territory and make them compact. But watch out! They may sometimes be out of date—still showing old, abandoned trails with no trace of the new ones. Write to the BLM at: BLM, Office of Information, Department of the Interior, Washington, DC 20240 for availability and pricing. Or call 1-800-USA-MAPS. They usually are available for the same price as USGS maps.

Hiking Club Maps

Local hiking clubs are another good source of maps. Clubs often compile maps about the trails they maintain. The best ones often provide useful information gathered from hikers and other trail users. Often, however, they are not detailed enough to meet professional standards. Still, they will often do the trick if you're traveling on a well-marked trail!

A good way to find out about hiking clubs is to contact your local sporting goods or backpacking store and ask them for more information. Specialty magazines and hiking books can also be a good source of information on where to find them. Another way is to contact the tourist information office or park headquarters for the area you will be traveling to and ask them to put you in touch with the groups. They can be a good source of information on how to get maps and usually know a lot about trail conditions. The maps can vary in price but are usually less than $10.

Profile Maps

Profile maps provide information such as the ups and downs of a trail, the mileage between important landmarks, and the steepness and length of climbs and descents. But profile maps are not topographic maps. Instead of using contour lines, profile maps convey information on a graph that measures elevation gained or lost per mile. A profile map provides the hiker with a simple formula that combines traveling distance and elevation; some backpackers find these maps helpful in planning each hiking day of their trips. Profile maps are less popular than the other types but they can sometimes be found in trail guides published by hiking associations.

Map Covers

Commercially available "raincoats" for maps can be a hiker's best friend—if it rains or you happen to drop your map into a river or lake, it won't be ruined. They can be folded up and kept in one of the outside pockets of your pack for easy access during your hike. A map cover can be obtained at most sporting goods or backpacking stores.

Reading Your Map

The *worst* time and place to learn how to read a map is when you're lost in the middle of a remote wilderness. The *best* way to learn is to take a map with you when you're on a well-marked trail. Start by trying to identify the map's landmarks in the field—such as mountain peaks or the mouth of a river. As with everything, the more you practice, the better you'll get at reading the map. On most maps the top is usually where North is. It's important to know that the longer the trip, and the more remote the wilderness, the more important a detailed map becomes.

Looking at the Legend

The most important tool to reading your map is the legend. The legend will tell you the scale of the map, and of course, this is important in helping you calculate distances between landmarks and planning your route.

The legend will explain the various symbols that can be found on your map such as bodies of water, railroad tracks, and trails or roads. It will also tell you how the trail you are following is indicated on the map.

Here's How
One of the most important features of a legend is that it tells you how the trail you want to follow is indicated on the map. On most maps hiking trails are indicated by a dashed line. Because these can sometimes be hard to see, some maps indicate the trails with a red line. If you like, take a pencil or a highlighter and reinforce your route line so that it is even more visible. This is especially important to do if you will be hiking without the benefit of a trail.

Contour Lines: The Tree Trunks of Maps

If you've ever seen the inside of a tree trunk, you probably noticed it has a pattern of rings. The more rings, the older the tree. Well, topographic maps are similar, but they have *contour lines* instead of rings. These lines don't tell you the age of the trail, but rather how steep or flat a section of it will be. Lines extremely close together mean the trail is steep, with deep slopes or cliffs. More distance between lines means the terrain is flatter.

Each contour line represents a certain amount of elevation, which may vary depending on the map. This unit of elevation is called a *contour interval*. For example, on a typical 7 1/2-minute USGS map (each inch on the map equals about 2/5 mile), each contour line represents another 40 feet of elevation. This means the contour interval is 40 feet. Always check your map legend to find out what the contour interval is; it can range from 10 to 100 feet. Don't ignore it! Otherwise, you might wind up doing a lot more climbing than you originally had planned, and could end up having dinner in the dark.

How to Figure Out Your Route

There are many things to consider when planning your route. You want a route that is scenic; challenging enough, but realistic considering your level of experience; and, most importantly, one that avoids unnecessary hazards. You also want your route to be practical, like making sure it takes you to that great fishing spot you've heard so much about.

The contour interval of maps can range between 10 and 100 feet.

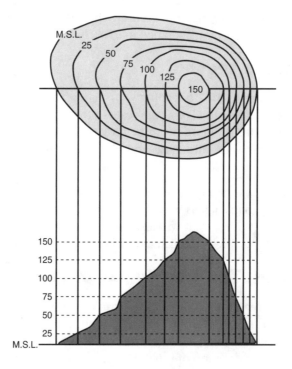

Are You Experienced?

The first thing to consider when planning your route is your level of experience.

Are you a beginner or an expert? If you're a beginner, long hiking trips through treacherous wilderness are NOT recommended. It's better to start small and get a feel for hiking, taking short day hikes on well-traveled trails. This type of hiking only requires a light daypack with some essential equipment, and is a great way to practice using your map and compass (which I'll discuss in the next chapter).

With more experience under your belt, you might consider setting up camp after hiking a few hours into the woods. Then, using your campsite as a base, you could try several more challenging day hikes, but without a burden of a heavy backpack. Finally, you might consider a serious backpacking trip, where you hike and climb 10 to 20 miles a day, then set up and break down camp each night.

After several of these types of hikes—and only then—I challenged myself to a five-day backpacking excursion through the mountains of Gros Morne National Park in Newfoundland. On that trip there was no marked trail; I had to depend on only a map and compass. Whatever your level of experience, the trick is to plan a trip and route that match it.

> I'LL TELL YA!...
>
> **Conventional Wisdom**
> If you're going to take a day hike, it might seem like just a light jaunt. But there are still a few essential things to bring in your pack. Extra clothing, such as a warm sweater or extra socks are good in case you happen to get wet. Extra food for quick energy such as some gorp and at least one freeze-dried meal. Your space blanket. A flashlight. A tarp that you can use to have lunch on or for an emergency shelter. Always bring your first-aid kit. Bringing along your raingear, even if it is just a poncho is usually a good idea.

How Long Have You Got?

Always think realistically about the kind of hike you can do in the amount of time you have scheduled for your trip. If you have only a weekend, it might be possible to do a loop trail where you set up camp after three to six hours of hiking, and then come back. But it wouldn't be wise to hike so deep into the woods that you have to rush to get home in time. *Anything can happen on the trail*; it's always best to be conservative about what you can do in a day. It's important to pay close attention to your map when doing this. Many hikers have looked at a map thinking that they could cover 20 miles in one day, only to find out they could do half that much because the whole hike was uphill!

Physical Conditioning

As with any sport, the more fit you are, the more you'll be able to do. If you're in great physical shape, you may not find a three-day backpacking trip difficult—but if this is the only exercise you've done all year, it could be disastrous. And the longer the trip, the more stuff you need to bring, and the heavier your load will be. When planning your route, ask yourself whether you're really in good enough shape to climb that 6,000-foot mountain peak or cross rapids or difficult terrain with a backpack on. The best course of action is to adopt an exercise regimen *before* heading off (see Chapter 20 for more). For a serious hike, frequent cardiovascular exercise is recommended. You might want to try running, biking, swimming, or squash several times a week. You want to build up your endurance before you leave so that you can enjoy yourself on the trail. Weightlifting can also be good to build up strength, especially exercises to strengthen the legs and the back, which will be stressed during your trip.

Even physically fit people can succumb to blisters, which can really slow you down. Unfortunately, there is no way to train for those, but you *can* make sure you have the right socks, that your boots fit well, and that you've properly worked them in (see Chapter 13). Don't forget that certain medical problems you may have (such as asthma) must be taken into account when you plan your route. You should also visit the dentist if you're going on a longer trip to make sure no unforeseen dental problems come up.

As far as altitude goes, a few thousand feet incline won't affect you too much. But 10,000 feet will. The higher the altitude, the thinner the air is, the less oxygen there is in it. You'll have to slow down to keep feeling good. There is no rule of thumb, just ask the ranger or people familiar with the trail what you can realistically expect to accomplish.

Looking for Helps and Hazards on Your Route

Your map provides you with a wealth of essential information for planning your hiking trip. The more serious the hike, the more important the map becomes. A good hiker will learn to identify rivers, lakes, ridges, valleys, and mountains on the map. When I was just a beginner and took a hike through Kluane National Park in the Yukon, I planned a three-day hiking route—failing to see on the map that a treacherous river stood in my path. Luckily, a park ranger told us about it before we left and advised us to take another route. No matter how good or detailed your map is, it's always best to review your map with a park official before leaving on your trip. He'll help point out hazards that might not even appear on the map, such as fallen tress that are blocking your route or flood waters.

A map also tells you about elevation levels and features of the landscape—which must be considered when you plan your hiking route. Hiking 10 miles on flat land in one day is a reasonable goal, but 10 miles uphill is a very different story. If your route involves crossing rivers or rapids, be sure to allow extra time; crossings are more difficult than walking on dry land, and only recommended for the experienced back-packer. Bushwhacking through the wilderness also takes longer than hiking on a well-maintained trail. A map can also be useful when choosing your camp-site. Many people find it convenient to camp near lakes and rivers; a map can often help you find just the right spot.

Safe Camping

CAUTION

Backpacking can be tough physical exercise; hikers should be drinking a lot of water to make up for all the sweating. On some trails there is an abundant supply of water. On others water sources can be scarce. It's very important to look at your map to find out where the water sources are to fill up your water bottles regularly. Treat all water for drinking.

Calculating Your Hiking Mileage Per Day

There is no sure fire method of calculating how much you can expect to hike in one day. There are just too many variables. Instead, most experienced hikers like to plan their hikes on the basis of *hiking hours* instead of mileage.

On flat terrain, usually a fairly fit person can walk about two to three miles per hour with a backpack weighing about 40 pounds. But various factors—bad weather, elevation, trail conditions, and fatigue—can take a toll on how much you can hike.

Your map will tell you a lot about the terrain, but you'd be wise to talk to the forest ranger to get up-to-date weather and trail conditions. If you are bushwhacking, you'll frequently have to stop, look at your map, and get your bearings—all of which will slow you down.

Most people like to take a 10-minute break every hour to drink and have a little rest. And don't forget breaks for snacks, lunch, and going to the bathroom. So even in ideal conditions, it's not realistic to plan to hike more than two miles per hour. Then it's up to you to decide how much you want to do in one day. Many trail maps will tell you not only about the experience level required for a particular hike, but also how long it will gener-ally take. Unless you are superhuman, you should *not* attempt an 18-hour hike—possibly 30 miles under fairly good conditions—in one day.

A hiker with some experience may find that hiking 10 miles in five to six hours is a reasonable goal in the right conditions. On my Newfoundland trip, the weather was so bad, and the terrain so difficult (we had to cross bone-chilling rapids and climb steep mountains) we often hiked more than 10 hours a day and barely covered one mile an hour.

Remember also that *a hike is not a race* unless you want it to be. Take the time to have fun on the way. Some trails are as beautiful as anything on earth. Following the trail to where you are going is usually better than getting there.

Weathering the Weather

When I hiked through the mountains and fjords of Gros Morne National Park in Western Newfoundland, I was confronted with every type of weather imaginable. It would hail for an hour. Then the sun would beat down on us for a few hours more. Then the rain would come. The ever-changing conditions meant we had to stop frequently to change our clothes; this slowed us down more than we planned. Hiking in the rain is also much slower than hiking when it's nice and sunny. When planning your route, consider seasonal and local weather conditions—in some cases, they may even alter the route you want to take. A snow-covered trail may not only slow you down but make it impossible to travel on. Remember that in the mountains, weather conditions can be radically different from those at lower altitudes. Ask the local ranger what the weather conditions will be like for the trail you have in mind. Check your map to find other possible routes or shelter to turn to if bad weather makes travel on your primary route impossible. Talk to the ranger about it.

To Trail or Not to Trail

When you have no maintained trail to follow, planning your route is even more important. One of the key differences is that you want to make sure you camp in areas that are easily recognizable to you so you'll know you've accomplished your objective and you're still going the right way. For example, on Day 1 you know you're camping at Big Pond. On Day 2, you have to reach Small Mountain. Talk to the ranger about the route you're planning and make sure there are no obstacles in your path. Have him look at the route with you to make sure it's OK. I highly recommend drawing in your route with a pencil or highlighter before you leave, and then putting your map in a map cover and keeping it in the outside of your pack for easy access.

What Your Map Won't Tell You

A good map, especially a topographic one, is essential for the serious backpacker. It will help you visualize a detailed, accurate picture of the terrain you are traveling through, and it's useful when you're planning your hiking route. If you have the misfortune to get lost, a map is probably your best means of getting unlost. (In the next chapter, I'll discuss using a map and compass together, and how they can help you find your way home.)

But a map will not tell you *everything* you need to know to plan a successful hiking trip. Some maps are out of date and won't indicate recent changes in the terrain. But there is some information that even the best, most up-to-date, professional topographic maps can't provide. And it's information every backpacker should know.

A ranger can tell you a lot of things that a map can't. He or she spends a lot of time in the woods and is familiar with the terrain and trail conditions. Give the ranger a pretty good idea of how much backpacking experience you have; ask for advice about which trail is suitable for you. A ranger will tell you about the weather conditions on the trail, how hard the rivers are to cross, and whether the water is good for drinking. You'll also learn about the animals in the area. On serious hiking trips in the backcountry, be sure to tell the ranger where you're going and when you expect to come back. That way a search crew can be sent for you if something goes wrong.

Discuss these variables when planning a trip and when you arrive at a park and speak with a ranger:

➤ **Weather.** No map can tell you about recent weather conditions in the area you are hiking, or how they have affected the trail. If a storm hits, it can turn what looks like an "easy" hike on a map into an obstacle course. Fallen trees, mud, deep snow, icy paths, and rain can make travel much more difficult and will slow you down. Talk to the ranger, and listen to the radio or watch television for up-to-date weather forecasts.

➤ **Trail Maintenance.** Some trails are regularly maintained, others are neglected; maps won't tell you anything about this. They won't tell you what color the trail markers are, whether the bridges or walkways are broken, or whether the trail is littered with fallen trees or big rocks (as is common after a storm). The best way to find out about this is to ask your local ranger.

➤ **Trail Traffic.** Some trails are more popular than others, especially during peak tourist seasons. In some cases, it's even necessary to reserve your trail months in advance if you plan to go camping in the backcountry. A crowded trail not only cuts down on the number of available campsites, it can also slow your pace. Ask your ranger or wildlife officials about whether you can expect company on the trail.

> **Conventional Wisdom**
> I'LL TELL YA!..
> Certain areas may be home to animals such as deer, bear, porcupines, rabbits, and moose, just to name a few. They are usually more scared of you than you should be of them. Still, it's necessary to take some precautions if you think you'll be encountering wildlife on the trail. It's best to ask the ranger for his advice on dealing with them.

The Final Decision

In the end, it's up to you to decide just how challenging you want your hiking trip to be. A map will tell you how high a mountain is, but it won't tell you whether you are experienced or eager enough to climb it. You'll have to discover that on your own.

The Least You Need to Know

➤ Always bring a good map with you on a hiking trip. If you plan to travel in the backcountry, take along a topographic map and a compass.

➤ Always read the legend on a map to determine its scale, contour interval, landmarks (such as abandoned roads and railroad tracks), and where to find good campsites.

➤ Contour lines on a topographic map are not complicated; just think of a tree trunk. If the lines are close together, you'll find higher elevations. Lines that are farther apart mean flatter land.

➤ Always talk to the forest ranger before taking a serious hiking trip. You can find out quite a few things that even the best maps can't tell.

➤ Invest in a good waterproof map cover. After all, a map is a backpacker's best friend; any essential tool on a hiking trip should be protected and cared for.

Chapter 10

Compass Basics: Definitely Worth Learning

In This Chapter

➤ How to use a compass

➤ Adjusting your compass

➤ Taking a bearing

➤ Finding your way

In the last chapter, we talked about how a good map can be a backpacker's best friend. Well, another useful tool, one that goes hand in hand with a map, is the compass. There are many good reasons to bring your compass along on a backpacking trip.

As with a map, the more serious the adventure, the more important your compass becomes. Suppose you're on a trail and you come to a mountain peak that you can see on your map. Your compass will help you find landmarks (such as other mountain peaks or lakes) that can help guide you. If you know how to read a map and you get lost anyway (it happens), a compass can help you determine exactly where you are. It's always good to take a map and compass along—even on a short hiking trip on a well-marked trail—just in case you happen to lose your way. And if are traveling through the backcountry, a compass can help you get to a destination you can see clearly on a map, but not with your own eyes.

This chapter introduces you to your friend the compass and teaches you the basic techniques of using it. As with using a map, practicing the skills you'll learn here will help your hiking trips be safe and trouble-free.

What Is a Compass?

A compass is an instrument with a magnetic needle that points north. Army engineers, hunters, fishermen, and canoeists use many different types of compass, but the one best suited to the backpacker is the *modern orienteering compass*. It consists of three basic parts: the magnetic needle, the revolving compass housing, and the base plate. A compass may sound complicated when explained, but is actually quite easy to use. The best way to learn about a compass is to get your hands on one and look at it while reading this chapter. First, let's take a look at the parts of a compass and how they help you navigate. Readers should use an orienteering compass (one with the whole ruler attachment) while reading this chapter. If you don't have one, purchase one for between $15 and $70, depending on the model. This will make it much easier to understand the chapter.

Basic parts of an orienteering compass

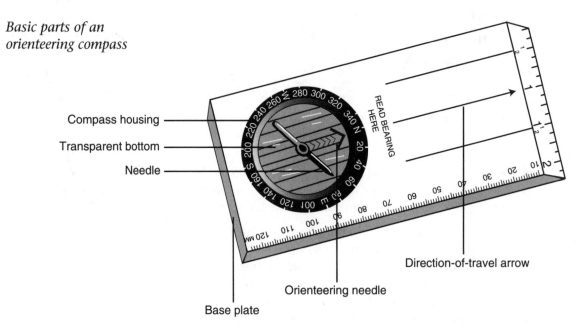

Compass housing

Transparent bottom

Needle

Direction-of-travel arrow

Orienteering needle

Base plate

The Needle

The needle is made of iron and is magnetized. It balances on top of a sharp point where it swings freely in all directions. The needle swings because of its magnetic properties being pulled by the magnetic properties of the earth. The north end of the needle is pointed like an arrow and is painted red—on some models, the point even glows in the dark. The needle is submerged in a non-freezable fluid so it will work even in sub-zero conditions.

Compass Housing

The revolving compass housing is a plastic dial that looks something like the one on a diver's watch. The upper part of the compass housing dial displays the letters N, E, S, W, representing North, East, South, and West. The lower part of the dial is divided into 360 degrees. The degrees match the longitudinal and latitudinal lines that divide the earth. If your compass is pointing to the 40, that means you're traveling in the direction of 40 degrees NE. Markings appear at every 20 degrees around the circle, numbered from 20 to 360. Between the numbers, tiny lines represent increments of two degrees each.

Look under the needle and you'll see a big black arrow pointing directly to the N on the compass housing. This is the *orienteering arrow*. On the transparent bottom of the compass housing, several thin, engraved lines run parallel to the orienteering arrow; they'll be important when you learn how to orient your map (stay tuned for more on this subject later). The compass housing is attached to a base plate that lets you turn it around easily.

Base Plate

The base plate is a transparent rectangle of plastic with several useful markings on it. The front edge of the compass is a ruler divided into inches and fractions of inches. The opposite edge is a metric ruler divided into centimeters and millimeters. Use these rulers to measure distances on your map.

Two engraved lines in the center of the base plate run parallel to the ruler. These lines (which glow in the dark on some models) are designed to help you travel in the right direction. The line with the arrow at the top of the compass is called the *direction-of-travel arrow*.

True North and Magnetic North

Everyone's heard about the north pole—but not everyone knows that there are really two of them. One is the *magnetic* north pole; the other is the geographical, or *true*, north pole. The true north pole is a place located exactly on the "top" of the world. It's the frame of reference for all maps. Magnetic north, on the other hand, is actually about 1,300 miles from true north, located around Canada's Ellesmere and Bathurst Islands.

To navigate effectively with a compass, you should understand that your compass' magnetic needle points towards magnetic north. Regardless of what you've been told, however, the pole does *not* attract it. Earth's magnetic fields align the compass needle in that direction.

Adjusting for Declination

You've just learned that your compass is telling you that north is in one place, but true north is actually somewhere else. The difference between where your compass says north is (magnetic north) and where north really is (geographic north) is called *declination*. This term may sound purely technical but it's actually important on a hiking trip. The declination will vary for different geographical areas in the world, and is measured in degrees. Your topographical map will tell you the declination for its area. In some cases, the amount is slight; in other cases, ignoring declination could put you severely off course. The longer the trek, the more important a set declination becomes.

One type of compass is easy to adjust for declination, as explained next. The legend of your map will tell you the declination, in degrees east or west, for the area you will be traveling through. In one area of the White Mountain National Forest in New Hampshire, for example, the declination is 16 degrees west. That means the magnetic pole is 16 degrees west of geographic north; therefore, you must make an adjustment of this in order to go in the proper direction.

> **Here's How**
> One rule of thumb that's quite useful when calculating declination: West is best and East is least. Always add degrees to the course you're following if it's a westerly declination and subtract degrees from your course if it's an easterly one. This is one of the easiest ways to stay on the right track. Of course, it's even easier if you have a compass with a built-in adjustment for declination.

Look for a small diagram like this on your topographical map to identify the degree of declination.

Mag. N

16°

The best compasses have a hassle-free feature that you can adjust for declination as you begin your hike. It usually involves turning a screw on the compass housing to move the orienteering arrow in the direction of the declination. This adjustment will move the arrow either left or right and the compass can be read in a normal fashion. I highly recommend that you buy a compass with this feature. It may cost a little more, but it will save you the trouble of calculating the declination yourself every time you take a bearing. (We'll learn about taking a bearing, and calculating declination manually—without this kind of compass—later on.)

Orienting Your Map

Imagine you're walking through a strange city. You want to hold the city map in the proper way, aligning it correctly with the landmarks and streets it shows. That way you know that streets that appear to be coming up on your left on the map, are *really* coming up on your left.

It's the same thing in the backcountry. When you turn your map so its landmarks line up the way they actually do on the terrain—instead of holding the map so that north is toward the top—you have *oriented* it. Doing so makes your map much easier to use, landmarks on the trail easier to identify, and the way easier to follow. In the city, you don't need a compass to orient your map because the landmarks are well identified. But in the backcountry—where rocks, mountains, and trees normally don't have signs that identify them—a compass gives you an excellent way to orient your map.

Here are some simple steps you can take to orient your map by using your compass:

1. Place your map on a flat surface.

2. Put the compass on the map. Check your legend to find out which direction north is on the map. (On most maps, north is at the top.)

3. Make sure that north (N) on your compass housing is pointing toward north on the map. If you use a topographical map, line up the ruler on the compass base plate with one of the vertical gridlines on the map. If your map has no gridlines, just line up the compass ruler with the side or margin of your map.

4. Turn the map until the magnetic compass needle falls completely inside the orienteering arrow. The map is now oriented.

Orienting your map

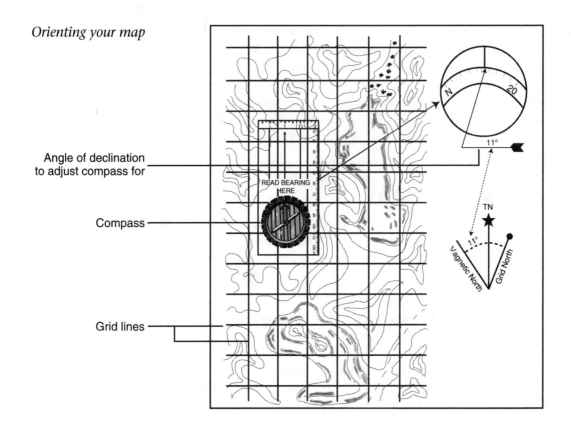

Angle of declination
to adjust compass for

Compass

Grid lines

READ BEARING
HERE

Taking a Bearing Using a Map and Compass

Orienting your map is always helpful, no matter what type of hiking you're doing. But when you begin to take longer hikes in more remote areas, taking bearings with your compass is essential. That means determining your direction, in degrees. My five-day backpacking trip through the mountains and fjords of Newfoundland provides an example. Our route was planned, no marked trails were available. At the beginning of our hike, we knew that our next goal was to reach the peak of a mountain. Being in the valley, we could see the mountain peak represented on our map, but not yet as part of our surroundings. The only way we could reach that peak was to take a bearing on our compass. Once we had our bearing, we knew what direction to hike in. In our case, taking a bearing was the best way to follow our route and get to our destination.

But taking a bearing is also a good precaution when you're deep in the wilderness, even on marked trails. That way, you don't have to worry about getting lost if a section of trail is poorly marked.

Here are some easy steps to follow to show you how to take a bearing using your map and compass:

1. Locate where you are on the map. Identify where you want to go.

2. Put your compass on your map. Line up the ruler on your compass so it makes a straight line between your current position on the map and where you want to go. Make sure the direction-of-travel arrow is pointing toward your destination.

3. Locate the thin engraved lines in the compass housing under the orienteering arrow. Turn the compass housing to line them up with the vertical gridlines on your map. If you don't have a topographical map with gridlines, use the margin or side of the map.

4. The number on the compass housing that lines up with the direction-of-travel arrow is your bearing. If you have a hassle-free compass with a built-in declination feature (and have already adjusted it), then this number is your *true bearing*; you can go on to step 6. Otherwise, go to the next step (5), to calculate the declination.

5. If you don't have a compass with a built-in declination adjustment feature, you have to factor the declination into the bearing yourself. It's easy to calculate: If the declination is to the west, *add* the declination number from your bearing; if your declination is to the east, *subtract*. For example, let's say you're hiking in White Mountain National Forest in New Hampshire. You want to go from Point A to Point B, about a two-mile hike. You find that your bearing, without accounting for declination, is 88 degrees. Your map legend says that the declination for that area is 16 degrees west. Now add 16 to 88: your true bearing is 104 degrees. If your declination is to the east, you would *subtract* 16 instead of adding it to 88, to arrive at 72 degrees. Remember this saying: "West is best, east is least." At any rate, after you take your bearing, add the degrees of declination to the west or subtract the degrees of declination to the east to find the true bearing.

6. Your true bearing will help you determine in which direction to hike to arrive at the next landmark on your route. Without moving the compass housing dial, take the compass off the map and rotate the compass until the red magnetic needle is aligned correctly with the orienteering arrow. The direction-of-travel arrow will now point in the direction you should be walking.

Using a Compass to Stick to Your Path

You now know how to use a map and compass to take a bearing, and figure out which direction to hike to get to the next landmark on your route.

But even though your compass is telling you the right direction to travel, the land or its conditions may not let you go there directly. Let's say, for example, that your compass is telling you to travel 88 degrees to get to Point A in White Mountain National Forest. You walk about a mile in that direction; when suddenly you find that a large tree has fallen during a storm and is blocking your path, or the trail has been completely washed out in a bad rainstorm and is now a pond of muck. You realize you have to change your route to get around the obstacle, but are afraid that doing so will cost you your bearings.

The solution to your predicament is a *careful* detour (as described next): to get back on track, you'll alter your bearing temporarily by following a new landmark.

Taking a Detour

If you must take a detour, you can be sure to get back on track by doing the following:

I'LL TELL YA!...

Conventional Wisdom

You might think the wilderness is a good time to leave your pad and paper at home. Well think again. On longer hiking trips, taking notes of your journey and keeping track of landmarks can help prevent you from getting lost. You can also take notes in another section about how much hiking you're doing and how you're handling it, what you forgot to bring, and what you like and dislike about your gear, and what you should bring next time. If you've purchased a GPS, keep track of how accurate it is. Another interesting use: inspiration may hit you when you are out in the woods. Who knows what you'll come up with.

1. Figure out where you are on the map *before* you take any detour.

2. Mark your detour on a map.

3. Pick a new landmark that you can identify on the map.

4. Using your map and compass, take a bearing of this new landmark.

5. Hike in the direction of the new landmark.

6. When you get there, take a new bearing on a major landmark included in your original route.

7. Hike to that point.

Now you'll be able to resume your trek to your original destination, having bypassed any obstacles in your way. If you encounter another obstacle, repeat the detour process.

A good way to avoid making unnecessary detours is to read your topographical map very carefully in the first place to make sure there are no permanent obstacles (such as treacherous rapids) before you hit the trail.

Captain's Log

When hiking in the backcountry, keep referring to your map; take frequent bearings on the new landmarks that come into sight on the trail. Spread out your map and orient it in places that give you the lay of the land. Mountain tops, for instance, let you see a lot of terrain. These steps can prevent you from finding out that you've been walking for hours in the wrong direction. Some hikers keep a logbook of the landmarks they've reached and the bearings they have taken along the way. If they happen to move the compass housing dial accidentally, changing their bearing, they still have an accurate record of what bearing they took.

A logbook is also a good place to make notes about landmarks that may not appear on the map—such as a big rock, a fallen tree, or a large nest. Having a record of these smaller landmarks can help get you back on track should you happen to lose your way.

Orienteering in Bad Weather

During a hike through Gros Morne National Park, sometimes the fog reduced our visibility so much that we could see only about 15 feet in front of us. In these conditions, I found it useful to pick a prominent object—such as a large rock—in my intended direction of travel, and hike toward it. When I got there, I would check my compass to make sure I was still traveling in the right direction. I would then pick another large object in my intended direction of travel and move toward it; I kept repeating the process until I got to another major landmark that was on the map. Then I would take a new bearing on my intended day's destination. (I mention this to show you how bad weather conditions can cause you to take more frequent compass readings, and how you can use small landmarks that are not on your map to guide you.)

Carry Your Compass

The best way to learn about using a map and compass is to carry them with you on your next hiking trip and, well, *use* them. Even if you're just going on a short day hike, get a topographical map, orient it, and use it to help you distinguish landmarks on the trail. To practice for longer hikes, take bearings of landmarks on the trail using your map and compass. This is a safe and excellent way to learn about orienteering, and to prepare yourself for trips in the backcountry.

The North Star Can Tell You Where You Are

Identifying the North Star, known as Stella Polaris (or just Polaris), is a good way to figure out which way north is. Its bearing will never be more than 2 degrees from true north—unless, of course, you're in the Arctic or just a few hundred miles south of the Arctic circle. In that case, the bearing will be different. A good way to find the North Star is, first, to locate the constellation known as the Big Dipper. It's made up of seven stars in the northern part of the sky, with the last two forming the lip. You'll find the North Star in the center of the Big Dipper.

Conventional Wisdom

If you know where north is, you automatically know where south, east, and west are. If you know you've been traveling west for the last two hours, and that's where the road was, then you now also know that you need to go about two hours east to get back. It's rough and approximate, but eventually you are bound to hit a road.

The Big Dipper

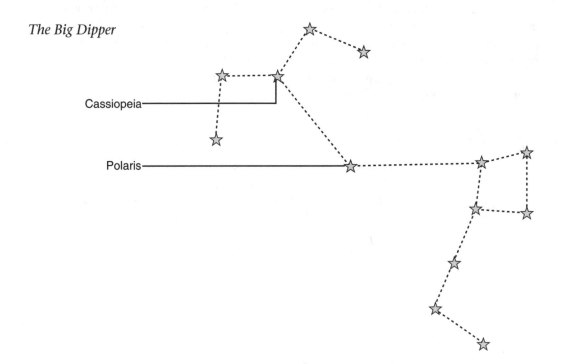

Objects Can Help

If you want to orient your map but don't have a compass, it's possible to use objects instead. But you have to know your position on the map—and be able to identify the position of a clearly identified object. To figure out where you are: Look for clues like rivers and streams in your environment, find your position on the map, and then turn it until it corresponds with the layout of the ground.

Going Global

Modern technology has made it almost impossible to get lost, but such peace of mind comes at a cost. Hikers can now use a high-tech tool called the Global Positioning System (GPS), originally set up by the military. To use it, you need a special (and fairly pricey) hand-held receiver that pinpoints exactly where you are, anywhere in the world. The little gadget picks up signals from orbiting satellites; these tell you your latitude, longitude, and elevation above sea level. You'll still need a map to make the readings meaningful—and you should know how to use a map and compass in case the system breaks down or runs out of batteries. GPS units cost between $200 and $600.

Conventional Wisdom

People are both inputers and outputers. At work, we often spend a lot of time sending out information to others. When we go into the wilderness it's best to get out of send mode and into receive mode. Pay attention to the environment. Take a good hard look at landmarks and your map. Listen to what nature has to say. Being observant will help prevent you from getting lost.

A Global Positioning System (GPS) receiver

Getting Lost and Unlost

If you're hiking on a well-maintained trail that gets a fair amount of human traffic, your chances of getting lost are pretty slight. But in the backcountry, things change. Trails are not always well marked; sometimes a fork in the trail will come up and you will have trouble figuring out which direction to go. Using your map and compass correctly will reduce the odds of getting lost.

But hey, it still happens—sometimes even to experienced hikers. I got lost once during my trip to Gros Morne. I was walking in the right direction, but mistook one hill for another. When I crossed over the hill, I got to the river I was expecting to cross—but instead of crossing water a few feet deep, I met with some pretty tough rapids. It wasn't until I had crossed them (about an hour later) that I looked closely at my topography map and realized I had strayed from my route. The route I had intended to follow crossed the river at a much shallower and safer area.

Getting Lost

It's always important to pay careful attention to your environment, and to your map. And if you have a hunch that you might be lost, don't be afraid to investigate it.

These warning signs may indicate you're straying from your intended path:

➤ Your trail is marked frequently (with ribbons, signs, ax cuts on trees, piles of rocks, and so on) and the markings suddenly stop.

➤ Your trail is well maintained and then deteriorates.

➤ Landmarks do not appear as they are represented on the topographical map.

Just because you notice one of these warning signs doesn't necessarily mean you're lost. There may be another logical explanation for what's happening. Perhaps you crossed into a wilderness area where the markings are less frequent. You may have entered a new park or wildlife area that is not well maintained. Your map may be old or not detailed enough to represent the landmarks accurately.

Getting Found

If you can't find a common-sense explanation for changes in your surroundings, and still feel uncomfortable with your location, you might be lost. The best strategy to take, at that time, is to *stop hiking* and think carefully about your next move. The worst thing you can do is keep walking. You may only be just slightly lost; if you keep marching on, you will only make a small problem worse.

Above all, don't panic. Most hiking trails are usually not that far off from civilization. Here are simple suggestions to help you get back on track.

1. Pinpoint your last known location and identify it on the map. How long ago were you there? How long have you walked since then? (This is another good reason to keep an accurate logbook.) Now draw a circle around your last known location. Use the distance you walked since then as your radius.

2. Carefully observe your surroundings. Look at your map and try to see if you can identify any features, such as a big river, in the circle you've drawn on the map. It can be useful to climb to a higher point to get a more complete picture of the terrain. But don't forget to bring your pack with you. Getting lost with your pack is not a disaster; getting lost *without* it could be. If you can locate a landmark on your map, you'll probably be able to figure out where you are.

Getting lost can be stressful, so don't make it any harder on yourself. Give yourself extra time to get back—about twice as long as it took you to get where you are. You will be traveling on unfamiliar territory, so the going will be slower. And remember to think clearly. Your mind is the most important tool you've got. Don't worry—you'll be home before you know it! Remain where you are if you can't get back on track.

The Least You Need to Know

➤ A compass is a tool that tells you which direction north is. Always bring a good orienteering compass with you on a hiking trip. The more serious the hike, the more important the compass becomes.

➤ Don't wait until you're lost in the backcountry to learn how to use your compass. Practice using your map and compass by taking bearings on easier, well-marked hiking trails.

➤ You might want to practice using a map and compass without the aid of landmarks to orient yourself before you head off.

➤ Remember that your compass points toward magnetic north and not the true geographic north pole; the difference is called declination.

➤ Look on the legend of your map to find the declination for the area you'll be hiking in; adjust your compass accordingly. If you don't have a compass with a built-in declination feature, remember to calculate the figure yourself.

➤ In fog or other weather that reduces visibility, use smaller landmarks to help guide you on your hike. Check your compass readings more frequently to ensure that you're still traveling in the right direction.

➤ If you get lost, don't panic. Try to remember your last known location and how far you've walked since then. Draw a circle on the map around that area. You're probably somewhere in that circle. Look for large landmarks in the circle on the map and try to find them in your surroundings. This will help you pinpoint your location and get back on track. If you can't figure out where you are, *stay put!* It is more difficult for rescuers to find someone who keeps moving.

Chapter 11

Weather Matters

In This Chapter

➤ Tips for predicting the weather

➤ Taking cover in stormy weather

➤ How to read various cloud formations

➤ How the weather works

Vacationing outdoors doesn't mean you'll always be dry and warm. Mother Nature can have her way—and certainly will—sometime during an outdoor trip.

Predicting the weather, even for professionals, is an imperfect science at best. Checking out the forecast for your chosen hiking-and-camping area doesn't guarantee good conditions when you arrive, even if forecasters give an all-thumbs-up several days before. If you're planning a trip that is far from home—in another state, or across the border— research what the typical weather conditions are for the time of year you're going. Phone the visitor center, the state or provincial tourist office, or a chamber of commerce near where you'll be traveling. You can consult precipitation charts and all manner of geological data in publications like *USA Today*, but the best and most reliable information comes from someone on the scene.

When the weather turns bad, there are some safety considerations too. A windstorm can send things flying around a campsite and can wreak havoc if you have left camping items around the campsite. But bad weather can be bad news too. If you become wet and cold and your body temperature drops you could become a victim of hypothermia—a life-threatening condition that is very dangerous. If you're hiking in an open area or canoeing on an expanse of water, lightning may pose a danger because it looks for the tallest thing around to strike—which means you, in these examples. If a thunderstorm blows up, take cover immediately.

Reading the Weather

Weather is changeable and pretty unpredictable. The best defense against getting rained out is to listen to weather reports before getting underway. If yours is a weekend trip, and your destination is fairly close, you might want to head out there in spite of a bad forecast. A couple of hours can make a big difference in the weather, and your destination may have a climate of its own that big-city weather forecasters have neglected take into account.

Weather reports are often concerned with large urban areas rather than the outlying boonies. In addition, the destination you have in mind may have a *microclimate* all its own. How many times, on long driving trips, have you driven into bad weather—and then out of it again? Your chosen destination may, in fact, be in such a good-weather zone. A bad forecast may also help keep trails and campgrounds free of people.

Of course, there is bad weather, and then there is Bad (with a capital "B") weather. A periodic light drizzle is a lot different from heavy rain, thunder, and lightning. Serious campers are seldom scared off trails by a light drizzle, and even embrace the refreshing effect it has during hot summer months. In some regions of the country, rain and drizzle are givens. Rain in Maine, for instance, is part and parcel of most summer trips in the state.

What if you've planned a trip months in advance, and the forecast calls for heavy showers and generally wet conditions for the entire stretch of time you'll be there?

CAUTION

Safe Camping
Really "good" weather—hot weather—can take its toll on outdoor vacationers. Sun and heat can rob the body of extraordinary amounts of water, especially if hiking is added into the mix. Be sure to carry an adequate supply of water at all times: The body will need from *four to six quarts* a day.

You have several choices: Consult the other members in your group to see whether they want to postpone the trip to another (more pleasant) weekend. If there is a consensus to go anyway, hikers and campers should equip themselves accordingly with the proper rain gear and equipment (see Chapter 15). At the very least, you'll want to be wearing waterproof hiking boots, a rain jacket that acts as a water-resistant shell and allows perspiration to escape, and some kind of hood or hat. Rain shells made of Gore-Tex, a specially formulated waterproof fabric used in outdoor gear that allows body moisture to escape, are ideal in wet weather. Cheap plastic ponchos don't work very well for active hikers because they trap body perspiration.

Weather Reading on the Scene

Weather is hard to predict because it changes so quickly. Just think how often TV weather reports change or are wrong. In the woods, you may have to rely on your own weather-predicting abilities—especially on longer trips where professional forecasts are few and far-between. This means being aware of your environment and reading the signs of upcoming changes in the weather. The most basic weather-predicting skills involve learning to read what the clouds are telling you. Specifically, various cloud formations reveal what kind of weather is in store for the day. To start learning to predict the weather by using clouds, ask yourself these questions:

➤ Can you identify the cloud patterns in the sky?

➤ Are the clouds getting more or less numerous?

➤ Are they getting lower or higher in the sky?

Typecasting the Clouds

Cloud-reading is fun, and can be very useful in understanding how weather systems work. There are three main types of clouds to keep an eye on: billowy (cumulus), layered-looking (stratus), and wispy-looking (cirrus).

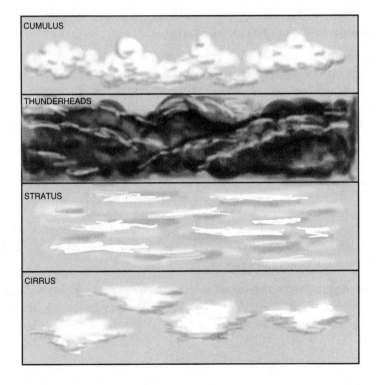

CUMULUS

THUNDERHEADS

STRATUS

CIRRUS

Looking at the clouds can help you predict conditions.

Formation 1: Cumulus Clouds

Puffy white *cumulus* clouds typically indicate good weather, though they can sometimes turn—quite quickly—into darker clouds, which means that thunder and lightning will become the order of the day. When they are *anvil-shaped*, they are called *thunderheads*, and foretell of impending bad weather.

Formation 2: Stratus Clouds

Keep an eye on *stratus* clouds—the thin, layered clouds prevalent on hazy days. Typical on hazy days, they may become thicker and get dense enough to block the sun. If this happens, a light rain may ensue. Should they turn dark and get lower in the sky, heavier rain may be on the way.

Formation 3: Cirrus Clouds

Cirrus clouds have turned-up ends that give them the nickname "mare's tails." If they get dark and seem to descend from the sky, rain can result. These are the most elusive of clouds, and can keep you guessing as to what they will do.

Winds of Change

In combination with clouds, several other variables can indicate whether you should stay put at a campsite or trek on to the next location on the map.

Hot air rises and cold air falls. Wind is created when this happens; combining this knowledge with your observations of clouds, you can guess the coming weather fairly well. When clouds are moving fairly quickly across the sky, conditions can change quite rapidly. If the temperature gets cooler as clouds are getting darker, there is a pretty good chance that foul weather will follow. If cumulus clouds appear in the distance and temperatures are on the rise, count on fair weather.

Humidity and Fog

How often have you heard others—or yourself—complain that "it isn't the heat, it's the humidity" that is most irritating about hot spells? Humidity results from a lot of water in the air and can indicate the coming of showers. Hikers who notice greater humidity in combination with a darkening sky should prepare for rain.

Fog is an extreme form of water-saturated air; in fact, it's a cloud that has formed down near the land because conditions happen to be right for it. Fog may become so dense that vision is limited (or, worse, nonexistent); identifying the landmarks shown on your maps may become impossible. Some areas—for example, locations next to the ocean—are notoriously (but naturally) foggier than others. In such regions, campers and hikers should keep an eye on their progress and be able to reasonably estimate their locations at all times. In this type of weather, sometimes it's better to stop and set up camp if you can't see where you're going.

Conventional Wisdom

Inexpensive battery operated weather radios are recent additions to the arsenal of prediction methods. These pocket-size radios pick up broadcasts from the National Oceanic and Aeronautical Administration (NOAA) from transmitters across the country. Short- and long-term weather forecasts are regularly broadcast 24 hours a day.

Conventional Wisdom

Some parks and campgrounds continually broadcast weather information along with fire conditions and other facts on designated AM/FM radiowavelengths. Signs along access roads in these outdoor recreation areas will indicate where to tune radios.

Red Sky at Night, Sailors' Delight . . . . The Proverbs and What They Mean

Weather proverbs, wherever they came from, have been traditionally attached to the world of ships and boating, and were reliable in times before the advent of modern forecasting methods. Outdoor vacationers can try to use some of the proverbs to predict the weather on their more landlocked adventures by looking at the underlying phenomena that governs how the weather moves.

Red sky at morning

Sailors take warning;

Red sky at night,

Sailors' delight.

Weather patterns tend to move from west to east. A red sunset is caused by the sun's rays filtering through dust particles and pollution. Since the weather in the west will most likely reach you the next day, and a red sky indicates dry conditions in the west, the weather should be good the next day. A gray or yellowish glow indicates wet weather is on the way. A red sky in the morning shows the sun lighting up high cirrus clouds, which may lower later on—a warning that wet weather may follow.

Mackerel skies and mares' tails

Make tall ships carry low sails.

Skies filled with mares' tails (cirrus clouds) indicate that a storm may be on the way. Scattered, high-altitude cirrus clouds usually indicate good weather unless their wisps (mare's tails) point up or down, which foretell possible rain.

Sound traveling far and wide

A stormy day does betide.

If voices seem louder, or the clink of pots pans against the side of a rock or pack are more shrill than usual, this may foretell an approaching storm. As clouds lower in the sky, sound waves hit them and bounce back faster than usual. You may think your hearing has become more acute. Once the clouds have lifted, sounds will return to normal.

The moon with a circle brings water in her beak.

A halo around the sun or moon tells of approaching rain. The halo is the refraction of light off ice crystals in cirrus clouds. When cirrus clouds lower in the sky, rain may follow.

Rainbow in morning,

Sailors take warning;

Rainbow toward night,

Sailor's delight.

Rainbows seen from the east in the morning where the sun rises and shines on moisture in the west, indicate the approach of wet weather. By the same token, an evening rainbow seen in the east is being illuminated by the sun setting in the west—which suggests that wet weather has already passed.

Lightning from the west or northwest will reach you,

Lightning from the south or southeast will pass you by.

Storm clouds and thunderheads come from the west or northwest and move east. If you see lightning in the south, the storm system has missed you; there is little likelihood that the storm will travel north to your location.

> *If smoke goes high,*
>
> *No rain comes by;*
>
> *If smoke hangs low,*
>
> *Watch out for a blow.*

Smoke rising from a campfire in a thin, vertical spiral reveals a high-pressure system, therefore good weather. Smoke will stay close to the ground in the presence of a low-pressure system, which may mean rain.

Follow these general guidelines for predicting the weather in your neck of the woods:

Good Weather

➤ A clear sky, (or nearly cloudless) sky

➤ High-altitude clouds moving across the sky

➤ Light breezes and winds

Bad Weather

➤ A halo around the moon

➤ A halo around sun

➤ Thunder and lightning to the west

➤ Increasingly black clouds on the horizon

➤ A red sunrise

Taking Cover in Serious Weather

When rain and high winds hit—and they *will*, at some point—you want to be dry and secure within your tent, or at least reasonably comfortable and protected from battering rain and winds. When thunder and lightning catch up to you on the trail, you may wish you were lying on the living-room couch at home instead of feeling like a doll in nature's toy trunk. These feelings won't help you ride out bad weather; fortunately, it usually passes fast.

If you're lucky enough to be nestled inside a tent (properly staked and set up, of course) when the rain starts to fall, you might consider curling up with a good book until it's subsided.

Tips for Avoiding a Lightning Strike

If you're hiking and a bad storm happens, take cover immediately in the lowest, driest place around. Then decide whether you're going to try to ride out the storm without setting up your tent. A tarp is ideal to use in these situations; everyone in the group can huddle beneath it until the storm clears. If the storm is truly awful and you can't count on getting any more hiking done, resign yourself to the fact and set your camp up for the evening. (In places with designated campsites, you may have to push on anyway, even when bad weather comes up.) Hikers should look for a stand of timber that's even in height and in a low area away from water. It's also best to stay clear of trunks and roots. It's unsafe to hide under tall trees and isolated trees, because lightning seeks out the tallest object in a given area. In spite of these warnings and precautions, the odds of being struck by lightning are pretty minimal—about 1 in 600,000.

Safe Camping
If bad weather keeps you tent-bound, and you need to heat up soup or tea to keep warm, remember that *stoves should never be used inside the tent*. If you must, lean out the tent entrance and use the stove there. If your tent has a vestibule, then you have a covered, protected area in which to cook.

Take cover under trees that are lower than others around you; lighting will likely strike the tallest object around. Metal attracts lightning, so remove metal-framed backpacks and place them at distance from you. Plant yourself down on something that can insulate you from lightning, such as a rubber sleeping mat or hiking pack.

If you're hiking in areas above the treeline and along trails with sparse vegetation, lightning can strike somewhere close by and travel along the ground. If there is a chance of *ground lightning*, take the precautions just described—but avoid taking cover under rocky overhangs. Try to insulate yourself by sitting on mats or packs, or set yourself down on rocks that are naturally piggy-backed on top of each other. The more obstacles in the way, the less likelihood of exposure to lightning.

The Least You Need to Know

➤ Listening to the weather forecast before you embark can help keep bad weather from throwing a wet blanket on your outdoor adventure. If you are traveling far from home, phone ahead to find out the weather forecast.

➤ Some parks and camping areas broadcast their own local forecasts on designated frequencies. Look for signs along access roads telling you where to tune in.

➤ Find out in advance if there are any particular weather conditions that you should know about where you'll be camping and hiking. Some regions, particularly in coastal areas, can become socked in with fog.

➤ There are three main cloud formations to look out for when attempting to predict the weather: Cumulus, stratus, and cirrus. Learning which ones are which helps you plan for good and bad weather.

➤ Clues in nature can help you tell how the weather will turn out. These include signs of impending rain; one such indication is a halo around the moon and sun.

➤ In bad weather, the best advice may be to *stay put*. If thunder and lightning occur, take precautions against getting struck by a lightning bolt.

Chapter 12

How to Identify Trees and Other Green Things

In This Chapter

➤ Learning how to be an amateur naturalist

➤ Identifying trees and plants

➤ Finding wild berries for dessert

Hikers and campers look out for nature in the form of birds and other wildlife. What they usually neglect to notice is the variety of plants growing everywhere—from trees and bushes in the forests to the wildflowers that add a splash of color to all the greenery. Appreciating the plants around you can be a delightful part of the outdoor experience.

Wouldn't it be fun to be able to identify the different trees and plants around you? By stopping to smell the flowers (so to speak) and looking more closely at plants often trampled underfoot, you may come to realize that forests and wild areas are filled with a huge range of life that doesn't walk on all fours. And you may even be amazed at what all the green stuff does.

At first, trees may resemble nothing so much as giant broccoli stalks growing out of the ground. You may not even know the difference between a conifer and a deciduous tree. If you fall into this category, start off by looking at the natural world around you; try to count the types of plants you see. Here's a hint that should give you a head start in plant identification. You should know these six basic kinds of plants: flowers, ferns, plants that bear cones, mosses, algae, and fungi.

Different types of plants often prefer different locations. The redwood tree, for instance, only grows on the West Coast; hikers in that region encounter these towering *conifers* (cone-bearing trees) along trails. Generally speaking, western forests are populated by evergreens and eastern forests by *deciduous* trees. Depending on which region provides the setting for your hike, you may notice exceptions to this rule.

Although this chapter only touches on plant identification, there are detailed field guides that describe just about every type of vegetation, from flowers to trees, for specific regions in the country. Look to your local library or outdoor store for a guide to the types of plants you're interested in. Furthermore, the camping and hiking brochures you write away for will point out particular vegetation and trees for specific regions. On-site rangers can explain why a particular species grows in that place, and why it doesn't grow in others. Ask questions about the plants around you. The answers can be very revealing!

Brochures from parks will explain what vegetation is special in the area you're visiting.

Sequoia

Look at the Big Things First

Tree identification is a popular place to begin. There are two types of trees to consider: coniferous and deciduous. Coniferous trees produce cones and have needles. They are what people usually call Christmas trees. Cones from conifers harbor seeds, and when the cones fall to the ground they are picked apart by animals in search of the yummy seeds inside. Examine the accompanying profiles of coniferous trees. With a little practice, you may soon be able to identify a range of trees in your neck of the woods.

You can identify *deciduous* trees by their shape and by their leaves, at least in seasons when they're still attached. A fall camping trip to such Northeastern regions as Vermont, New Hampshire, and New York will offer spectacular vistas of blazing colors as the leaves get ready to fall just before the cold weather arrives (an excellent time for an outdoor vacation).

You can size up a tree as coniferous or deciduous by starting with its shape. This is an inexact science, because younger trees don't often resemble their parents, and they'll look different—especially coniferous types—depending on the season. Like many other plants, particular tree species show up in regions of the country that have the environment, weather, and soil conditions they prefer or have adapted to. You might not locate trees that have the exact shapes shown and listed here, but you are certain to find some that are pretty close:

> **Conventional Wisdom**
>
> I'LL TELL YA!...
>
> Talk about the majesty of the vegetable kingdom! The largest living thing on earth is not a whale, or even an animal. It is the giant Sequoia. This species of tree grows only on the west slope of the Sierra Nevada. The General Sherman Tree in Sequoia National Park, California, is between 2,300 and 2,700 years old; its largest branch is close to seven feet in diameter.

➤ Pyramidal (coniferous) (spruce)

➤ Conical (confierous) (cedar)

➤ Columnar (coniferous) (poplar)

➤ Spreading (deciduous) (dogwood)

➤ Vase-shaped (deciduous) (elm)

➤ Broad (deciduous) (cottonwood)

➤ Round (deciduous) (oak)

Tiptoeing through the Leaves

The next thing to notice about trees are their leaves. Some trees have needles for leaves, and others have what we might think of as "real" leaves. Leaves on trees fall into six general categories, detailed in Table 12.1.

*Common tree
shapes*

Pyramidal   Conical   Columnar   Spreading

Vase-shaped   Broad   Round

**Conventional
Wisdom**

California's Sequoia
tree may be more
massive, but the
Redwood claims the
title as the tallest tree
in the world. Trees of
this western species reach 300 to
350 feet toward the heavens.

Pine trees are coniferous trees and have needles that
remain evergreen throughout the year. Maple trees, on the
other hand, have broad leaves, that turn color and fall to
the ground in the autumn. Some trees have other things
that fall to the ground: Acorns fall from oak trees. Chest-
nuts fall from chestnut trees. And of course, we've already
mentioned cones that fall from coniferous, or evergreen
trees. In sub-tropical regions, such as Florida, the trees and
leaves will be very different from those seen in northerly
climes. And the things falling from the trees may be
coconuts instead of acorns. Watch out!

Table 12.1 Types of leaves to look for

Leaf	Type	Example Species
A	Needle leaves	Pine tree
B	Lobed	Oak

136

Leaf	Type	Example Species
C	Unlobed	Birch
D	Compound	Honey locust
E	Broad leaf	Balsam poplar
F	Simple	Beech

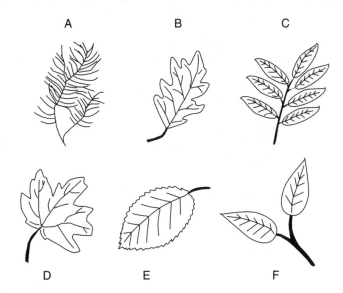

Going Wild for Wildflowers

As you eye your surroundings more closely, you'll find that trees are only one part of nature's mix. Start at the top, with trees, and work your way down to ground-level plants. You'll open a doorway to appreciating the vegetation around you. Nearer to the ground, you'll find many more plants than you'll be able to identify. The ones you'll probably notice first are the many colorful flowers that seem to bloom everywhere—in fields and meadows, among shrubs, and next to ponds and streams. In the right seasons, Nature is bursting with color!

Some wildflowers may be eaten or added to salads. Dandelion leaves are good added as greens to salads, as are lady's thumb leaves and flowers. Some recipes incorporated red or white clover flowers, violet leaves and flowers, and hosts of other wildflowers in the mix. Look in recipe books that have an organic theme to them, or pick up one of the many herbal recipe books available for wild wildflower recipe ideas.

Wildflowers are the most plentiful plants on earth. Two-thirds of all known plants are classified as wildflowers, so named because they are uncultivated by man and grow freely wherever they can.

The sole purpose of any flower is to propagate by dispensing its seeds. Flowers achieve this by attracting pollinators such as bees, other insects, and birds, which carry off the seeds and spread them elsewhere. Flowers appeal to pollinators through color and smell. Red flowers, for instance, are known to appeal to hummingbirds, though some red flowers emit a fetid, rotting smell that attracts flies. Others smell nicer.

Flowers usually have two or more *petals*, which are known collectively as the *corolla*. They are also characterized by the following parts:

➤ **Sepals.** A division, or leaf.

➤ **Stamens.** Male fertilizing organs of a flowering plant.

➤ **Petals.** Enclose the reproductive parts of the flower.

➤ **Pistils.** Female organ of a flower.

Like trees, flowering plants also are characterized by leaf shapes. Table 12.2 illustrates several of the leaf shapes.

Parts of a flower

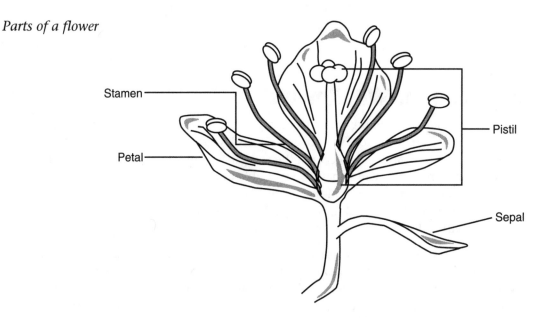

Table 12.2 Leaf shapes for flowering plants

Leaf	Type	Example Species
	Palmate	Gold thread
	Pinnate	Lead plant
	Toothed	Wild sarsaparilla
	Lobed	Round lobed hepatica
	Alternate	Butterly week
	Opposite	Wild bergamot
	Whorl	Indian cucumber root

Rules

Never strip branches or bark from a living tree for firewood! You may kill the tree, and the wood won't burn anyway—it contains too much moisture. Look for fallen, dry wood on the forest floor, preferably away from your campsite.

Magical Mushrooms

Fungus has less to do with athlete's foot and more to do with mushrooms when you're talking about plants in the wilderness. These kinds of plants aren't green (but they can be quite colorful) because they don't contain chlorophyll, and therefore don't produce oxygen the way other plants do. Wild mushrooms are interesting to look at, but don't risk eating them. There are indeed many edible varieties on the forest floor, but poisonous varieties are also spread generously around. Unless you know *exactly* how to identify edible mushrooms—absolutely and positively—you should never eat them!

Conventional Wisdom

If you suffer from hayfever, make sure that you take along the appropriate medication to deal with sniffles, itchy eyes, and the other irritations that go hand-in-hand with hayfever. Avoid smelling flowers up close.

Other kinds of fungi in nature occur in the form of *puffballs*. These are tumor-like plants that can grow to a foot in diameter. They often have interesting designs on their surfaces. After encountering one of these babies, you may end up asking yourself how nature could be so unkind in making such an ugly plant. They are the vegetable kingdom's Elephant Man, and they are truly not animals.

Safe Camping

Don't eat any mushrooms you find in the forest. Many varieties are extremely poisonous; even tame-looking mushrooms (like the ones you buy in supermarkets) may be harmful when plucked directly from nature. It's fun to identify the different kinds pictured in the wonderful field guides available, but when in doubt—*any* doubt—don't touch.

Wild Berries

Many plants in nature *are* suitable for eating. Among the most popular are wild berries that grow in many parts of the country: raspberries, strawberries, blackberries, and blueberries. Raspberries grow on 6- to 8-foot-high woody stalks; blackberries grow on prickly branches 2 to 8 feet high. Typically, strawberries and blueberries grow close to the ground (though one species of blueberry grows over 14 feet tall).

Different berries appear at different times of the year and in different habitats. Blueberries, for instance, can be found in bogs, woodlands, rocky barrens, and on mountain slopes. They tend to thrive in places that have acidic soil, and can be had for the picking in a lot of harsh conditions. They ripen between June and September, so look for them then. Strawberries, on the other hand, don't have such a long growing season—typically about two weeks around the summer solstice (June 21). Wild strawberries are smaller than the commercially grown variety and grow in open, sunny places, in the woods, and along forest borders. Raspberries grow readily in thickets, and along trail borders and are ripe for the picking in midsummer. Blackberries ripen later in the season.

Rules

Don't pick a berry plant dry. Leave enough for animals and other wildlife, which will disperse the seeds in the berries and create new plants in the process. Similarly, don't pick the flowers. Many of the more colorful wildflower varieties are rare and need all the help they can get to survive.

If you're lucky to find any of these berries on your wanderings, pick a cup or two as a snack or an after-meal treat. Wild berries won't taste the same as the cultivated berries you'd buy in the supermarket, but that's part of their charm. It makes them a true delicacy.

Although other edible berries grow in the woods as well, remember—some varieties are poisonous. As with anything you consume, make sure you know what you're eating *before* you pop it into your mouth.

Conventional Wisdom

I'LL TELL YA!...

Before collecting flowers and other plants, make sure that you're not destroying a protected species or removing an attractive sight for someone else. Unless you're planning to put your flowers in a vase in camp, why would you want to pluck them anyway?

Rules

Remember to use only dry groundwood for campfires if you must light a fire and they are permitted. But make sure you can use groundwood in the area where you are traveling—in some regions using any found wood is prohibited.

Not all plants are our friends, and poison ivy, poison oak, and poison sumac are relegated to the outdoor adventurers' Hall of Shame. Most hikers and campers who come in contact with one of these plants will suffer from a severe skin irritation—an itchy red rash filled with blisters, this ugly mess is caused by the chemical urushiol on the plants' leaves and stems. The lucky few who don't develop a rash when they come into contact with these plants aren't necessarily safe from a reaction in the future. Most who come into contact with the leaves and other parts of these plants will develop a rash within 24 to 48 hours of contact.

The best advice is to avoid these plants—know what they look like. Poison ivy and poison oak have three shiny, toothed or lobed leaves and grow as drooping vines or shrubs. The plant may have berries that are white or slightly green. Poison sumac grows as a small shrub and has a leaf grouping of seven to eleven leaves on each stem. It grows in sandy, coastal conditions around the Great Lakes and other coastal areas, but also thrives in wet, swampy conditions. Poison ivy and poison oak grow across the country in various locations.

The Least You Need to Know

➤ The range of plant life in the backwoods is truly amazing. Outdoor vacations that include plant identification lead to a deeper appreciation of nature.

➤ You can learn to identify conifers, deciduous tress, wildflowers, and leaf shapes. Becoming more of an amateur naturalist adds to outdoor fun. Guides are available to help you learn more about various species.

➤ Most regions will be home to particular types of plants and trees. These are plants that proliferate in certain areas. Brochures and hiking guides to different regions point out these plants, and casual observers will probably notice particular types of vegetation growing in different regions.

➤ Although many edible varieties of mushrooms exist, it's better to be safe than sorry: Don't eat any mushrooms unless you are *expert* in identifying them. The same goes for anything you pluck and plan to pop into your mouth.

Part 3
Gearing Up

Whether it's a weekend jaunt or week-long excursion into the deep woods, no camper can enjoy the outdoors without a few essentials. Specifically, you'll need suitable outdoor clothes, decent footwear, some comfort gear, and a good pack to put everything in.

Accessories such as flashlights and lanterns are essential. Not only are they basic safety devices, they're convenient when you have to find your way on dark paths and trails. Speaking of necessary trips in the dark, portable outdoor plumbing can add comfort to your trip.

As with all outdoor equipment, you'll find a wide range of choices—with a wide range of price tags attached. Choosing and using the right clothing and outerwear can mean the difference between a successful outdoor vacation and a sorry slog with vivid memories of tired feet and rain-soaked nights. High-tech materials and fabrics offer adventurers a great deal of comfort, no matter what the weather—but all new developments bring a new vocabulary. Learning the terminology and determining which fabrics are superior can give you a whole other adventure in language acquisition. But with a little knowledge and determination, you'll be ensured of getting the right stuff for an enjoyable trek into the woods. And enjoying it is what it's all about. Right?

THEY'RE A LITTLE BIG...

Chapter 13

The Dirt on Hiking Boots

In This Chapter

➤ Choosing the right hiking boots for your trip

➤ Boot care and repair

➤ Choosing socks, sock liners, and other wearing matters

➤ Treating blisters

Cinderella had it easy. A dashing prince showed up, tried a glass slipper on her foot, and then carried her off to his palace. Choosing a pair of hiking boots for the trail will seem more like Cinderella's chores, but a little time spent choosing the right boots will rescue you from the agony of sore and tired feet on the trail. Selecting appropriate footwear may be integral to your successful outdoor vacation.

Of course, if you're not going to be doing substantial hiking, you may need no more footgear than a pair of decent running shoes. However, if your plans include anything more than a 2-hour hike away from camp, then you should look into a pair of good hiking boots to get you where you're going, safely and (just as important) *comfortably*. This chapter provides a look at the available types of footwear; get the gear that's right for your needs.

The Hook on Hikers

Hiking boots are different from work boots and snow boots because hiking boots are designed specifically for walking and supporting your feet as they grapple with uneven terrain, excessive moisture, and rugged conditions. Hiking boots must be built for comfort, even in the face of harsh conditions, and this means they must be as light as possible without sacrificing their ability to provide support for your feet. Work boots which may look similar, are designed to protect the wearer's feet from the hazards of a construction site. These boots are often reinforced with metal toes and heavy, thick leather to prevent damage to the wearer's feet from falling planks, rough surfaces, and the vagaries of construction sites. Hiking boots wouldn't be appropriate in the construction business, and work boots aren't appropriate on the trail. Hiking boots feature treads that work well with the trail and encourage natural foot movement, as much foot support as possible for their weight, and comfortable insides that are kind to a hiker's feet as he or she makes their way down the trail.

If the Shoe Fits, Wear It

As with buying any pair of shoes, you need to visit a reliable outfit specializing in hiking boots and outdoor gear to get a feel for what's out there, and to figure out the differences between models and features. Shopping for hiking boots isn't much different than shopping for shoes when you come right down to it. You really want to make sure that what you're buying really does suit you. Check out magazine reviews to see what features are available in addition to reviewing the information here.

Start off by trying on boots that match your shoe size and then work from there. As with most footwear, a 9 ½ in one brand and style of hiking boot doesn't always translate into the same size when trying on another brand or model. Some boots made in Europe are sized according to a different numbering system (see chart on following page); women's boots, obviously, don't translate to men's sizes.

When you've put on a pair of boots that feel promising, test them by walking up an inclined surface. On a steep slope, your feet should slide toward the front of the boot just a little—just enough to allow you to fit a finger between your ankle and the collar of the boot. On a flat surface, your toes should be about a thumb's width from the front of the boot. If there is more or less room than that, consider moving to a different size.

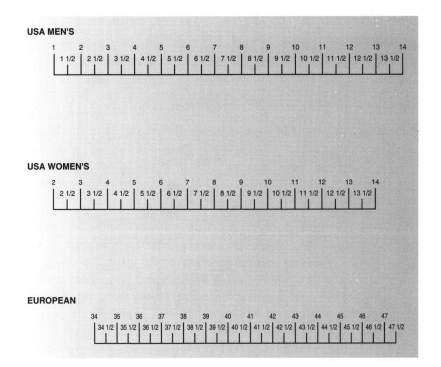

Footwear size conversion chart

If you purchase your boots from a mail-order outlet, you can trace the outline of your foot with a pencil or pen and send the tracing to the store. This is obviously more risky than trying before buying, but if you do find a good pair of boots this way, you can usually rely on the size and fit of similar boots in the future. Most reputable outfits, mail-order or not, will make an exchange or refund if the boots you purchased don't work out (assuming, of course, you've worn them for 50, and not *500*, miles of walking).

Keep in mind that you may be wearing thicker socks with your boots, especially if you'll be doing some serious hiking. You may need to go one-half to a whole size larger to accommodate the extra material you're expecting to ram into your boots. Instead of guessing, bring the socks you'll wear on the trail, and try out various boots with these socks on.

General guidelines for footwear selection aside, you probably know your feet better than anyone else. One foot may be wider than the other, one may be longer, or they both may fit comfortably into only certain shapes and sizes of boot. You'll encounter three types of outdoor footwear: Lightweights, midweights, and heavyweights.

Sound a bit like a boxing match? Well, there won't be much of a fight getting into the shoe that fits.

Before you start shopping, take a few minutes to inventory your anticipated needs. Ask yourself the following questions:

➤ Will you be using your boots for day hiking, weekend trips, or extended backpacking?

➤ What kind of terrain will you be walking on? Trails or backcountry terrain?

➤ What season will you be doing most of your trekking in?

➤ Do you need boots that are waterproof?

I'LL TELL YA!...

Conventional Wisdom

Softer soles are easier on the environment and fit into the low-impact camping ethic. Wear lighter camp shoes or wilderness sandals that allow your feet to breathe after being bound inside boots all day; they're also easier on the ground beneath you.

I'LL TELL YA!...

Conventional Wisdom

Try before you buy. Then wear your hikers for a few days to make sure they don't cause undue irritation. You may look funny in a suit and hiking boots, but nothing is funny about sore feet on the trail.

Lightweight Boots

All things considered, lightweights may be the way to go for most casual outdoor adventurers. Lightweights, made from a combination of natural and synthetic materials (including suede), weigh in at under 3 pounds for the pair. Many models resemble running shoes; no surprise—many big manufacturers of athletic shoes make them. Typical lightweights offer added support in the ankles, softer, cushioned linings, and reinforced eyelets for heavy-duty laces. Such boots are the best bet for summertime use and hiking in hot climates (plain running shoes may be best for desert areas). Lightweights, however, are not very waterproof. That makes them a poor choice for spring and fall hiking on muddy ground—unless they have Gore-Tex liners, which allow feet to breathe while fending off external moisture. Gore-Tex works extremely well, but no boot is completely waterproof.

When trying on lightweights, pay attention to the kind of support you're getting at the ankles. Try to picture how the boot will "handle" on the trail when confronted with uneven turf, small stones, and exposed tree roots. Lightweights are made by most athletic shoe manufacturers, and cost between $70 and $90.

TAHOE II
Raichle's lightest hiker is the best outdoors value today! 2.0mm waterproof, split grain leather and NatureTex 100 recycled polyester fabric in lightweight pattern • recycled polyester lining • recycled nylon shank • PU midsole and Raichle's Positrac Hiker sole made with 40% recycled scrap material • Quick Dry covered PU footbed • cemented construction.

Sesame/Olive	MS 7–12, 13
Brown/Navy	MS 7–12, 13
Olive/Burgundy	LS 5–10
Grey/Navy/Burgundy	LS 5–10

Lightweight hiking boots with manufacturer's description and sizing information

Midweights

When you expect wetter conditions where you'll be hiking, all-leather midweights may be required, if only as a waterproofing measure. This class of boot weighs in at 2 $^3/_4$ to 4 pounds for a pair. Unlike most lightweights, these boots can often be resoled, have more water-resistant seams, and generally last longer. Because they are somewhat less flexible than lightweights (but not as inflexible as heavyweights), midweights require some softening up before you wear them on a long hike. To work in new boots, follow the "50-mile rule"; wear them for at least 50 miles, or until you're confident that they won't give you blisters. Let the boots get to know your feet. These kinds of boots cost between $125 and $225.

Midweights are characterized mostly by what they are made of. Most will be made of suede or nubuk because they tend to be lighter than other types of "finished" leather. Nubuk has a suede-like appearance, but is hardier than suede. You may, however, encounter midweights that are made from a combination of synthetics and leather, as well as models made from more polished leather. There are simply too many style variations to make broad generalizations about material-related configurations.

Most hiking boots are made from top-grain leather, basically the best kind of leather available. If a hiking boot is made from "nubuk leather" it means that top-grain leather has been roughened in the finishing process to give nubuk its suede-like appearance. Suede is top-grain leather that has been split, and its "rough" finish results from this process. This is to say that suede is half the thickness of nubuk (or any other top-grain leather), and therefore lighter than nubuk. Suede is not as durable, however, because it is

> **Conventional Wisdom**
> *I'LL TELL YA!...*
> Remember that feet expand as they heat up and over the course of the day. Shop for hikers in the afternoon or toward the end of the day.

> **Conventional Wisdom**
> *I'LL TELL YA!...*
> Human feet are very complex things. There are more than 52 separate bones in each foot and more than 250,000 glands. It's no wonder they sweat so much, and tend to get sore after so many miles on the trail.

not as thick. When you see smooth leather hikers, you're probably looking at silicon-impregnated leather that appears polished. You'll find this kind of leather in midweight and heavyweight hiking boots.

Midweight hiking boots with manufacturer's description and sizing information.

RAVINE
For the traditional heavy-duty backpacker, 85 years of classic design. 3.5mm Galluser Montan, waterproof leather upper • full leather lining • center folding gusset tongue • stainless, non-rusting hardware • Norwegian stitched welt • steel shank • dual layer leather midsole • RRaichle mountaineering sole • shock absorber heel plug • Climate Zone footbed • strap crampon compatible.

Classic Brown   MS 7–12, 13, 14

Heavyweights

This third class of hiking boot weighs in at over 4 pounds and belongs in the domain of the very serious mountaineer. We mention them here only because you may wonder who on earth would choose to wear such cumbersome—let alone heavy—boots. These boots are often characterized by their one-piece design, meaning that there is no stitching, and therefore no chance of water penetrating sewn stitch lines. (This is not to say that a number of midweights don't share this feature too.)

Heavyweights are designed primarily for mountain climbers who require thick soles and extreme ankle support. Most of these oh-so-serious boots also allow climbers to attach *crampons*—metal treads for walking on ice. If you're considering an adventure that calls for gear this hefty, you probably don't need this book. If you feel you have to own a pair of heavyweight boots, consider that it will be a long time before you feel comfortable in them. Often they require a *long* break-in period. Heavyweights are more pricey too. They cost between $120 and $180.

Caring for Your Boots

A little attention to your boots will help them last for many trips to come. All boots should be kept clean between trips. Dried mud and dirt can be brushed off; many of these boots may be washed on outside surfaces with saddle soap and water. Don't toss your boots into a washing machine; you may ruin them.

When boots are new, you can treat the seams on lightweights with a sealer (available commercially) that can be applied directly from a tube or with a toothpick. Also apply the sealer at the points where the seams meet the soles. The fabric and leather parts of lightweights need to be treated with a silicone treatment like Biwell Green (it comes in a green box). Apply a thin coat with a toothbrush and allow the boot to dry for at least

24 hours. Treat your boots again after each two weeks of use. Use a stiff brush to remove dirt; allow your boots to dry completely before you apply another waterproof coating. Spray-on waterproofing treatments are generally not as good as those rubbed on, even though the convenience in application may seem worth it.

Leather boots should be broken in and then treated with a recommended leather protector. Before treating your boots, wash them thoroughly with saddle soap, be sure to rub off any dirt, dry them off using a rag, and then place them in a warm place to dry out completely. Treat the seams separately with a sealer, and then apply a sealer designed for either nubuk or smooth leather. (Also apply the sealer at the points where the seams meet the soles.)

Nubuk Leather

If you're applying a coat of nubuk leather treatment to boots of this type, allow the sealer to dry before you go over the boots with a suede brush (which should return them to their original appearance). Lightly wash the boots with saddle soap, making sure you allow adequate drying time before you reapply the waterproofing treatment.

Smooth Leather

A number of preparations are available to protect smooth leather boots: Some spray on; others you rub in with a cloth, an old toothbrush, or a sponge ("elbow grease" is the secret ingredient). Some hiking boot manufacturers are fussy about the protector their products like best, and will recommend you apply one particular brand.

Many retailers recommend a product called Biwell Red (it comes in a red box and is the sister treatment to Biwell Green). Applied sparingly, it penetrates smooth leather boots and replaces essential oils—keeping leather soft, supple, and waterproof. Who could ask for more?

Wash and reapply leather protectors after every two weeks of use.

Here's How

Never place your boots next to a campfire or other heat source to dry them! Heat can seriously weaken leather and deforms synthetics. To dry out boots, remove the insoles (if any), loosen the laces, pull out the tongues, stuff them loosely with newspaper, and place them in a dry, warm location. If your boots are completely soaked through, they may take several days to dry.

Rocks Around the Socks (and Liners, Too)

Comfortable boots go hand-in-hand (or should we say foot-to-foot?) with wearing the appropriate socks and foot liners. The goal is to keep your feet warm and dry. You want a sock that wicks perspiration away from your feet and allows it to evaporate. And, you want your socks to be comfortable and provide extra padding too. Experienced backpackers wear a pair of liners (polypropylene, Capilene, or Thermax brand) under heavy or slightly lighter wool socks. Other one-piece hiking socks are designed to be worn without liners and provide wicking action, and padding to cushion bumps in the road.

Don't wear cotton socks or cotton liners! As a matter of fact, avoid cotton garments in general when adventuring in the outdoors. Cotton will sop up foot perspiration, stay damp, and cause blistering. Wool, on the other hand, acts as a foot cushion and wicks away moisture. Even in hot climates, experience teaches that wool socks are best. Carry extras, or try to rinse out (and dry!) your socks and liners every day.

Good wool socks for hiking and backpacking will have smooth seams and soft fibers. Some sport reinforced heels and toes for extra durability. Gore-Tex boot liners and sock covers are also available, though somewhat expensive; this miracle material may be the right choice if you're wearing lightweights without adequate water protection.

Conventional Wisdom
Calf-length socks can be rolled over the tops of hiking boots to prevent laces from becoming untied. On longer trips, it's a good idea to re-tighten boot laces after about an hour to ensure a good fit.

Although most of us don't give it much thought, socks do come in different sizes, though sizing information is somewhat baffling in relation to how footwear is sized. Choosing the right size of sock can be nearly as important as choosing a sock in the right material. A sock that is too small will bind your foot or be too small to layer with other socks. Socks that are too large will bunch up and cause uncomfortable rubbing. Table 13.1 shows you how sock sizes compare to boot sizes; choose the sock size that's right for you.

Table 13.1 Sock-and-boot conversion chart

Kids	Boot Size Women	Men	Sock Size
10–12			7
	2–4	1–3	8
	5–6	4–5	9
	7–8	6–7	10

Kids	Boot Size Women	Men	Sock Size
	9–11	8–10	11
	11	12	

Treating Blisters

Blisters are an inevitability. Grin and bear it.

Certainly you can reduce the chance of blisters by wearing liners and wool socks, taking your boots on a break-in tour of duty, and insisting on the right fit when you buy your boots in the first place. But what if you've taken all these bits of advice to heart and *still* feel a blister coming on as you head down the trail?

The first thing to do is to stop, sit down, and take off your boot.

The second thing to do is to treat the blister or blister-in-the-making (the sore, red spot where it hurts) with some sort of blister medicine.

Blister treatments are not really "medicines" per se; normally they cover the blister and cushion it against further irritation. The most relied-on blister treatment is moleskin, available at most outdoor specialty stores, shoe stores, and drug stores. It comes as a flat strip of padded adhesive that varies in size, color, and thickness. You trim it to cover the affected area and a little bit more.

If possible, dab the blister with an antiseptic and allow the affected area to dry before application. If the blister has filled with water (resulting in a white, yucky-looking bump) it should be drained before covering it. To accomplish this, lance the blister at the edge with a needle sterilized in rubbing alcohol, or by positioning the tip of the needle in a flame of a match or butane lighter.

Conventional Wisdom
Discolored toenails are a sign of ill-fitting boots or long toenails. Keep your toenails trimmed and make sure your boots are the right fit.

I'LL TELL YA!...

Here's How
Stubbed toes can create a blood spot under a toenail. To lessen pressure and speed healing, heat a needle or tip of a safety pin until it is white-hot, and then *gently* pierce the affected toenail to release the trapped blood. The heated needle should effectively "melt" a small hole in the nail—a painless procedure (believe it or not) that can be used for fingernails as well.

Then peel away the backing from your prepared moleskin patch to expose the adhesive; stick the patch over the affected skin. To protect the area even further, put another moleskin patch on over the first one, or you can cover the moleskin with medical tape.

Another blister remedy is a product called 2nd Skin, manufactured by Spenco in Waco, Texas. These sheets of friction-reducing jelly can be applied to the blistered area and held in place with a strip or two of adhesive tape, a Band-Aid, or the self-sticking adhesive netting supplied with the product.

Whatever method you use, never set off on a trip—even a short one—without some kind of blister treatment. Blisters can become very painful and can ruin a trip. As soon as you detect any discomfort, remove your hiking boots and have a look. Try to locate the source of the friction (bunched sock, pebble, and so on) and remove the problem. Then treat the blister as just described.

The Least You Need to Know

➤ Choosing the right hiking boots for the type of trekking you do is important. What really counts, no matter which model you choose, is that it fit properly. Make every effort to try out as many different boots as possible before you settle on a particular pair.

➤ Always wear wool socks; and steer away from anything made of cotton. Wool wicks away moisture; cotton holds moisture, encourages chafing, and can cause blisters.

➤ Never embark on any hike, whether for a day or for longer, without carrying a treatment for blisters like Moleskin (Dr. Scholl's) or 2nd Skin (Spenco). As soon as you feel any foot discomfort, remove your boot and remedy the problem.

Choosing the House for Your Back

Admittedly, the picture of a hiker with a loaded backpack conjures up images of a snail, turtle, or other cold-blooded animal that carries its house on its back. The image is not so farfetched, considering that that's what you're effectively doing when you strap on one of these monster suitcases and head off into the woods. To avoid becoming a sweating beast of burden for all your stuff, you need to know how to select, load, and wear a backpack. This chapter teaches you how to do just that.

Conventional Wisdom

No pack is completely waterproof. If you'll be traveling in areas where it is known to rain frequently, make sure that the pack has some kind of waterproofing (typically a urethane coating) and that clothes and supplies are packed in water resistant stuffsacks.

Ideally you'll be able to visit a store that offers a range of backpacks in different sizes, capacities, and colors. It's the same old story: Try before you buy. This sage advice is as important for backpacks as it is for hiking boots; these two pieces of equipment determine your overall comfort outdoors—and in some cases, the very success of your outdoor adventure.

Considering that both boots and backpacks will constitute two of the biggest expenses in your camping-gear repertoire, you should be as picky as possible about how a backpack fits and feels when fully loaded. And as with all outdoor gear, you'll be confronted with a host of options—and ultimately tradeoffs—when it comes to what your bank account can bear. Keep in mind that you can *rent* backpacks when you're first starting out. Road-testing (or should we say *trail*-testing) backpacks this way gives you some insight into what's out there; you can gauge the features you like and dislike. Most experienced backpackers keep going back to the same makes and models; if you seek advice, don't be surprised if the people you ask are adamant about the brands they use, even if you find their choice uncomfortable (or unbearable) when you try it on yourself. Ask for advice, but don't be stymied by one person's preference.

Conventional Wisdom
Choose backpacks with a high-thread count, and look for extra strength in the pack's bottom and along the seam lines. Stress points—where seams meet each other—should be reinforced with extra stitching.

Getting the Best Backpack

Backpacks are divided into two main categories: Internal-frame and external-frame models. Casual backpackers may want to purchase an external-frame model, which is distinguished by an exposed aluminum or rigid support system, if only for price alone. Decent external-frame backpacks start at about $149. Day hikers can stick to smaller packs designed to carry only the essentials needed for the day.

Take some time to pick whatever backpack you ultimately choose. A good backpack should fit properly and feel somewhat comfortable to carry—remember you'll be wearing it for long stretches of time. It should also feel well-balanced: Follow the advice given here for determining how to choose the right backpack for you.

External-Frame Backpacks

These backpacks are becoming fewer and fewer on trails everywhere as internal-frame backpacks improve in design and comfort, though they are still more expensive than internal-frame models.

External-frame models are distinguished by three components, namely the frame, packbag, and suspension system. Without making too much of it, the idea behind any frame is to distribute the load of the pack onto the wearer's hips, thereby eliminating weight on the more fragile back muscles. The exposed frame of this type of backpack is made from seamless aluminum, or another high-tech alloy. External-frame backpacks, compared to internal-frame models, place the pack's load up high, thereby concentrating the center of gravity on the hips. The advantage of this setup is that it permits the wearer to stand straighter while walking, which is less tiring than having to slouch forward when transporting a load of clothes, cooking equipment, a tent, and bedding. You get the idea.

External frames also hold the pack away from the wearer's back, which allows air to circulate, and by extension, is a cooler alternative to having the backpack right up against your back. Depending on what the temperature is, the type of terrain you're walking on, and your general level of fitness, your back may come to resemble a small waterfall anyway. And on uneven terrain where you lose your footing from time to time, the high load may make you look like a drunken camel. On established trails where the high load won't snag too many branches, and where the ground is relatively level, external-frame backpacks may be good choices for both expert and novice alike, but the majority of salespeople will tell you that in the long run an internal-frame model is best. It is easier to travel with, can fit into a canoe more easily, and is better for carrying laundry when called into action in an urban environment.

> **I'LL TELL YA!...**
>
> **Conventional Wisdom**
> However rugged they may be outdoors, backpacks with external frames are less durable than internal-frame packs when checked as baggage on commercial flights. The exposed frame invites damage into its open spaces on conveyor belts and baggage carousels.

An external-frame pack concentrates the center of gravity for the load on your hips.

Internal-Frame Backpacks

Internal-frame packs are worn closer to the body and have a lower center of gravity than their external-frame siblings. The frame in these packs is integrated into the pack itself, which means that it is hotter to wear, but the load is more manageable on uneven terrain. The frame is usually made from two aluminum strips that conform to the shape of the wearer's back over time and is concealed in parallel sleeves that are stitched into the back of the pack. In fact, the frame may already be slightly bent when new; some designs also taper slightly inward as they reach the bottom of the pack. Other backpacks have combination stays and a plastic sheet that give the packs their stiffness. In this setup there may be only one stay running through the center length of the pack combined with a plastic sheet. Other models may have two stays and a plastic sheet.

As with an external-frame pack (but not as efficiently), this structure transfers the weight of the stuff inside the pack to the hips. Internal-frame packs are not as rigid as external-frame models; they allow a certain amount of flexing and movement in tandem with the wearer's body. High-tech designs may be molded for comfort and extra strength; they conform to the back more precisely.

Internal-frame packs are less rigid and better when you're hiking on uneven terrain.

So Discreet: Travel Packs

One interesting variation on the internal-frame pack is a pack that converts to a sort-of-suitcase. This *Get-Smart*-meets-007-style backpack has a zippered panel to conceal its belts and straps, as well as a front-loading panel that permits easy access to the pack's contents. For shorter jaunts, or where the appearance of a real backpack may be out of place (say, if you're taking off for a hike from a ritzy hotel), these backpacks may fit the bill if you don't mind losing some performance characteristics of a real backpack.

Fit, Form, and Function . . . Putting It All On

Unfortunately, you can't just throw the thing over your shoulders and dart off into the woods. Most backpacks, whether internal- or external-frame models, require that you give some thought to fitting. Correct fit depends on the size of the pack and its type of suspension.

Backpacks are rated according to height (tall, medium, and short). The height of the pack corresponds to the length of the wearer's torso, or the measurement from the hips to the shoulders. Needless to say, people are shaped differently, and a tall person may have a shorter back than someone who is short. Determine what length range you're in (have a friend measure you, or ask a salesperson at your local camping/hiking supply store); try on a number of different packs to find a good fit. Keep in mind that *no* backpack feels very comfortable when you first put it on; they need adjustment. Also, over time an internal-frame pack's frame will bend to take on the contours of its master's back.

Cubic Inches or Liters: A Matter of Capacity

Packs are sold according to their capacity, rated either in cubic inches or liters. Depending on where the pack is manufactured (much of the world still isn't metric), you'll need to use one of these two measurements to determine how much room you're working with. For example, a 4,271-cubic-inch (70-liter) backpack has the volume you'll normally need for treks that last over five days. Use the following tables (14.1 and 14.2) to convert back and forth between liters and cubic inches.

Table 14.1   Converting liters to cubic inches

Liters	Equivalent in Cubic Inches
10	610
20	1,220
30	1,831
40	2,441
50	3,051
60	3,661
70	4,271
80	4,882
90	5,492
100	6,102

Table 14.2   Converting cubic inches to liters

Cubic Inches	Equivalent in Liters
1,000	16.4
2,000	32.8
3,000	49.2
4,000	65.6
5,000	81.9
6,000	98.3
7,000	114.7
8,000	131.1
9,000	147.5
10,000	163.9

Backpack Capacity for Different Trips

Ovenights (1–2 days) 2,800–3,000 cu. in.

Weekends (2–4 days) 3,000–4,000 cu. in.

Longer Trips (5+ days) 3,800–4,800 cu. in.

Expeditions (10+ days) 5,000–6,500 cu. in.

Although you can rate packs according to total volume, another important issue is how much a particular design—and hiker—can carry. Bigger is not always better, especially in the case of backpacks. An extra-large capacity pack is great, but think seriously about the amount of weight *you* can actually carry mile after mile. Most adventurers can tote only about 40 pounds; if you have to carry more because the length of your trip demands it, the general rule of thumb is that backpackers should plan to carry about 30% of their weight on their backs. This means, for instance, that a 160-pound person should be able to load up with about 48 pounds, and a 110-pound person about 33 pounds. Comfort and fit are key qualities.

Suspension Systems

We're not talking about shock absorbers or independent suspension here. In the world of backpacks, the *suspension system* refers to the hip belt, shoulder straps, and back support. A pack's suspension should be attached to the frame to distribute the load correctly. A properly adjusted suspension system will transfer up to 80 percent of the pack's load to the hips, which are (it bears repeating) much stronger than the shoulder and back muscles.

Ways to Be Hip

Because the hips are designed to take on most of the body's weight, the *hip belt* is the most critical part of a backpack's suspension system. Look for packs that feature well-padded belts that are also shaped to fit around the hips. Ideally, the upper ridge of the hip belt should be positioned about 1 inch above the hip bone.

Shoulder Straps

Shoulder straps are designed primarily to stabilize the pack while at the same time absorbing some of the pack's weight. Look for shoulder straps that are adequately padded and contoured to fit the curves of your shoulders; check to make sure you can comfortably position them where they get close to the neck. On large-capacity packs, *tension straps* at the tops of the shoulder straps are designed to pull the load in closer to the shoulders.

Loosen and tighten these straps while walking with the pack to determine the correct tension, and to transfer weight to the shoulder blades. In addition, a *sternum strap* fastened across the chest will prevent the weight of the pack from pulling your shoulders back. The sternum strap keeps the shoulder straps from splaying out into your armpits; be sure to position it comfortably.

Back Supports

For maximum comfort and ease of carrying, your pack needs padding in the shoulder straps and hip belt. Internal-frame back packs also use a *lumbar pad* to provide back support and protection from any hard objects inside the pack. In many models, the lumbar pad can be moved up or down for optimum performance. External-frame backpacks employ a piece of fabric or a similar lumbar pad stretched between strategic points on the frame tubing to provide similar support.

Conventional Wisdom

Packs made for women assume a narrower back: Men with narrow shoulders should check out a women's backpack for comfort, and women with wider backs should try packs designed for men.

A Matter of Construction

Quality backpacks will be hard-wearing and hard-working pieces of equipment because they have to be. You'll be offered two types of materials to choose from: Cordura and nylon packcloth. Each has its own look and feel, and you'll have to evaluate one over the other according to your budget, the type of trip you're undertaking, and how long you expect to be on the trail.

Cordura Nylon

Backpacks that boast of being made of Cordura or another strong nylon like it are very durable and rip-resistant. Cordura should be incorporated in backpacks for those traveling off-trail and in the deep backcountry; it's made from large-diameter nylon fibers. Cordura is rough and textured to the touch, and ideal for heavy-duty conditions that demand durability. Cordura is typically coated with urethane to make it waterproof. Kodra is the offshore version of the Cordura-brand material, meaning that it is not made domestically.

Nylon Packcloth

Nylon packcloth is smoother to the touch and somewhat more waterproof than Cordura because waterproof coatings bond better. Nylon packcloth backpacks are quite durable and feature high thread counts (meaning that the fabric is tightly woven and durable). The standard weight for packcloth is 250 to 270 grams; good backpacks will feature these numbers.

Fine-Tuning the Rig

Few backpacks feel good when you first put them on. As you get to know your backpack, you'll be able to tweak a strap here and tighten a belt there to get it to feel right. Before you plunk down the cash for a backpack, try loading it up in the store with a bunch of items (at least 25 pounds for serious backpackers) to simulate a load you might carry on the trail.

First, secure the load by fastening the *compression straps* tightly (these straps on the outside of the pack hold the whole parcel together). Put on the backpack and fasten the hip belt around the hipbone so it's snug. Then adjust the shoulder pads so that most of the weight in the pack is borne by your hips. If the pack has a sternum strap, tighten it to help minimize shifting. Try to get the pack as close to your back as possible.

To ascertain the comfort and fit of a pack, go on a little tour around the block with the loaded pack. Good camping and hiking outlets will oblige and wave you through security at the exit. On your mini-hike, adjust the various straps and see how the pack responds.

You should be able to get the backpack to feel fairly comfortable on its trial run. If it doesn't, try on other models when you return to the store; keep looking and testing until you find one that feels right. Remember that the stays of an internal-frame pack will conform to the shape of your back over time; the pack should become even more comfortable with use. Some stays can be extracted from their sleeves and bent by hand, but this is a job for experienced backpackers (and those more familiar with backpacks in general).

If you're looking for ease of adjustment, an external-frame pack may be for you. There are fewer factors to consider, and certainly fewer adjustments to make. The trade-off is a less precise fit. With an internal-frame pack, you'll need to make adjustments almost daily when backpacking. This isn't a chore, but something to think about as you go through the motions of trying on different packs before purchasing one.

> **Conventional Wisdom**
> No backpack is rainproof, no matter what it's made of or coated with. If you expect to be backpacking in rainy weather, pack items that should stay dry into a number of color-coded stuffsacks; cover the pack with a waterproof cover.

I'LL TELL YA!...

Day Packs

On short day-long hikes a simple, inexpensive *day pack* (like those commonly seen on college campuses) is the answer. These small packs should have enough room for guide-books, cameras, binoculars, and lunch—enough carrying capacity to get you through the day with just enough creature comforts to keep you happy. Many day packs come with waist straps and extra padding for stability and greater carrying comfort. They may also have zippered pockets for storing the smaller things that need to be carried along. These packs can serve as an adjunct to bigger backpacks when day-long excursions away from a base camp don't require all the goods and services you'd normally lug in a full-size pack. Also consider strapping on a *fanny pack* when you wear either a day pack or a full-size backpack. They offer easy access to matches, knives, lip balms, and the like.

Rules

Day hikers are, in some ways, prime candidates for hypothermia—a condition that sees the body temperature drop to dangerous lows—because they are not carrying the appropriate equipment to protect them from all the elements. Day hikers should carry an emergency blanket under which to nestle if the weather unmakes their day, the temperature drops, or they find themselves lost and cold.

Ways to Pack a Backpack (Say That Five Times in a Row Out Loud)

Backpacks are designed either to be loaded from the front or loaded from the top. Because zippers allow access to panels in front-loading packs, there is an increased risk that the zippers will break (although top-quality packs will offer an iron-clad guarantee). In addition, zippers are potential entry points for water. Top loaders are therefore more water resistant, but there is a tradeoff in accessibility to the contents of the pack. Don't take a chance on waterproofness: Get a rain cover to fit over your pack.

Generally speaking, heavy items should be packed up high in the pack for balance while walking. Also, toiletries and things you may need to use during the day (like toilet paper, insect repellent, blister covers) should be placed where they can be easily unpacked. Place your sleeping bag in the lower portion or compartments *inside* the pack (strapping it to the outside leaves it exposed to the elements). By placing soft things in the lower part of the pack, you create a foundation for the rest of your equipment while adding lumbar support in packs with little or no lumbar pad.

Place heavier items (stoves, food, pots, pans, extra boots, and so on) in the center of the main compartment. Ideally, the heaviest part of the load should be above the hips and below the shoulders. As you get to know your pack better—including the way it handles on your back—you may want to move heavy items upward or downward in the pack to get the best weight distribution.

Backpackers don't universally agree on the best way to pack equipment; only your own acquired experience will settle the matter for *you*. But by loading heavy items in the middle to upper part of the pack, you maintain your natural center of balance and ability to negotiate slopes and uneven terrain.

Place clothing and lighter things inside and on top of the rest of your stuff. Once your equipment is packed, batten down the hatches (or pull the top closed, in plain English). Use the top and side pockets for emergency gear and supplies, first-aid kits, water, and toilet paper. The tent should be packed in the lower part of the pack, along with the sleeping bag, but tent poles contained inside a stuffsack can be lashed to the outside of the pack, along with a Therm-a-Rest mattress (or another rolled up sleeping mat).

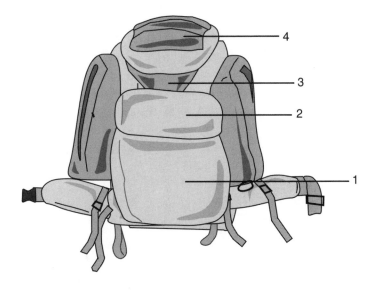

Packing a backpack

1. Sleeping bag, clothes, soft items, and tent

2. Heavier items, stove, and extra boots

3. Need-to-have clothing, rainwear

4. Pockets: emergency supplies, first-aid kit, water, toilet paper

Safe Camping

Don't forget about the bears. If you're carrying any kind of food in your pack, whether it be a chocolate bar or bag of granola, suspend your pack (along with any other foodstuffs) from a high branch when you stop for the night. Put it out of the reach of bears. Even the smallest whiff of food can be an invitation to a marauding bear. And that's a hell of a way to wake up!

Backpack Packing Checklists (Essentials)

Day Trips

Snacks

Sandwiches

Water (4 quarts per day, minimum)

First-aid kit

Toilet paper/tissues

Insect repellent

Topo maps

Pencil

Hat

Self-sealing sandwich bags

Compass

Watch

Sunscreen

Raingear

Whistle

Hiking boots

Appropriate clothing

Matches/lighter

Moleskin

Overnight

Tent

Groundsheet

Stove

Fuel

Cutlery•

Pots, pans, kettle

Sleeping bag

Sleeping mat

Water bottles

Water (4 quarts per day, minimum)

Water filter/purification tablets

First aid kit

Toilet paper

Insect repellent ✦

Topo maps

Pencil

Biodegradable soap

Flashlight/candle lantern/extra batteries

Hat •

Camp shoes (sneakers)

Sunglasses

Hiking socks

Self-sealing sandwich bags

Toothbrush

Toothpaste

Razor

Shaving cream

Signal mirror

Rope (50 ft. length)

Compass

Watch

Sunscreen

Food

Snacks/energy food (Power Bars)

Raingear

Whistle

Hiking boots

Tarpaulin

Appropriate clothing

Garbage bags

Matches/lighter

Towel

Portable bladder shower

Moleskin

The Least You Need to Know

➤ Backpacks come in basically two configurations: External- and internal-frame models. External-frame backpacks require less adjustment, but place the pack's load up high—which may make them less stable than internal-frame models in rough terrain.

➤ Try on as many backpacks as you can to find the one that fits just right. Don't be shy: Load up the backpack with at least 25 pounds of stuff and go for a walk around the store (or, if possible, for a longer walk outside).

➤ Play around with the various straps and adjustments to find out what they do. Get a pack that will break in well; never purchase one you're uncomfortable with.

➤ The most important part of the suspension system on a pack is the hip belt. It transfers most of the pack's weight to the hips, which are stronger load-bearers than any of the back muscles. Ideally, the upper ridge of the hip belt should be positioned about 1 inch above the hip bone.

Ways to Dress for Success in the Outdoors

The outdoor look is in.

This chapter isn't really about fashion, even though the height of urban chic means wearing clothes that typically belong in the outdoors, or at least on a hunting expedition in the deep woods. In most cases, looks really are deceiving; most people who wear outdoor apparel will come about as close to the outdoors as a walk in the park. This is not to say that outdoor clothing isn't dandy to wear in normal, everyday circumstances (it can be extremely comfortable and durable). But choosing the right clothes for an actual outdoor excursion is very different from suiting up for a safari in the concrete jungle, as you'll learn in this chapter.

Although style and looks are more important in the urban world, wearing the right clothes can make the difference between a comfortable outdoor vacation and one that is cold, wet, and miserable. In essence, "dressing for success" in the outdoors really means protecting yourself from the vagaries of wind, rain, and cold. Add to this list heat and sun, and you realize that clothes are really your first line of defense against a whole slew of things that nature can throw at you.

Conventional Wisdom

Choose quick-drying synthetic materials when purchasing camping and hiking clothes. Not only are they lighter, they tend to be more durable for outdoor use. Gore-Tex fabric is designed to keep you dry in a rain storm while still being "breathable"—allowing perspiration to pass through the fabric to the outside. Other synthetics may be waterproof too, but prevent perspiration from passing through the fabric to the outside.

Before synthetics, outdoor adventurers had only a small choice of materials to wear in the outdoors. Today, modern synthetics abound, many specially formulated for active outdoorsmen and nature-lovers who are willing to endure a bit of bad weather in their quest for adventure. But suiting up for the outdoors doesn't mean that you have to wear garments made of Space Age materials. Wool has never been matched for its ability to sustain both bad weather and physical abuse; the same is true of other natural fabrics and insulators. If you combine some of the old with some of the new, enjoying the outdoors is no problem at all.

Layering—Peeling for Pleasure

Experienced outdoor adventurers will tell you that the key to dressing comfortably is to *layer your clothes*. This is not a complex concept, as anyone who has lived in a colder climate already understands. When venturing into the frigid outdoors, people typically wear a shirt, a sweater, and then some kind of insulated jacket to stay warm and comfortable. Simply put, layering means covering the body with several layers of clothing that can be removed or added as temperatures or weather conditions change. But it doesn't have to be cold for outdoor adventurers to benefit from layering.

Conventional Wisdom

Summer weather conditions may warrant loose-fitting clothes and shorts. But remember, nighttime temperatures can drop, so plan for colder weather in warmer weather.

Vigorous activity makes the body work harder and get hotter. The body tries to cool things down by perspiring to maintain its ideal temperature range (between 97 and 100 degrees Fahrenheit). In the outdoors, the surrounding temperature can rise and fall—and you exert yourself differently depending on the terrain and the amount you are carrying. In response to these and other factors, your body makes an effort to maintain what it thinks is normal. You feel this adjustment when you detect the discomfort of being too warm or too cold.

To stay comfortable in the outdoors, the idea is to help the body maintain its normal temperature. Ideally, wearing three thin layers of clothing—which you can shed or add, depending on how cold or hot you feel—should do the job. Peel down to a lighter layer to cool down; add a layer to warm up. That's what it means to peel for pleasure—and that's how simple layering is.

> **Conventional Wisdom**
> I'LL TELL YA!...
>
> *Anoraks*—originally invented by the Eskimos—are shells that pull over your head and can be tightened with a drawstring. Synthetic versions are made of urethane-coated nylon. More advanced types may be coated with Gore-Tex. Because they have no full-length zippers running down the front, anoraks are completely wind-resistant; and often they feature a large closable pocket across the front, with side pockets that offer sanctuary for cold hands.

The Inner Layer (Psychiatrists Take Note)

I'm not trying to delve too deep into your psyche in this section. The *inner layer* refers to the first layer of clothing that any outdoor adventurer should be concerned with. We're talking about underwear, of course, but not the kind you find in a Victoria's Secret catalog. Specifically, we're talking about long underwear, or some variation on it.

In a system of layered clothing designed for colder weather, underwear is critical. Underwear must wick moisture (in the form of perspiration) away from the body and transfer it to the next layer of clothing, where it can evaporate. The fabrics that do this best include polyester and polypropylene, which are quick-drying and durable.

The importance of staying dry cannot be overstated: Wet clothes against the skin draw out heat from the body at an amazing rate because water is especially good at conducting heat. Improperly dressed campers

> **Conventional Wisdom**
> I'LL TELL YA!...
>
> Synthetic underwear usually comes in light, medium, and heavy weights. Lighter weights are used for backpacking, medium weights for general-purpose camping, and heavy weights for cold weather when insulation is important.

can suffer from *hypothermia*—a potentially life-threatening condition in which the body falls dangerously below its normal temperature. Hypothermia can strike in temperatures above freezing, and any camper's underwear should be designed with one purpose in mind: To remove moisture in the form of perspiration and move it out to the next layer of clothing. Recommended fabrics include spun polyester, with Lycra for extra stretch, and silk, which is less durable but feels great against the skin. Look for outdoor-grade underwear where you purchase outdoor gear.

The Middle Layer

The function of the *middle layer* is to draw moisture from the inner layer and encourage it to dissipate as quickly as possible. Look for shirts that provide enough freedom of movement and insulation qualities to do a good job of keeping you both warm and unhindered as you go about your outdoor activities—whether backpacking, hiking, or just hanging around the campsite. *Pile*, which is made from polyester (and also from various blends of nylon and acrylic), has proved itself an ideal material for the middle layer.

Conventional Wisdom

Jackets and shirts not only protect you from the cold, they can act as a barrier to biting insects in mosquito and black-fly season if you turn up the collar and tightly button the cuffs.

Good fabric choices at this stage in the game include wool and some of the newer synthetics. Wool is not as efficient as synthetics in encouraging moisture to evaporate; its fibers have a tendency to take on moisture and hang on to it. Although wool can help fend off a light drizzle, it takes time to dry; synthetics dry extremely quickly. Wool is also bulkier compared to most synthetics. Combination fleece-and-pile garments are good alternatives to wool.

You should be able to count on the middle layer to help keep you warm, but it should also be adaptable to warmer temperatures. Look for buttons, zippers, or other openings that can provide extra ventilation.

The Outer Layer

The *outer layer* or *shell* can vary according to the severity of the weather in the region where you're traveling. It can be a lightweight jacket, stuffed away in a backpack's pocket and brought out at the first sign of a sprinkle—or it can be an insulated parka designed for the foulest and coldest of weather. Your shell should do two things well:

➤ Protect the wearer from rain and wind

➤ Permit body moisture to escape

Remember that water is a highly efficient conductor of heat; wet clothing will draw heat from the body like nothing else. Therefore the more waterproof the outer layer, the better. The outer layer should also permit body moisture to escape, and have slits or other openings that can be opened and closed depending on the temperature.

In warmer conditions where there is little chance of rain, a thin nylon shell may be all you need to deflect the wind as it passes by you. In more severe conditions, you'll need to be wearing something made from more durable and water-resistant materials.

Waterproof Breathables

This is where Gore-Tex fabric steps in and the other waterproof breathables take a bow.

Gore-Tex fabric is a high-tech textile that has become one of the premier waterproof breathable materials in outerwear. Its chemical name is polytetrafluorethylene. Used in everything from hiking boots to parkas and socks, Gore-Tex has earned a sterling reputation among serious outdoor enthusiasts everywhere. This performance fabric allows body moisture to escape while preventing moisture from the outside (whether pelting rain or light drizzle) from entering through to the inside.

How is Gore-Tex fabric both breathable and waterproof, you ask?

Concentrate for a moment and take this in: Gore-Tex fabric is actually a membrane that is bonded to other materials such as polyester and nylon. Every square inch of the membrane has about 9 billion microscopic pores. These pores are smaller than the smallest drop of water, but about 700 times bigger than a water-vapor molecule. Voilà! Water from the outside can't get through the membrane, but water *vapor*—perspiration wicked away from the inner and middle layers of clothing—can. Now isn't that unfair?

Gore-Tex membrane is not only bonded to shell fabrics. You can find it in a range of outdoor clothing, from sock liners and hiking boots to parkas and gloves. To top it all off, Gore-Tex fabric is very durable and resistant to oil-based lotions, insect repellents, and a host of other goodies that might be smeared over clothing during a camping trip or outdoor excursion.

Sound like an ad for Gore-Tex fabric or outerwear? Try it—you'll like it.

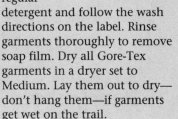

Here's How
Gore-Tex outerwear should be kept clean. Use regular detergent and follow the wash directions on the label. Rinse garments thoroughly to remove soap film. Dry all Gore-Tex garments in a dryer set to Medium. Lay them out to dry—don't hang them—if garments get wet on the trail.

Gore-Tex keeps wetness out, yet lets perspiration evaporate. (Courtesy of W.L. Gore & Associates, Inc.)

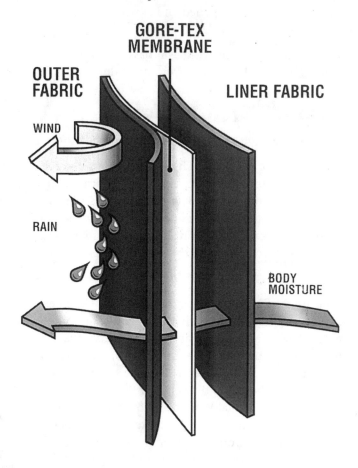

A Smorgasbord of Materials

When you're shopping for outdoor clothing, you'll run into a smorgasbord of different fabrics. It pays to understand the features and merits of each kind of fabric so you can choose the one that will work best for you. Don't be confused by the number of fabrics on the market, just pay attention to what each is designed to do—whether it's trying to keep you warm or dry, or cool and sweatfree. Ask questions and get the answers. Don't let fabric techno-babble get you down.

➤ **Cotton:** This natural fabric should not be worn in the outdoors except in the warmest conditions. It is extremely absorbent and soaks up moisture from perspiration.

➤ **Cotton/Nylon and Cotton/Polyester:** Blends of cotton and nylon, and cotton and polyester, are more wind-resistant than 100 percent cotton, but still should be avoided by serious outdoors people.

➤ **Wool:** This fabric is a favorite of outdoor travelers. It can be less soft to the touch than cotton, but it absorbs a good deal of moisture before it feels sodden. Once soaked, wool takes a long time to dry.

➤ **Wool Blends:** Blends are less warm than 100-percent wool, but may be more durable and less expensive.

➤ **Nylon:** Compared to cotton, nylon is lighter and more durable.

➤ **Uncoated Nylon:** Wind-resistant and breathable, but not waterproof.

➤ **Coated Nylon:** Water-resistant, but tends to "lock in" body moisture.

➤ **Ripstop Nylon:** A grid of threads strengthens garments made from ripstop nylon, making them more durable.

➤ **Nylon Taffeta:** Moderately water-resistant, this material is strong and often used in the manufacture of tents.

➤ **Cordura:** A heavy, coarsely woven nylon material, abrasion-resistant and strong. Coatings improve water resistance, but they don't bond as well to Cordura as they do other materials.

➤ **Pile:** More warmth but less protection from wind and water. Pile is a good alternative to wool as a middle clothing layer.

➤ **Plastic:** Not suitable for outdoor apparel because it stops body moisture from escaping.

➤ **Neoprene:** Strong, but weighty. Typically used in clothes made for paddlesports.

➤ **Urethane or Polymer:** Adds weight and water resistance as a coating on nylon or polyester.

➤ **Gore-Tex Fabric:** As described earlier, this is a miraculous waterproof and breathable membrane that is bonded to nylon fabric.

Fills and Insulators

No matter what kind of material or fabric you use, staying warm has a lot to do with the type of fill incorporated into the creation of a garment. Fills will be either man-made or synthetics, or natural or down, respectively.

➤ **Down:** This natural insulator—the feathers of geese—is the best insulator on a per-pound basis. Down is rated according to its *lofting* ability in cubic inches per ounce. A loft of 500 to 550 is good; 600 to 700 is excellent.

➤ **Synthetics:** Cheaper than down and not as long-lasting, but synthetics absorb less moisture and retain some of their insulating powers when wet. Thinsulate is less bulky than other synthetics but offers good insulation. It is used in gloves, mitts, hats, jackets, and a range of other cold-weather apparel. Other synthetic fills include Hollofil, Thermoloft, and Slimtech.

Singing in the Rain—A Heavy-Weather Alternative

The only bad thing about Gore-Tex is its cost, which can seem quite high when compared to other waterproof coatings and materials. If you're starting out and don't want to sink a lot of money into your outdoor clothing yet, you'll need at least some kind of protection from a potential downpour. The best that a little money can buy is a *rain poncho* to drape over the other layers in the clothing mix.

Although a poncho isn't breathable, it will allow air to circulate from the opening underneath. Some ponchos also have vents under the arms that provide more ventilation. In windy conditions, ponchos are prone to flapping, and therefore are less waterproof than a "closed" waterproofing system. You can, however, get double-duty rain protection from a poncho if you drape it over both your backpack and you. In a severe downpour, you'll have to decide who stays dry as you set up the tent—you or your backpack. (I know which I'd choose.)

Here's How

Keep outdoor clothing as clean as possible, and follow label directions for cleaning procedures. Wash outdoor clothing in the warmest possible water shown in the range to help remove dirt and grime. Wash wool clothing by hand in cold water with mild soap, or with a detergent recommended for delicate fabrics. Down-filled fabrics may be washed by hand or in a washing machine. Do *not* dry-clean down or synthetic-filled apparel.

Suiting Up for Colder Weather

If your outdoor activities take place in frigid conditions you'll need another layer under your rain- and windproof shell. Consider wearing some kind of down- or synthetic-fill vest or jacket under the shell. This layering configuration is an alternative to wearing a much heavier parka or insulated coat; your arms will probably move more easily.

As with sleeping bags, air warmed by your body can seep through a coat's zippers. When purchasing outdoor apparel for use in colder weather, select coats and other outerwear that feature flaps you can secure over the zippers to prevent heat loss.

Gloves and mittens keep hands warm, but can encumber movement and dexterity. Gloves obviously free up fingers for non-exacting tasks like collecting firewood, but often you need to remove them to strike a match or turn the flint on a lighter. Mittens are warmer than gloves, but prevent the fingers from moving much. Both may be made from a wide range of materials, including wool, leather, and a variety of insulated synthetics. Fingerless gloves leave fingertips exposed and ready for action, and are great if you want to look like Fagin in the movie version of *Oliver Twist*.

Don't Join the Cotton Club

Serious backpackers contend that cotton has no place on the trail. It has no redeeming qualities because when it gets wet it loses its insulating properties completely. It also takes longer to dry than synthetics. That means, jeans, T-shirts, socks (especially socks) are off the list when it comes to cotton and the outdoors. The only exception to this rule is when there is absolutely no chance of rain and the weather is extremely hot. Even then, a sweat-soaked T-shirt will cling to your back like a strange creature from outer space. Look instead for the special fabrics such as polypropylene designed to get rid of moisture given off by the body and encourage it to dissipate.

Pants

In fair weather, a good pair of shorts will help keep you cool and comfortable. Specially designed shorts for the outdoors incorporate extra material, and have more room in the rear and around the waist than other kinds of shorts. For comfort on the trail look for hiking pants that have simple, unadorned waists—belt loops and belts may get in the way of your pack's hipbelt and cause chafing. They should also feature extra-big pockets for storing pocketknives and the accouterments (like rolled-up trail maps) that go along with an outdoor trek. Some shorts feature Velcro closures in the rear pockets, which can be more secure than a simple button closure.

In mosquito season, or on more treacherous trails, shorts may be out of the question. In these cases, you'll have to wear a pair of long pants to ward off scratching branches and the probing proboscises of mosquitoes. Long pants should offer some of the same things as a good pair of shorts: Extra room in the rear (to make bending and crouching easier) and extra-deep, sealing pockets. Long pants should also be thick enough to protect against bramble bushes and scrapes from tree bark. Choose long pants that are made from rugged and quick-drying nylon, and have features such as bellowed thigh pockets (for maps) and tight-fitting cuffs to stave off biting insects.

CAUTION

Safe Camping

Protecting yourself from the sun's harmful ultraviolet (UV) rays means more than just covering up with clothing and wearing a hat. In all outdoor conditions, whether sunny or overcast, apply sunscreen lotion to exposed skin. Sunscreen should have a rating of at least 15 SPF. Wear sunglasses that provide protection from ultraviolet rays. The lenses on cheaper sunglasses often don't offer adequate protection.

To Top It All Off . . .

No outdoor vacation is complete without head protection in the form of a hat or bandanna. In this age of ozone depletion, summer hikers should don suitable headgear—not just to keep the sun out of your eyes, but to keep ultraviolet radiation off your skin. A hat also keeps flying and biting insects off your head (you'll find that insects are attracted to an uncovered coif like moths to a lightbulb).

There are a number of styles and options to choose from when looking for a good hat. Baseball caps will do the trick, but longer "duck-billed" caps are better able to stop the sun from beating down on your face. In foul weather, a hat is another form of waterproofing you don't want to be without. A traditional "sou'wester" is an old tried-and-true standby; often made of coated nylon or cotton, it offers good protection from rain. Many shells and ponchos have hoods that can be called into service during a downpour.

Less constricting, and offering a bit of "Crocodile" Dundee dash, Australian-style bush hats are attractive and functional protection against sun and rain. They are also good in windy conditions; a chin-tie keeps the hat in place. These hats are often constructed from heavy canvas and can be cleaned fairly easily. In bug season, a handkerchief can be tucked inside the back of a hat at one end and left to hang (or tucked into a shirt collar) over the back of the neck—another favorite spot for mosquitos and black flies in search of blood.

In cold weather, a wool toque or stockingcap of some sort is a warmer option for those adventuring in the outdoors during winter or fall. A wool cap can be worn during the night to help keep heat from escaping the body. In winter, a balaclava can be worn like a hat under an insulated hood, providing optimum comfort in extremely cold conditions.

Fun in the Sun

Fashion considerations aside, sunglasses belong on the trail to protect wearers from the sun's ultraviolet (UV) rays, and from the glare and eye fatigue brought about by squinting in bright conditions. Your choice of sunglasses depends largely on personal preference, and if you wear prescription lenses, contact lenses, or have perfect vision. Clip-ons are convenient for eyeglass wearers, but may not be as good as a pair of prescription sunglasses—though clip-ons are less costly. Some of us with perfect vision just have to choose a pair of sunglasses that look good and offer adequate UV protection.

Quality sunglasses should be treated with a UV-absorbing system, which means being dark enough to offer some resistance to bright light. UV light has been shown to damage the eyes, namely the cornea and retina. Look for sunglasses that offer UV protection and carry a label stating that they conform to ANSI (American National Standard Institute) requirements.

> **Safe Camping**
> See an eye doctor about recommendations for eyewear if you've had cataract surgery. Some drugs such as tetracycline increase your sensitivity to the sun's rays: Consult your physician if you are taking medications and plan to go on an extended outdoor trek.

The Least You Need to Know

➤ Outdoor adventurers should dress in layers—at the very least, underwear, a middle layer, and rain- and windproof shell. Layering allows the wearer to remove or add clothes as temperatures rise and fall, and is a great way to regulate body temperatures by allowing perspiration to evaporate.

➤ Cotton is bad news in the outdoors; it loses its insulating capability when wet. Choose from the newer synthetic garments available for backpackers and hikers.

➤ Wool is a natural material that does belong in the outdoors. It is a good insulator and can repel a good deal of rain. If it becomes completely sodden, however, it takes a long time to dry.

➤ Purchase the best rainwear money can buy. The downfall of many outdoor trips can be blamed on the misery produced by soaked-through clothing. Waterproof fabrics, especially Gore-Tex fabric and other waterproof breathables, offer good protection against rain while also being breathable.

➤ Get a good hat. Hats protect wearers from sun, rain, and cold. You can choose from a wide range of styles and materials.

Chapter 16

Comfort Gear for Your Home Away from Home

In This Chapter

➤ How to live comfortably outdoors

➤ Gear that helps you see in the dark

➤ Learning about alternative lighting methods

➤ Taking along a portable throne when a cat hole won't do

All hail the comfort ethic on the trail! The overriding theme of any vacation—whether you're spending time outdoors or relaxing by a pool—is comfort, comfort, and more comfort. Wearing the right outdoor gear has a lot to do with making yourself comfortable; so does the kind of outdoor gear that minimizes hassles and increases your possible range of outdoor activities.

"More gear?!" cries the backpacker who's trying to cut down the number of things that have to be crammed into an average-size pack. For the backpacker, weight is of obvious importance; it limits how many things, for comfort or not, you can carry along on a trip. But added gear isn't that much of a concern for many outdoor explorers who venture into or close to the woods for only a long weekend or a few days (or those who go camping by car). Both styles of outdoor vacation share the need for enough comfort gear to handle a number of needs.

Of course, one person's activities may require more specialized equipment than another's; fishing tackle is superfluous for someone who never intends to fish. Car campers who plan to hover around their vehicles all weekend won't have much use for a compass and topographical maps. A lightweight camp stove isn't as important to the car camper; a bigger portable two-burner will do the trick when weight isn't a concern.

When establishing priorities for what stays and what goes, each person will have a pretty specific idea of what's needed and what's not. Personal comfort thresholds are individual, but there *are* a few things that most campers won't want to do without. This chapter takes a look at those items.

Spotlight on Flashlights

A good flashlight is one of those essential camping items, and the available options are many. If you're a backpacker, weight will have a big part to play in your choice of lighting. Luckily, many makes and models are specifically designed for the rugged rigors of the outdoors.

Every camper, backpacker, and hiker needs a good, reliable source of light. Not only does a flashlight enhance your ability to see when the sun goes down, it's an important safety device that can be used to summon help. As a bonus, it also permits you to read at night, whether it's a Stephen King novel or trail maps for tomorrow's 10-mile adventure.

A good outdoor-quality flashlight has to be waterproof and durable. There's a good chance that the light will be dropped onto a rock at some point; you don't want the lens to shatter into a million pieces before you've had a chance to light your way down a slippery slope. In accordance with Murphy's Law, flashlights will inevitably also find their way into the drink. Nothing is quite so frustrating as watching a flashlight fall onto a shoreside rock, and then casually roll into a lake or pond. The shape of most handheld flashlights encourage this, and it is one of the reasons to consider purchasing one of the other shapes and sizes on the market. Around-the-neck straps may prevent you from dropping a flashlight, but may be a heavy burden to carry around the neck. In most cases you'll have to be holding the flashlight while trying to walk down a well-worn trail.

Headlamps

Based on the lights used on miners' helmets, headlamps for the outdoors are the way to go for many outdoor vacationers. Variations on this theme include handheld flashlights that fit into customized headband holders, and all-in-one versions (a dedicated flashlight and headband rolled into one). Both operate on two or more AA-size batteries and afford freedom of hand movement—plus the advantage of illumination in the direction the wearer is looking.

Some models may offer a tilting lamp head, which allows upward and downward adjustment of the beam so the light can be focused on the trail in the distance and up close. Headlamps are great when your hands need to be occupied with other activities. Cooking, which often requires the use of both hands at once, is an example. Pitching a tent is another. When you need both-hands dexterity, headlamps can't be beat for lighting the way. They are also excellent for locating worms as bait for fishing (see Chapter 7). These versatile lamps cost between $28 and $35. Try several models on to see which fits best.

Pinchable Flashlights

Small, squeezable flashlights about the size of a matchbox are sold by most outdoor retailers. These convenient lighting choices can be attached to a zipper and offer instant light in a pinch. One frequent traveler to the North swears by these "pinchable" lights, if not as a lighting source for the trail, at least as a safety beacon that warns snowmobilers in the night of her presence as she makes her way across the frozen, unlighted terrain. And for $2 or so, this kind of insurance is cheap.

> **Conventional Wisdom**
>
> I'LL TELL YA!...
>
> When storing your flashlight for long periods when you won't be camping or backpacking (say, over the winter), remove the batteries. They can leak if stored unused for long periods, resulting in permanent damage to the flashlight.

A Matter of Juice

A flashlight is only as good as its batteries. For this reason, always install fresh batteries before heading off on a trip. And carry extras! Backpackers may cringe at the prospect of carrying extra cells, but living without the benefit of light in the outdoors is no fun when you awake in the middle of the night and have to wend your way down an unfamiliar path to the campground's "comfort box" without the aid of a light (face the fact that you may not make it).

Whether you load your flashlight with fresh batteries or not, improperly packed flashlights may be switched on inadvertently when they rub against other objects in a pack. Some outdoor flashlights feature a twisting head that switches them on when rotated (the beam can be focused as well). Other models have a press-on, press-off switch; still others have a sliding switch. To avoid battery drainage in whatever kind of flashlight you use, it's a good idea to remove the batteries before packing the light. Another option is to turn one battery around the wrong way inside the light until you need to use your flashlight later in the day.

Rules

As with all garbage, be sure to pack out spent batteries. The contents of batteries are particularly poisonous to the environment, and *never dispose of batteries in a fire*. Rechargeable batteries that can no longer be recharged can usually be returned to their place of purchase for proper and safe disposal. Regular and alkaline batteries can be added to regular trash.

Types of Cells

Flashlights operate on a variety of battery sizes and types. Regular *carbon-zinc* batteries are the cheapest (and most often discounted) types available. Unfortunately, they don't last very long, though the "heavy-duty" ones offer a reasonable amount of extra energy. *Alkaline* batteries are a grade up and offer longer life, though they are more expensive.

Conventional Wisdom

Besides carrying extra batteries, carry extra bulbs for your flashlight. Some flashlights have places inside the units where extra bulbs can be stored. Maglites brand flashlights include an extra bulb under the end battery spring inside the flashlight. Pry away the spring to expose the bulb and pull it away. (Don't forget to purchase new replacements, though, or the next time you go looking, you won't be so lucky.)

Lithium batteries offer the longest performance in the outdoors; they are best for travelers who plan to be away from civilization (or at least stores that stock these often-rare batteries) for longer periods. Lithium batteries are considerably more expensive than other types; they belong in the realm of the serious (and seriously richer) outdoor adventurer. *Rechargeable* batteries are tempting from an ecological point of view, but they don't last as long as regular batteries and are therefore impractical for use in the outdoors. What's worse, they don't warn you when they're running out of juice. They are more appropriate for running toy bunnies.

In extremely cold weather, batteries may not work as well as they do in normal conditions. You may have to remove them from the flashlight and warm them inside your coat or jacket to "reactivate" them. If you're planning some winter camping where the temperatures drop below freezing, you should take steps to keep your batteries warm.

Choosing Alternative Lighting Methods

Flashlights and batteries are not the only solution in the quest for good outdoor illumination. A variety of other options burn some kind of fuel to produce light. Fuels include various forms of gas, and the meeker (and ever-reliable) candle—which, with a few modern improvements, is as good as ever for casting a glow over nighttime activities.

Candle Lanterns

As an adjunct, backup, or primary source of lighting, a small glass-and-metal cylinder containing a candle—known as a *candle lantern*—is a popular and reliable form of lighting for the outdoors. The principle here is simple: You place a special, dripless candle inside the holder, light it, and extinguish the flame sometime later. A specially designed add-on reflector attaches to the lantern so you can direct a beam of light where you aim it.

Candle lanterns are completely safe in the wide-open outdoors, but be careful when you take them indoors—that is, into your tent. The potential for disaster increases when you introduce *anything* with a flame into your cocoon. Good-quality candle lanterns dissipate heat very efficiently and are designed with safety in mind. But placing one of these lanterns on the floor of a tent is a *big* no-no. Often tents (particularly dome designs) feature a corded loop that dangles from the inside roof. Use this loop to suspend the lantern (or, for that matter, a flashlight) if you do use it inside the tent.

Candle lanterns offer a reasonable amount of light, but don't count on them as spotlights or to illuminate a huge area. They are good for general lighting needs, casting a romantic and ecologically friendly glow over whatever is around them. You'll have to remember to take along spare candles—the ones to use are sized and manufactured for particular brands of lamps. The cost is between $14 and $19, depending on the configuration you choose (with or without reflector). A package of three candles costs about $2, and each provides eight to nine hours of light.

Safe Camping
Never use any kind of exposed flame inside a tent. Although tents must be made of fire-retardant materials according to federal government regulations, a candle's flame can burn a hole in the tent's fabric. The bottom line: You don't want to *test* the tent's resistance to flames.

Gas-Powered Lighting

When weight isn't too much of a concern or you're planning to stay at one campsite for a longer period, gas-powered lighting offers bright and reliable light. Much like gas stoves (see Chapter 6) gas-powered lighting uses white gas or butane or propane canisters.

Like their cooking counterparts, gas-fueled lights should never be used inside a tent. Fire and oxygen depletion are real dangers. Use a battery-powered lamp to light up a tent.

Some campers find that gas-powered lamps are too bright. This is a personal opinion that may not be shared by those who prefer a large, well-lighted campsite. A bulky gas-powered light is also difficult to handle and aim; these lights are really meant to stay put. On car camping excursions, you can also use the headlights from the car when you need strong, direct, *temporary* lighting in a pinch. Big, gas-powered lights are quite a bit more fragile and heavier and bulkier than standard outdoor flashlights—major disadvantages.

The glass that surrounds the flame and mantle can be damaged if the lamp is dropped or accidentally hit. Propane lanterns cost about $25 and lanterns that burn white gas go for about $40.

Rules

Always pack out spent propane/butane canisters and dispose of them in suitable facilities. In keeping with the low-impact camping ethic, trailheads have begun to offer canister compactors that first puncture the gas canisters to release any residual gas, and then crush the can into a pancake of metal for disposal.

Fluorescent and Halogen Lighting

A decorator's dream in the home, fluorescent and halogen lighting has found its way onto the trail as well.

These types of lighting require gas-filled bulbs. Electricity sent through the bulb "excites" the gas to produce an extremely bright light. Fluorescent lighting in the outdoors is helpful in low-light situations, but may (as in office buildings and other places where fluorescents are most often used) cast a harsh glow that is inconsistent with the mood of a natural environment. Most fluorescent outdoor lighting options are dismissed by backpackers and others concerned with weight. Fluorescents are generally quite heavy due to the bulk of their batteries, and weigh in at three pounds or more. Some models feature batteries that can be recharged from regular household current or from a car-lighter socket.

Halogen flashlights look and function like regular lights. The light created is extremely white, but less harsh than fluorescent lighting. Typically, they use standard batteries, which gives them a weight advantage over fluorescents. On the downside, halogen bulbs are quite a bit more pricey than standard bulbs and must be handled with extra care when replacements are installed. Avoid touching the bulb with your skin; natural oils left on the bulb can weaken the glass and cause it to fracture. New bulbs should be handled with a lint-free cloth or gloves, and wiped clean if they touch the skin on your fingers. Fluorescents retail for about $40. Halogen lights run in the $15 range.

Portable Outhouses

No amount of lighting will save you from the call of nature, and waking in the middle of the night with pressing matters to contend with will undoubtedly have you reaching for a flashlight as you're heading out of the tent to locate the nearest outhouse or box privy to sit down on. But what if you're uncomfortable about heading a good ways down an unfamiliar path, there simply isn't any kind of outhouse or box privy around, and you aren't up to digging a cat hole (see Chapter 8)?

Portable Privies

Among the choices of portable outdoor toilets, there are a range of receptacles suitable for those who find the prospect of going *au naturel* simply too much. These portable bathrooms range in design from the simple to the more complex. Experienced outdoor adventurers will likely dismiss these items altogether, and backpackers will rule them out because their weight is unmanageable. Still, for those without the fortitude, and those who are operating from a base camp for a number of days, the extra weight and hassle of lugging portable privies around may be worth the inconvenience of "the convenience."

The most basic of these receptacles is the portable commode, essentially a folding frame that holds a waste-disposal bag under a plastic seat. Once filled, the bag may be wrapped up and packed out to a traditional garbage-disposal site. Similar in concept, but without a bag, another configuration utilizes a seat that snaps onto a rigid plastic bucket. The seat may be removed and the contents of the bucket poured into a conventional toilet or outhouse on the return to the trailhead.

A more complicated setup uses a holding tank, and flushes away waste with the use of a piston-powered water pump that draws on a small reservoir. An indicator on the outside of the tank tells the level of the tank's contents. A third type of portable loo relies on chemicals to digest waste, and is basically a portable septic-toilet tank. One model features a toilet-paper holder in the lid, and a removable waste receptacle that lifts out to empty into a permanent toilet facility.

Portable Showers

The possibility of a hot shower in the middle of the woods?

The concept is not as far-fetched as it sounds.

Here's How
You can make a portable shower from a collapsible plastic water jug. Attach a light plastic hose to the jug. Fill it with water heated in a pot on a camp stove or fire. Hang the jug from a tree branch above where you want to bathe. Control the flow of water by putting a nozzle on the hose end or by using the jug's lever.

The reality of a hot shower after several weeks of bathing in cool lakes and streams (or without the benefit of any bathing facilities), can be realized with the use of a commercially available solar water heater. In this setup, you fill a specially made plastic bladder with cold water and leave it in the sun for about three hours. The bladder is designed to absorb heat from the sun and transfer it to the water inside, which is heated to around 180° F. An indicator on the bladder tells bathers when the water is hot. Once the water has reached its appropriate temperature, you string the bladder from a branch or other natural hook. You turn on the shower by pulling on the nozzle. More modest people can even set up a shower enclosure designed to work with the solar shower.

Solar showers really work! Backpackers worried about weight will be unlikely candidates as users, and others may find that water taken from lakes and other natural water bodies is just as suitable for washing up.

Rules

When bathing outdoors, use biodegradable soap for lathering up and rinsing down well away from natural water sources. All-purpose biodegradable soap is available in liquid form, stored in handy bottles and tubes, and can be purchased where you buy outdoor gear and supplies.

Chairs and Cushions—Supporting Bottoms and Brains

Tired of sitting on rocks and bare patches of ground? Want a chair to sit on in the outdoors? Sound like an odd concept? Well, take heart, there are a variety of portable chairs available for the outdoorsman, and not the bulky, heavy kinds found on decks and patios in the suburbs.

Although not within the domain of the weight-conscious backpacker, there are portable, fold-up chairs that weigh in at anywhere between 1 1/2 and 4 pounds, depending on how they are built. Such chairs usually feature lightweight steel tubing over which weather-resistant fabric is stretched. A variation camp chair includes camp stools that may be collapsed at a moment's notice. And from the great minds concerned with comfort comes an ingenious design that features a canvas-like envelope into which you slide an inflatable Therm-a-Rest mattress. With a few straps secured, the mattress converts into a chair.

For real comfort mongers, no camping trip would be complete without a pillow. You can make your own by filling a stuffsack with clothes, but self-inflating models and half-size camping versions of the ones you sleep on at home are less cumbersome alternatives to carrying a real pillow along on a trip.

The Least You Need to Know

➤ Flashlights are necessary camping items, allowing you to see at night when navigating trails and setting up camp. Backpackers normally choose small, lightweight flashlights; car campers and those setting up a base camp will often use heavier units with fluorescent tubes.

➤ Lighting in the outdoors is not necessarily battery-bound. Portable candle lanterns and propane/butane-powered lighting afford auxiliary or primary sources.

➤ Portable outhouses can take the sting out of going to the bathroom outdoors. Some campers may find a bring-along bathroom worth the trouble of lugging one of these weighty setups into the wilderness and packing out the waste.

➤ Taking a hot shower in the outdoors is not as impossible as it sounds. Portable solar-heated bladders of water can be strung from a tree and used when lakes, rivers, and ponds are too cold or unavailable.

Part 4
Getting There

Getting to the ultimate campground often involves more than driving to an established location in a car. Sure, the first part of most trips will involve packing a car, climbing in, and taking off. But for more advanced outdoor vacationers, a trip in a car is only the first part of getting there. And "there" is a relative word.

There may be an established car campground you visit every summer. Or it may be a destination at the end of a two-day canoe trip. In fact, canoeing, kayaking, or biking to a destination are ways of getting there, and can be a big part of any outdoor vacation in themselves. Not only does traveling by other means give your feet a rest, but it can be as exciting as arriving at the destination itself. Bike camping lets riders sightsee as they glide through the countryside, is a good form of exercise, and is faster than walking. Canoes and kayaks allow campers to pack in a lot of stuff and get to places that are inaccessible by foot or pedal power.

Whatever mode of transportation you use to get there, a minimum amount of planning and preparation is needed to put such a trip together—including some special skills you should practice before taking off into the great beyond. Suffice to say that nothing is beyond the reach of the intrepid traveler, whether the mode of transportation you choose is a bicycle or a canoe. The point is getting to "there," and hopefully proving wrong Gertrude Stein, who said, "There is no there there."

Chapter 17

Trailblazing Made Easy

In This Chapter

➤ Special considerations for the wilderness backpacker

➤ Backcountry preparation and planning

➤ Tips for wilderness hiking

There are some special considerations for planning a trip that takes you miles away from civilization on foot, not the least of which is making sure that you are up for a trip of this kind, both physically and in terms of experience. If you're lucky, you'll be able to go along with somebody who has done it before. This person can act as a mentor before you embark on a longer trip of your own. If not, try pushing the limits on less serious trips by going farther and farther into the wilderness for a day or two when hiking in more populated areas.

When you've been by yourself (hopefully with a hiking partner) for four or five days without seeing anyone, you'll know that you've done it and can take a longer trip next time. You'll get an idea of what solitude and self-reliance is all about—no doubt having gone without something that you should have brought along on your trial trips—and you'll plan accordingly.

This chapter helps you take a specific look at what you need to know and how you need to prepare for a backcountry hiking and camping trip.

Defining True Wilderness

As our cities and towns get bigger, the wilderness is getting smaller. Still, there are some areas in the world that have not been developed by man. These areas, some of which are protected (like national parks), provide us with the best chance to see nature in its purest form.

It's always great to get out of your car and go hiking, even if only for a short trip. But many different kinds of trails—and trips—are possible. Perhaps you have stopped at a national park office and asked for information, got back in your car, and driven to your campsite. Or maybe you've taken a short hike on a trail in the woods with other people nearby. But there is another part of the park that most visitors will never see: the wilderness.

You won't find parking and rest areas here. But you might see the silhouette of a moose standing on the top of a mountain. There are great hiking trails—and even campsites—to be discovered in the wilderness. But remember, the campsites here are *primitive*: You won't find showers, toilets, or cooking facilities. You might find this idea of a life without amenities a bit daunting, and decide that this kind of trip is not for you. But with some preparation, the wilderness can still be comfortable, even it means packing in your own comfort gear to make it that way. The "real" wilderness offers the ultimate chance to get away from the hectic pace of modern living and experience the raw beauty of nature.

Rules

If you will be hiking in a national park and plan to camp in the backcountry, you will need to get a permit. You can usually get one from the park's on-site office. This is also a good time to talk to the ranger about trail and weather conditions. You will have to inform the park office how long you will be going into the backcountry, what your route will be, and when you plan to return.

Backcountry Rules

The following is a list of the most important things to remember when you're hiking in the backcountry. The key principle is respect: Treat the wilderness as if you were a considerate guest in someone else's home. Enjoy the trail, but don't leave even the slightest hint that you were there. This way others can enjoy it just as much as you did.

➤ Get a permit for overnight backpacking.

➤ Fill out appropriate forms for mapping out your itinerary, especially if you are hiking solo.

➤ Leave all natural, prehistoric, and historic features undisturbed.

➤ Carry plenty of drinking water—at least one gallon per person per day.

➤ Pack out all your litter—that includes cigarette butts, toilet paper, and sanitary items.

➤ You should get a permit for backcountry camping at the national park office. If you are not traveling in a park, you can usually obtain a permit at the ranger's office.

Rules

Pack it in and pack it out. The cardinal rule of traveling in the backcountry is that whatever you take into the wilderness should come back out with you. Empty fuel cans, food wrappers, and other garbage should be brought back to civilization with you. Keep a plastic bag for your garbage in your pack. Don't spoil the wildness of the wilderness.

➤ Bury human waste six to eight inches deep, 250 feet away from camp and any water source.

➤ Camp at least 100 yards away from any water source—being too close may frighten wildlife and damage fragile vegetation.

➤ Prepare for emergencies. Bring the essentials, which include equipment for emergencies and foul weather: First-aid kit, compass, topographical map, extra food, water, knife, flashlight, rain gear, and spare clothing.

➤ Notify friends or family of your itinerary. They can contact officials if you fail to return.

➤ Notify the park office about your route and how long you will be in the backcountry.

➤ Build fires only where and if permitted.

➤ Don't bring your pets; they frighten wildlife and are often not permitted off established campgrounds.

➤ Some animals, like coyotes, have been known to attack dogs. The best policy is to leave them at home.

➤ Avoid smoking while traveling—if you do, only light up where you can't start a fire.

➤ Don't bring firearms into the backcountry. They are illegal in many areas.

➤ Don't rock climb, explore caves, or participate in any other "adventure" activity unless you have the experience and proper equipment.

Rules

Purists may disagree but some wilderness hikers may be interested in bringing a cell phone or a small two-way radio (of the kind obtainable at most electronics stores) with them on a hiking trip. These can be useful devices to prevent you from getting lost if they are used correctly. Check with the ranger and your cellular phone line provider to make sure you will have service once inside the wilderness area you are visiting. If you will be using a radio, make sure you know what channel to tune in for help. Some national parks have begun to provide hikers in remote wilderness with a small transmitter that always keeps track of the hikers and makes rescue much quicker. If you are considering a hike like this, ask the ranger about it.

Tiptoeing through the Wilderness

Having a healthy respect for the power of nature will help make for a safe and successful backpacking trip. Remember, the wilderness is much bigger than you are, and has within it powerful rivers, strong winds, steep hills, and sometimes tough terrain. Be cautious. Trying to conquer and control the wilderness is a dangerous mistake. Instead, evaluate the environmental conditions around you and don't undertake anything that looks as though it could be hazardous—it probably is. You really shouldn't go into the backcountry alone, unless you've gained enough experience to feel that you could handle a serious mishap. Still, even the most experienced hikers can have accidents. Going with someone or in a group is a basic safety measure: If somebody should get hurt and can't continue hiking, someone else in the party can go and get help.

Preparing for Your Trip

There is an almost unlimited variety of possible hiking trips through the wilderness. What you choose to do should depend on your experience, the amount of time you have, and what your interests are. Some people are looking for adventure and solitude. I found that on my trip to Gros Morne National Park. The only person I saw during the five-day trip (besides my hiking partner) was a man who lived in a small cabin and monitored birds for a government agency. I like solitude, but doing that all year would be a little too lonely for me!

When planning a trip, be sure to establish what you want. Some crave the canopy of an eastern forest, others the starkness of a desert environment. If you're interested in magnificent and unique landscapes, perhaps a trip to the Grand Canyon is for you. Sure, this is a destination for camera-clicking car campers, but these places also offer outstanding trips through the backcountry too.

Requisite Research

Research the area you will be traveling to before your departure. For example, in the summer months, the temperature inside of the Grand Canyon can reach 140° F. This would make hiking unbearable and dangerous. But taking the same trip in the spring or fall, when the temperature is comfortable, is a completely different story. On the other hand, in these months the trail is so crowded that you may have to reserve a hiking permit as many as six months in advance. Write, phone, or fax to find out what the drill is: You could spend thousands of dollars getting to a destination, only to find out that there is no room on the trail for you.

Bookstores, outdoor clubs, libraries, national park offices, tourist associations, and even the Internet are good sources for locating information on your destination. If you will be traveling in a national park, try to contact the park's information office before you go. Refer to the list of U.S. national parks in Appendix A to get the phone numbers and addresses for the national parks in the United States and Canada. Ask what the trail and weather conditions are at the time of year you're planning to go. Most national parks will mail you information about hiking trails and weather conditions free of charge. However, for the most up-to-date information it's best to phone. That way you'll know what to wear, and be able to anticipate whether you'll need to carry extra water bottles or specialized equipment on your trip.

What to Bring on a Backcountry Trip

In earlier chapters, we discussed what every backpacker should take, depending on the length, complexity, and type of trip. Some essentials are a good-quality backpack, sleeping bag, tent, hiking boots, map, compass, and good rain gear. A *wilderness* hiking trip, however, has other special requirements.

Traveling in the backcountry is usually an overnight affair—but unlike an ordinary camping trip, it will have no supply or grocery stores nearby. This means you will have to *bring* everything you'll need to set up camp, cook, and hike in the wilderness. A good first aid kit is a must (Chapter 24). If you forget something on a wilderness expedition, you'll have to do without it. And because weight is a big concern when you're carrying stuff yourself, you'll want to bring only what is essential—nothing that will burden you with extra weight. This is one of the backpacker's biggest dilemmas. A can of beans might not seem very heavy, but after eight hours of hiking through the mountains, even a few ounces can seem like pounds. For this reason, freeze-dried or dehydrated dinners and dried soups are *de rigueur* for the wilderness traveler.

Clothing

Find out what weather conditions will be for the place you will be traveling to. Consult a temperature chart for the region to get a sense of the appropriate clothing to wear once you get there. The temperature in mountainous regions can drop into the 40s at night; then it can be a blessing to be wearing warm underwear. Polypropylene underwear is great; it transfers body moisture from your skin onto the next layer of clothing where it can evaporate, and it can serve as a great pair of pajamas in the outdoors. Silk underwear designed for the outdoors is also good. Dress in layers (Chapter 15), so you can remove a layer when you get hot or add an extra layer when it gets colder.

> **I'LL TELL YA!..**
>
> **Conventional Wisdom**
>
> Before you set out on your trip, be sure your boots are as waterproof as possible—and well broken in. A new pair of boots can give you a few blisters on a day hike, but they can be so severe on a long backpacking trip that they could stop you from walking. Moleskin blister bandages will help relieve the pain associated with blisters. You can wear running shoes when crossing rivers so your hiking boots stay dry.

Besides considering temperatures in the region where you'll be going, you will need a good water-resistant outer shell if it rains. Gore-Tex outerwear is ideal in rainy and windy conditions. Don't forget to bring a hat for protection from the sun, and sunglasses and sunscreen as well. When you are outside all the time, you can still get sunburned on a cloudy day.

Food

All the food you eat in the backcountry will have to be brought with you. You might catch a few fish or find some blueberries to eat, but don't count on it. The amount of food you bring will depend on how long you expect your trip to be. The longer the trip, the more carefully you have to consider how much each food item weighs, and how long it will last.

WEATHER ▬▬▬▬▬▬▬▬

Month	Average Maximum (F°)	Average Minimum (F°)	Percipitation Average	Percipitation Ytd Total
			(inches)	(inches)
January	60.9	35.0	.46	.46
February	66.2	37.8	.34	.80
March	77.4	45.3	.31	1.11
April	80.7	52.3	.70	1.81
May	88.0	59.3	1.50	3.31
June	94.2	65.5	1.93	5.24
July	92.9	68.3	2.09	7.33
August	91.1	66.4	2.35	9.68
September	86.4	61.9	2.12	11.80
October	78.8	52.7	2.27	14.07
November	68.5	42.3	.70	14.77
December	62.2	36.4	.57	15.34

Temperature charts provide clues about what to bring and how to dress for a backcountry adventure at the time you plan to travel.

Temperatures in higher mountain areas vary about 5-10 degrees below those shown, while temperatures along the Rio Grande run from 5-10 degrees higher. Sunshine is abundant the year round. Infrequent or brief periods of cloudy weather are confined mostly to the winter months. Snow falls very rarely and is generally light, lasting only a short time. Relative humidity is usually quite low. The "rainy season" extends from mid-heavy thunderstorms and some flash-flooding. The water recedes rapidly, however, and the rainy season is a delightful time to visit the desert.

A good camping stove, utensils, a pot and pan, water bottles, and a good knife or pocket-knife are all essential for cooking. Cans and bottles are cumbersome and have to be packed out; don't bother bringing them. It's the same for items that are perishable or need to be refrigerated. It's a good idea to plan every meal, including snacks, before venturing into the backcountry. And always plan for one extra day in case of an emergency.

Shopping for a backcountry trip can be done at the grocery store as easily as at a specialty hiking shop. Dehydrated meals are extremely light, but they can be pricey and the taste is sometimes lacking. One or two packages of instant oatmeal, weighing one ounce per pack, make a great breakfast. For lunch try 2/3-ounce packages of Knorr Swiss soups, which are very nutritious and tasty. Just-add-water soups weigh the same and can also be good, as can Ramen noodles, which weigh a couple of ounces per package. Pieces of dried salami can also make a nice tasty lunch. Bring along lots of gorp (a mixture of dried fruit and nuts; a good energy source) for snacks. For dinner, bring along pasta to supplement your dehydrated meals. These dehydrated meals weigh only a few ounces each, but you will probably need twice as much as the package recommends.

Conventional Wisdom

When you've finished your meals, you'll have to wash your dishes. First, be sure you wash your dishes away from your tent—the smells may attract animals. Use a scouring pad and some biodegradable soap. Never empty soapy dishwater into rivers or streams. Instead, rinse dishes with water from your water bottle; pour the dirty rinse water onto the ground as far as possible from rivers, streams, and lakes.

Both the camping stores and the grocery store can be good sources of backcountry camping food. Instant oatmeal (two normal-size packets are needed for one person's breakfast) and granola are good ways to begin the day. They are especially filling on a cold morning when eaten with some reconstituted powdered milk. For lunch, try some dry salami; it lasts for several days without refrigeration. For the first few days of a trip, sharp cheese and pita bread will also stay fresh without refrigeration.

Some backpackers swear by healthy dried soups like the Knorr Swiss variety, but stopping to cook three meals a day will slow you down. For dinner, many decent dehydrated and freeze-dried meals are available. They weigh next to nothing, take minutes to cook, and are fairly filling. Your local camping store usually stocks a wide variety; many mail-order outlets carry them too. If you need a change, pasta tastes great and is easy to make, but you'll need a ready source to boil it.

Fueling Levels

The key thing about cooking in the wilderness is figuring out how much fuel you will need to bring. Besides saving time, not cooking lunch on the trail saves fuel as well. On a five-day trip, cooking two meals a day, a stove full of fuel along with two full aluminum fuel bottles (about half a pint each), will usually do the trick. Before venturing into the wilderness, cook a few meals in your backyard (or on a short hike) to determine how much fuel you use for each meal. Buy food items that require less time to cook, such as dehydrated meals and instant oatmeal. Try to set up your stove in an area where there is little wind, or purchase a windscreen for your stove if it doesn't have one built in. Cooking your food without a windscreen wastes fuel because heat is used less efficiently.

Filtering Water

Never drink untreated water from any source in the backcountry. No matter how clean you think the water may look, chances are it isn't. Bring along some water-purifying tablets, liquid iodine, or a filter to purify your drinking water. Chemical purification works to kill most microorganisms, but filtering water is safer and doesn't add an unpleasant taste. Boiling water to purify it consumes time and fuel, and hot drinks are not always refreshing during a scorching hot day on the trail. Drink at least a gallon of water per day.

Water filters are best for making water safe to drink.

Simple Hiking Techniques

Let's say you've researched your hiking trip and packed everything you need. You've talked to the ranger about your route and you've gotten the okay. You know where the primitive campsites are along the trail, and how long it will probably take you to get to them.

Mark down your whole route on the map, including where you plan to stop for meals and set up camp each day. You will probably want to stop for about ten minutes every hour or so to rest, drink something, and have a snack. A good time to stop for lunch is at the halfway point in a day's hiking. If covering ground is important to you, try to do several things in one rest stop, like going to the bathroom, having a snack, and checking your bearings. Be sure you allow yourself enough time to set up camp before nightfall. It's best to set up camp and *then* cook and clean up, so you have nothing to worry about at bedtime.

Easy Route Finding

Most hiking trails into the backcountry are accessible from some point on a main road, are fairly well marked, and usually offer some place to park. If you are traveling on a "loop trail," which will bring you back to your starting point, your car will be waiting for you when you return. However, some backcountry trails will lead you to another exit that may be miles away from your vehicle. In these cases, it's best to arrange to have someone drive your car to the exit of the trail. One tip I learned from hiking in the wilderness is staying one night in a motel in a town close to the trail. For a fee, staff will often drive your car to the point where the trail ends so it will be waiting for you when you exit. This is preferable to having someone pick you up at the exit point and drive you back to your starting point. It's hard to plan exactly when you will be getting out of the woods, and either you'll end up waiting for a ride, or your ride will end up waiting for you.

> **CAUTION**
>
> **Safe Camping**
> One of the worst ways to end a breathtaking wilderness trip is coming to the end of a trail and realizing that you are stranded on the road. In these cases you might be tempted to hitchhike. Here, as with most things, prevention is the best cure. Make sure a car or a lift is waiting for you when you exit the trail before you depart. Hitchhiking with hiking gear is very difficult because many motorists will not want to put it in their cars. And you are taking a big risk getting into a car with a person you don't know—a lot more risky business than the wilderness adventure you just endured.

Marked Trails

Marked trails in the backcountry are usually marked by blazes—by paint markings on trees or rocks. On well-maintained trails, there is usually a path cleared of fallen trees and other objects that may get in the way. In most cases, you'll be fine if you stick to the path. If the trail is not well marked, it's best to keep checking your map and compass to be sure you're going the right way. Sometimes you'll get to a fork in the trail where a section branches off or a new trail begins. In most cases there will be a sign with arrows pointing in the right direction. If there isn't one, use your map and compass to be sure you stay on the right path.

Unmarked Trails

Unmarked trails are a totally different story. But just because there are no markings to follow doesn't mean there isn't a route. You should discuss this route with the park ranger beforehand. Often it will consist of sections of abandoned hunting routes and animal trails. Animals are a lot like people—once they've cleared the brush on a path, they like to use it again. Animals like to use our paths because they are convenient, so why shouldn't we use theirs? If you hike on animals trails, especially in bear country, you have to be very aware that there may be…well…*animals* on them. Do not startle them, and don't get between a sow and her cub, otherwise you could find yourself in trouble.

The route you choose should be simple enough so that you always know you are going in the right direction. It should cross major identifiable landmarks, like a green mountain or a large waterfall. Of course, unless you know the terrain like the back of your hand, it's impossible to navigate your way on an unmarked trail without knowing how to use a map and compass.

Losing Your Way

If you've filed an itinerary with wilderness authorities and you haven't returned when you said you would, officials will usually wait until you are one or two days late before sending out a search party to find you. Be sure to inform the park when you've ended your trip. When you exit the trail, there may be a box to deposit a card indicating that you have returned. If a search team is sent to find you and you've neglected to inform authorities of your return, you may have to pay for the expense of a needless rescue operation.

Conventional Wisdom

When you have to walk to the grocery store to pick up some food, you usually take the most direct route to get there. Well, animals are like that too. If an animal is thirsty and wants to drink at the river, it will also take the most direct and easiest path to get there. It is common to see animals on man-made trails or roads for this reason. Would you walk through uncomfortable brush if you didn't have to?

NAME OF GROUP LEADER:		PERMIT NO: N° 0153
MAILING ADDRESS:	STREET ADDRESS	No. PEOPLE:
CITY:	PROV./STATE	DATE IN:
COUNTRY:	POSTAL CODE/ZIP	DATE OUT:
HOME PHONE:	BUSINESS PHONE:	TRAIL/ROUTE:
VEHICLE MAKE/MODEL:	COLOUR:	SITE No. 1ST NIGHT
LICENSE ORIGIN/PLATE No:	LOCATED:	2ND NIGHT
SIGNATURE (GROUP LEADER/*CHEF D'EQUIPE*)	AMOUNT PAID: $	3RD NIGHT TENT STYLE/COLOUR

Staff: retain top portion

Name of group leader / *Nom du chef d'equipe*:	Date out / *Date de retour*

PERMIT No: N° 0153
NAME:
TRAIL:
DATE IN:
DATE OUT:
1ST NIGHT:
2ND NIGHT:
3RD NIGHT

Permit No. / *Numbero de permis*: N° 0153

A registration card such as this listing your itinerary may be required in wilderness areas.

In most cases, prevention is the best cure for getting lost. Notify family or friends when you expect to return and give them the number of the wildlife officials to contact if you fail to. The extra food you bring with you on the trail will enable you to wait for rescue. If it is permitted, build a fire at night. This will not only help you keep warm, but could help a search team find you. A small mirror can be used to reflect light, which can be shined on passing planes. If you see a passing plane or helicopter, run to the nearest clearing and move your arms and legs around as much as possible to attract attention. Stay calm. Refer to Chapter 24 for specific directions on summoning help if you need it.

> **CAUTION**
>
> **Safe Camping**
> Cold weather is probably one of the most serious concerns for the wilderness hiker. In case of emergency, carry a space blanket. This is an ultralightweight mylar sheet that, when wrapped around you, reflects most of your body heat back to you. This inexpensive form of insurance sheilds users against the wind and is waterproof.

Don't panic if you get lost. Assuming that you've alerted local officials to your trip and left a trip itinerary, a search-and-rescue team will usually begin looking for you a few days after you were supposed to return. If the search team doesn't find you, a helicopter may be sent to try to locate you as well. Flares are good in an emergency to alert aircraft of your location; when you hear or see a helicopter or aircraft, light them up.

Checking Out

Some wilderness management agencies have begun charging foolish hikers. There have been cases when hikers have not exited the trail on time just because they thought it was a big joke. The joke is on them when they are presented with the bill for the search team and the helicopter team. Be smart: Notify officials that you've returned from the backcountry. You may end up with an expensive bill for the operation of a helicopter during a needless search.

The Bear Facts

There will be some wilderness trails that are home to animals. Most will be more afraid of you than you are of them. Some hikers, when traveling in black bear country, make a lot of noise on the trail to scare them off. Grizzly bears (which can be brown or black) are more unpredictable.

The best advice when dealing with grizzly bears is to try to avoid them, and if you happen to see one, stay calm and avoid threatening them. Sometimes a bear will start charging, then veer off or stop abruptly. Bear experts recommend that you stand still until the bear stops, and then slowly back away. If you are attacked, play dead: Drop to the ground, lift you legs up to your chest, and clasp your hands over the back of your neck. For black bears you should raise your arms, join hands with a companion to appear really big, and talk to the bear in a low deep voice. "Go away, Mr. Bear," usually works. Never leave food or other strong-smelling toilet articles (like deodorant) in your tent; they may attract a bear. Always suspend your food in a tree when you set up camp. Consult wilderness authorities about the best ways to deal with bears in the regions where you'll be traveling.

The Least You Need to Know

➤ Be sure you know what you are getting into before you venture into a wilderness area. Consult the park ranger; research and plan your hiking trip carefully before you leave. Know the type of terrain and the weather conditions you will face.

➤ Make a checklist of everything you'll have to bring with you on the trail. You'll need different things depending on the length of your trip and where you will be traveling to.

➤ Always bring a map and compass with you into the backcountry—and *know how to use them*. This is a good rule to follow even if the trail is well marked.

➤ Remember to treat the wilderness with respect. Don't be rude to the wilderness by leaving your garbage there or altering the environment in any way.

➤ If you are entering the backcountry, always notify the park office of your route, how long your hike is, and when you plan to return. Obtain a permit. Be sure to notify park officials when you exit the trail.

Chapter 18

Planning an Outdoor Vacation on the Water

In This Chapter

➤ A canoeing and kayaking primer

➤ Packing and loading up gear

➤ Learning basic paddling techniques

➤ Hull shapes and paddle sizes—what's best for you

Backpacking by definition means limiting the amount of outdoor gear you can bring along on a trip. Car camping means you have to stay near your metal chariot in a crowded country car lot. And day hiking means that you stand the chance of meeting others on popular trails and paths. So how do you take along a lot of gear without having to carry it, leave your car behind, and get to a remote enough campground where other people are few and far between?

The answer lies in combining canoeing or kayaking with your plans for an outdoor vacation. Canoes and kayaks were invented by the Indians and Eskimos, and fit quite nicely into an excursion into the outdoors. They hold a tremendous amount of stuff, are easy to learn to paddle, and provide you with a comfortable way to get from A to Z (and points in-between). The biggest advantage, of course, is that they take you to the heart of nature, where no paths lead and where few people have traveled. As with any activity on the water, however, certain safety precautions must be taken. By taking to the water, you open many doors to adventure that the backpacker on foot may never enter—but you may also expose yourself to the whims of the elements. And there is one prerequisite for this outdoor activity: *You must be able to swim* in case the canoe or kayak capsizes.

This chapter introduces you to the pleasures of camping with a canoe or kayak.

Everything I Own Is Rented

If you don't own a canoe or kayak, take heart: Outfitters close to popular "put-ins" can supply you with all the gear you need for a modest cost. Outfitters may supply you with everything from paddles to life jackets and, of course, the boat itself. So how do you know if the place you're traveling to has canoes or kayaks to rent? The same research that goes into selecting your destination will often reveal where you can get your boats locally. Chambers of commerce provide pamphlets listing outfitters in the region you're traveling. State and provincial parks will also send along information on where rentals are available, and some may have designated or appointed outfitters operating within the wilderness area's bounds. In most cases it's advisable to phone ahead and reserve the equipment you want for a particular time. In the summer, it's advisable to give a week or even a month notice.

The advantages of renting a canoe or kayak at the put-in location are several: You don't have to worry about transporting your boat atop your vehicle, you don't have heavy layout of cash for your vessel, and you get to choose (usually) from a range of equipment to try out.

Preparation and Planning

You want to see the unvarnished wilderness? Take a canoe or kayak. In most cases you'll have to get a canoe-camping permit for specific sites along your paddling route. You may also have to get a parking permit for your car if you leave it in one of the wilderness area's lots while you're paddling.

Brochures and literature from the area where you'll be boating will typically provide route suggestions based on the length of the trip and desired travel distance. Remember, if you're just starting out, don't take on too much. Three hours of paddling per day is plenty for novices. Plan for bad weather and down time. And even though canoes and kayaks allow you to carry more than a backpack would, try to limit the amount of stuff you take along. Make packing lists. This is especially important advice for those who will be portaging their canoes and equipment over land. ("Portaging" means carrying your boat and supplies some distance over sections of land between two or more bodies of water on a trip.) Some consider a good portage an integral part of a canoe trip (you can't portage a kayak with ease); others don't like it. And certainly portaging belongs within the realm of the more serious outdoorsperson and shouldn't be tackled by beginners without some kind of instruction. Refer to later in this section for specifics on carrying a canoe.

> **Safe Camping**
> Paddlers must wear some kind of *personal flotation device* (PFD) as an important safety measure. Comfortable, modern PFDs mean there's no excuse not to wear one. Type III Coast Guard–approved PFDs offer safety in a comfortable sleeveless vest that gives paddlers freedom of movement.

Like any kind of backcountry trip, you should be up to the trip and skilled enough to be away from civilization for days on end. You should plan your trip so that you reach civilization of some sort at the end of the trip, however. There you can get a lift back to where you parked your vehicle at the put-in, pick up the vehicle, and return to pickup fellow travelers, canoes, and equipment. Some outfitters offer pickup services, or places where canoes can be left for retrieval later. Some may even take you and your canoe by speedboat to a distant location on a large body of water, then come to pick you up at a pre-arranged later date. Inquire, plan, and improvise.

Canoes versus Kayaks

Generally speaking, canoes are designed and fare well on lakes and rivers. Kayaks do well in freshwater, but are more stable in rougher waves such as those found in saltwater environments—coastlines and near-shore channels. But canoes are also used on calm saltwater, and kayaks on lakes and rivers. Choosing one vessel over the other comes down to a matter of personal preference, though canoes are really considered much better transportation on lakes and rivers. In some parts of the world, no differentiation is made between a canoe and kayak. They are both paddled, albeit somewhat differently, but the principle of getting from one place to the next is similar. Take note that when we are discussing kayaks in this chapter, we are talking about sea kayaks as opposed to whitewater kayaks. The difference between the two is that sea kayaks are wider than the whitewater versions designed for "shooting" rapids. Sea kayaks may also be referred to as touring kayaks, and this is the kind to look to for camping.

> **Safe Camping**
> Personal flotation devises (PFDs) should fit snugly around the torso and be easily secured with a couple of straps. Metal buckles may be troublesome if they rub against a paddler's arms while they are in motion. Try before you buy.

Canoe parts

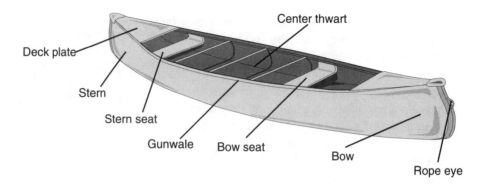

Center thwart

Deck plate

Stern

Stern seat

Gunwale

Bow seat

Bow

Rope eye

Kayak parts

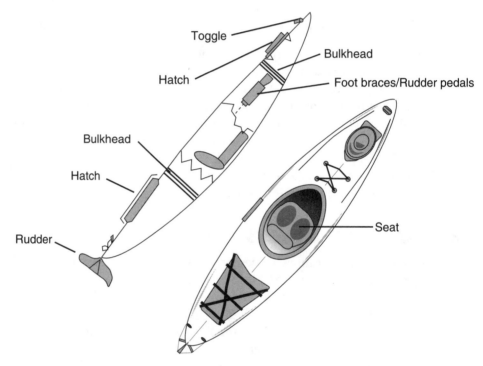

Toggle

Bulkhead

Hatch

Foot braces/Rudder pedals

Bulkhead

Hatch

Seat

Rudder

Canoes: Basic Principles

Canoes offer open cargo space for one or two paddlers and gear. Each paddler sits at one end of the boat (the *bow* or front and the *stern* or rear), facing in the same direction, with packs, food, and so on stowed between them. A third passenger may also sit in the middle of the canoe, although from this position it is difficult to use a paddle. You can tell which is front and which is back on a canoe very easily: The bow has more legroom.

The front paddler's role is to provide locomotion; he or she can switch paddling sides as the paddling arm tires. The stern (or rear) paddler also provides locomotion, but is also responsible for directing the canoe—either by paddling more earnestly on one side or by using the blade of the paddle as a sort of rudder to steer the boat at the end of a stroke. The paddler in the back of the canoe keeps an eye on the paddler up front, and generally switches paddling sides when the front paddler does. A solo paddler can sit or kneel near the back of the boat with the cargo stowed from the front (bow) back. In this situation, the bow may lift and catch a gust of wind, making solo paddling more difficult.

Kayaks: Basic Principles

Kayaks achieve their seaworthiness by virtue of their design. A paddler sits in a cockpit with legs and feet extended inside an enclosed shell. In tandem models, two cockpits are located along the length of the boat (offering couples a new opportunity for togetherness). In some cases a "skirt" around the paddler's waist connects with the shell to help keep water out of the interior of the shell.

Camping gear is placed inside sealed compartments at the bow and stern of the boat, where it remains covered and protected from rain and water. Water-resistant gear can be lashed to elasticized webbing on the outside shell of the boat.

Kayaks rely on a double-bladed paddle for locomotion. The paddle blades are offset at 90-degree angles. The paddler dips alternate paddle blades into the water one at a time, in a rhythmic right-left, right-left (or left-right, left-right) motion. As the paddler follows through in this way, either of the blades may be used as a rudder to direct the boat, depending on current and wind conditions—much as the stern paddler does to steer a canoe. In more complicated designs, the paddler uses an actual rudder (controlled by foot pedals in cockpit) to steer the boat. Because the paddler and gear are enclosed inside a waterproof shell, these boats are not easily swamped by rogue waves. And because the center of gravity is closer to the water than that of a canoe, a kayak is much more stable.

> **Safe Camping**
> Choose a kayak that's bright yellow, orange, red, or white—they're easier to spot in a rescue situation. The blue and green ones may look pretty on the showroom floor, but blend right into the water—not what you want if you're stranded somewhere.

Gripping Matters: Paddles

Choosing the right paddle, whether two-bladed (for a kayak) or single-bladed (for a canoe), is important for paddling comfort and ease of travel. A paddle of the right length should measure up to your chin; it can be a few inches shorter (see Table 18.1). Or you can select a paddle according to your torso size (the distance between your hip and shoulder), the length of your reach, and whether or not you're sitting or kneeling in the bow or stern (the bow paddler will often need a longer paddle to reach the water). Of course, the best thing to do is to *try* different-size paddles before you start a long trip. If you're renting a canoe from an outfitter, this is a good chance to figure out what feels best.

Table 18.1 Kayak paddle sizing chart

Paddler Height	Paddle Length
5' 4"	210 cm./6.9 ft.
5' 6"	210 cm./6.9 ft.
5' 8"	220 cm./7.2 ft.
5' 10"	220 cm./7.2 ft.
6' 0"	230 cm./7.5 ft.
6' 2"	240 cm./7.9 ft.

Paddles are made from wood, synthetics (usually some kind of plastic), or aluminum. Kayak paddles are most often available in synthetics; two-piece models fit together at mid-shaft and can be *feathered* (set off at 90-degree angles from each other) or used in an unfeathered configuration. Canoe paddles are most often made of wood; when you purchase a paddle, look for maple or ash—steer clear of pine and fir. Wooden paddles will have to be sanded and varnished from time to time; if you aren't up to this task and embrace a *laissez-faire* attitude, a lightweight synthetic paddle may be more suitable.

I'LL TELL YA!...

Conventional Wisdom

Paddlers should wear padded gloves (much like those worn for racquet sports) that reduce wear and tear on the hands. Kayakers can get specially made paddler's mitts known as *pogies*. These attach to the paddle shaft and allow for a good grip, but insulate the hands from wet and cold with neoprene or pile-lined nylon.

Single-bladed paddles have one of two kinds of grips: rounded or T-shaped. A rounded grip is a better choice if you'll be holding a paddle for longer periods of time; a T-grip gives you more push power in the form of leverage.

Another factor in paddle selection is the size of the blade. Paddle blades are classified as *narrow* (8-10 inches wide), *medium* (10-12 inches wide), and *broad* (more than 10 inches wide). The wider the blade, the more push power, but the less manageable the paddle. Blades come in different configurations as well: *round*, *rectangular*, and *square*. The bigger the surface area, the more efficient the paddle.

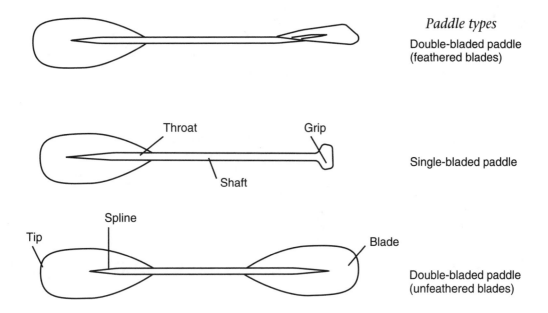

Paddle types

Double-bladed paddle
(feathered blades)

Single-bladed paddle

Double-bladed paddle
(unfeathered blades)

How to Pack Your Vessel

Whether your mode of transport is a canoe or a kayak, proper packing is extremely important, especially when you consider that an unbalanced load—especially in a canoe—can result in capsizing.

First off, you'll need to pack most everything in waterproof containers of one sort or another. Sleeping bags and extra clothing need the most waterproofing; serious canoe and kayak campers should consider using waterproof *dry bags*. These bags come in a range of sizes; roll-down tops, Velcro closures, and fastening straps and can make them completely waterproof. Most of these bags are made from thick PVC material, and actually can act as extra flotation in the unlikely event of a capsizing. Giant *Duluth bags* fit in the wide part of the canoe; you can carry them on land with the help of a headband known as a *tumpline*. Framed backpacks are not generally recommended for use in canoes because they aren't waterproof (besides being unmanageable around thwarts and seats); they also won't fit in a kayak's bilge. Delicate optics such as cameras and binoculars should be placed in sealable, rigid containers like those used for storing leftovers.

At the very least (or for short trips on quiet water), pack sleeping bags and extra clothes inside heavy-duty garbage bags. These won't stay waterproof for very long, but offer at least some protection against moisture in a wet and potentially hostile environment.

Packing Kayaks

The same general advice offered for canoes applies to packing kayaks as well. Like the floor of a canoe, the inside hull of a kayak will invariably invite some water to tag along, no matter how waterproof-looking the hatches are. And the size of hatch opening will discourage the kind of thinking that envisions cramming anything larger than a sleeping-bag roll into the boat. When you pack a canoe, a couple of large dry bags are preferable to many smaller ones; when you pack a kayak, the opposite is true. Careful paddlers should plan to pack a number of small bags into the boat's storage hatches. They should also apply the "need-to-have" principle used to pack a backpack: Keep things that you'll need throughout the day easily accessible. Sunscreen, snacks, maps, first-aid kits, drinking water, and rain gear should be near the top. Load heavier items so they are on the bottom to help maintain the boat's center of gravity.

Things to Consider when Choosing a Canoe or Kayak

➤ Aesthetics

➤ Maintenance requirements

➤ Repair ease

➤ Strength and durability

➤ Resistance to the sun's rays (ultraviolet light)

➤ A single or tandem model (for kayaks)

➤ Hull shape and storage capacity

➤ Cost

The Run-Down on Construction Materials

Kayaks and canoe may be constructed of different materials. The material choice depends on what the boat will be used for, its price, and the type of conditions in which it will be used. Most boats are made from one of the following materials:

Polyethylene is used to make the cheaper boats on the market. It is a fairly heavy material, but makes up for this deficiency by being extremely rugged and maintenance-free. In other words, ideal for occasional users who don't want to spend a lot of dough. Sunlight, however, can cause polyethylene to degrade over time; therefore canoes and kayaks made of polyethylene should be stored out of the sun. Canoes made from this material may have a layered structure with a foam core for increased flotation.

Fiberglass is durable and relatively heavy (though not as heavy as polyethylene); it requires very little maintenance. Cheaper canoes made of *chopped* fiberglass should be dismissed as possible choices because they degenerate quickly. If you'll be carrying your canoe over land a lot, a Kevlar boat may be a better option.

Wood has been largely replaced by modern materials in canoe and kayak construction. Making wooden canoes and kayaks is labor-intensive. Production of such vessels is often left in the hands of the skilled do-it-yourselfer (there are magazines devoted to the subject). Wooden boats are the most beautiful and ornate, but they need constant upkeep. They may be strip-built (discussed later) or made of plywood. These boats are better suited to cottagers who like to spend their time caring for their canoes.

> **Safe Camping** CAUTION
> Canoers traveling with a dog on board may want to outfit their animal with a life preserver. Man's best friend usually knows how to swim, but a prolonged dunk in the drink may tire the dog out. Specially made life preservers for dogs allow the animal to ride out the time it takes to get to shore in the event of a capsize. They cost around $40.

In addition to these materials, you may also find canoes made from the following:

Kevlar, another modern material, is used in the construction of high-end (and high-priced) boats. This lightest of materials is sandwiched (by various techniques) with other materials such as foam and nylon to increase the canoe's rigidity. Kevlar is quite durable, though it suffers the same malaise as polyethylene: in that it's susceptible to damage from the sun's ultraviolet rays. Kevlar is also less abrasion-resistant than fiberglass. A Kevlar boat may end up looking like a war-scarred battleship if you're not careful around rocks; take care when dragging the boat out of the water. The biggest thing Kevlar boats have going for them is that they are lightweight, for easy portages.

Aluminum is used in the manufacture of low-priced canoes and is the least aesthetic of materials for a number of reasons. First off, it can't be painted; you are always obligated to buy just one dull color—grayish silver. They are also heavy and amplify the lapping of water against the hull to an irritating level. But they are inexpensive and may be ideal for casual canoers who don't plan on portaging or using their vessels for long periods of time.

Royalex ABS is practically bombproof, but canoes made of it are quite heavy. Foam is sandwiched between two plastic coatings, on the inside and outside surfaces of the boat. The trim around the gunwales may be vinyl. These boats are inexpensive, but less nimble to handle than their sleeker fiberglass and Kevlar brethren.

Strip canoes are made from planks of red or white cedar that are covered with fiberglass. A canoe of this type is really a labor of love; it will have to be maintained with regular inspections and prompt repair of the hull if damaged. These types of canoes are popular with do-it-yourselfers who like to take on building boats as a hobby.

Digging the Design

Besides materials, you may want to consider the various hull designs available. Hull design is a major factor in how a boat will perform. No boat is perfect: A fatter (wider) boat will carry a lot of cargo and be more stable than a thinner (narrower) boat. A wider boat will be more stable, but won't track (steer) as well. A boat with a wider hull sits higher in the water than a boat with a narrow hull, meaning that the boat with the wider hull will catch the wind more easily—and may be blown about in windy conditions. A longer boat tracks better and travels faster than a shorter boat; thinner-shaped vessels create less resistance at the bow in the form of waves.

Rocker refers to the amount of curvature in the keel (the point where the bow and stern meet the water at each end of the boat). The more rocker, the easier the boat will turn because there is less resistance. A boat with more rocker may turn more easily than a boat with less, but it doesn't travel as fast or track as well.

Portable Boats

Folding kayaks feature a wooden frame with an ingenious hinging system that allows a waterproof shell to be stretched over the wooden frame. Everything fits into a couple of big duffel bags for ease of transport. What you gain in storage and portability, you lose in rigidity and tracking ability. But for apartment-dwellers, others with limited storage, and jetsetters who want to bring their boats along in the belly of an airplane, folding kayaks may be the way to go.

Decking and hull are made of Hypalon or some other heavy-duty waterproof fabric. Fabric-shell boats are quite heavy and require extra push-power from paddlers. They come in one- and two-person models, and can be put together in about 30 minutes with a little practice.

Inflatable canoes and kayaks may also be *considered* portable, but are really meant more for running rapids than for a week of flitting from one campsite to the other. Cheap inflatables are really more useful close to a cottage than as a mode of transportation for an outdoor vacation.

Your Backpack on the Water

The true advantage of traveling by canoe or kayak is the tremendous luxury of room for all the comfort gear you can possibly cram into your boat. There's room for just about every conceivable item—from two-burner camp stoves to several changes of clothing, as well as a day pack for short hiking trips. The added bonus is that something else transports *you*, rather than you having to transport your stuff. Of course, there *is* some work in paddling, but often the relaxing sound of the water lapping against the side of the boat and the passing scenery can make up for the extra exertion of arm muscles. The extra space afforded by a spacious hull should not be taken for granted; but paddlers, too, should consider the extra weight of bringing less-than-necessary items. Arms will get more fatigued on a long trip—which will seem vastly longer if the boat is packed to the gills with everything *including* the kitchen sink.

Different Strokes for Different Folks

A number of basic paddle strokes will get you from point A to point B. The strokes described next should be practiced before you set off on a trip. More advanced paddling strokes can be learned as your skill levels improve and you become better acquainted with your boat.

Holding and Handling the Paddle

To get from point A to point B you'll need to learn a few strokes first, and you should learn how to hold a paddle properly. Grip the top of the paddle so that it feels comfortable and use the other hand to hold the shaft about mid-way between the paddle grip (at the throat) and the beginning of the blade. When you are in the water, plant the paddle blade forward in the water and pull the paddle back toward you. The paddle blade should be at a 90-degree angle all the way through the stroke. When you get to the end of the stroke, angle the blade slightly so that it slices out of the water. Plant the paddle blade in front of you, and start over again.

You'll notice that by paddling on one side of the boat the boat will turn in the opposite direction (paddle on the right and you'll turn left). This means that to stay on course you'll have to change paddling sides from time to time. To do this, follow through on the basic forward stroke and as you end it (when the paddle is out of the water), let go of the grip. Use the hand holding the throat of the paddle to transfer the

> **Safe Camping**
> Stay close to shore if it's your first time out. Canoeing and kayaking are not hard to learn—but until you get the feel for the balance and motion of riding in a canoe, it's best to stay close to shore. Avoid fast-running water, and set out only in optimum weather conditions.

paddle to the other hand, then grip the throat of the paddle with one hand, and grip the paddle grip with the other. Plant the paddle blade in the water and paddle until you need to switch sides again.

Forward canoe stroke

Plant the blade toward   Pull the blade out of the
the bow and draw back.   water.

The *J-stroke*, so named for its shape, allows the stern or solo paddler to correct the direction of the boat's travel without changing paddling sides. The blade of the paddle is used to push the boat forward, but is "pushed out" at the end of the stroke.

Canoe J-stroke

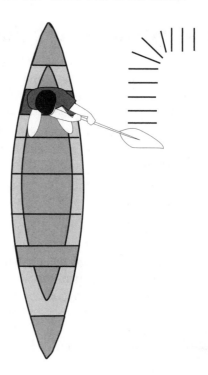

The *draw stroke* enables you (and your fellow paddler, if there is one) to move the whole canoe in a sideways direction. Plant your blade sideways, as far away from the boat as you can reach and not lose power, and pull the paddle toward you. The boat will move toward land, a dock, or away from an obstruction in the water.

Canoe draw stroke

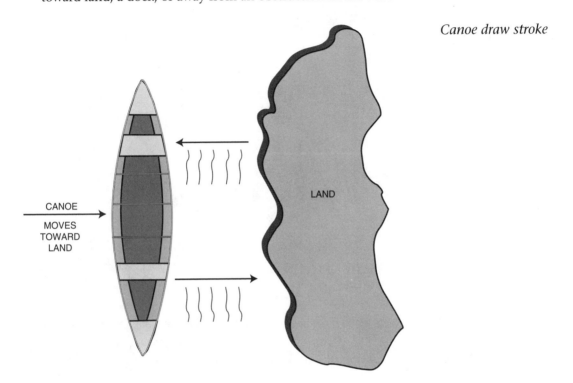

Kayak Strokes and Maneuvers

The Forward Stroke

Practice makes perfect, and you should aim in kayak paddling for a fluid, powerful stroke. You'll find that over time you'll develop a style of your own. The fundamentals involve gripping the paddle at a comfortable distance from the blades closest to the drip rings. You should strive to reach as far forward as possible when planting each one of the blades in the water. Start on one side, then transfer to the other. Your wrists and hands should move naturally—try not to concentrate too much on what's going on, but try and keep the submerged paddle blade perpendicular to the boat. Use the hand closest to water for power, but also try to use the power from your torso to add extra push power. Hold the paddle at a comfortable distance from your chest—and not too close. At the end of each stroke, rotate the blade a little to allow it to slice out of the water cleanly, and plant the other blade in the water on the other side of the boat. Avoid rocking from side to side as you switch from side to side.

219

To perform the basic forward stroke with a kayak paddle, position your blade to slice the water at the bow.

Follow through from the bow to the stern, then lift your blade out of the water and start over.

Kayak forward stroke

Lift the blade out of the water.   Position the blade forward and draw back.

Lean to the side of the boat opposite to the way you want to turn.

Turning

Paddling harder or more often on one side of a boat will cause it to turn. But if you face stiff winds and currents, paddling this way can disrupt the fluidity of your paddling motion. Another alternative is to lean to one side of the kayak while following through on your stroke. If you want to turn right, lean to your left; if you want to turn left, lean to your right. Keep leaning in the opposite direction to where you want to turn until you have put yourself back on course, paddling in as fluid a motion as possible.

Using a Paddle as a Rudder

Another turning technique involves using the paddle as a rudder to direct the boat. At the end of a stroke just before you pull the blade from the water, angle the blade to control your direction of travel. Push out on the left side of the boat to turn right; pull in to turn left. Push out on the right side of the boat to turn left; pull in to turn right. Every stroke will be either a push or a pull, and where you place it first determines where you'll move.

To turn, lean slightly against the turn direction.

To move sideways, plant your paddle blade in the water and pull the blade toward you.

Kayak draw stroke

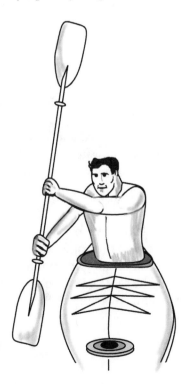

Use your paddle at the stern of the boat to make a tight turn. Draw the paddle toward the stern to move the bow in the opposite direction.

Kayak stern draw

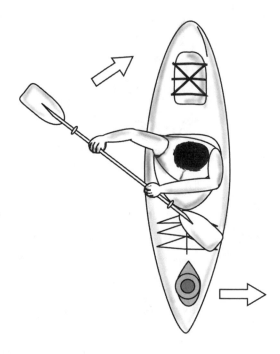

Rescue Techniques

Even the best canoers and kayakers end up in the water after capsizing. In fact, an important part of learning how to canoe and kayak *should* be self-inflicted dunkings in shallow water to learn how to right a boat in the event of a spill. If you are close to land and your canoe or kayak is heavily loaded, it's best to hug the boat and kick-paddle the whole rig back to shore where you can empty flooded bilges of water in shallower conditions. If the boat's load is lashed to thwarts and seats, the canoe may stay afloat (the load will act as extra buoyancy, believe it or not)—in which case, you may still be able to be paddle it ashore, even if the boat is completely filled with water.

In open-water conditions such as in the middle of a lake or bay, you may have to take more drastic measures—usually involving the help of another canoe or kayak. In the case of a canoe, you'll have to cut the load free and transfer it to another canoe. Then, with one or more paddlers still in the water, slide the capsized canoe up over the gunwales of the helpers' boat so that the cockpit on the sunken boat faces the water. Once the water has emptied from the canoe, the helpers in the rescue boat should turn the canoe the right-side-up and slide it back into the water. With the boat upright and stabilized next to the rescue boat, the dunked passengers should be able to climb back into their canoe. Use paddles extended from the rescuers' canoe across the formerly dunked canoe to help stabilize it. Remember that a paddle can be used to reach out to help someone who's lost balance and fallen in the drink.

Canoe-over-canoe rescue

With one or more paddlers from the sunken canoe in the water, slide the downed canoe over the gunwales of the rescue canoe to empty it. Then rotate the canoe into an upright position and slide it back into the water.

Kayak Dunking

The same emptying procedure used for canoes can be used for a kayak whose cockpit has filled with water. But because kayaks are less likely to fill with water (their bilges are sealed), loads will not have to be cut free during the righting procedure. The chances of completely flooding a kayak are also greatly diminished because there is less opportunity for water to get into the boat. (Of course, an open-cockpit recreational kayak will capsize much more like a canoe, as opposed to a *touring* kayak, which has completely enclosed bilge and sealing hatches.)

When a dunked passenger has to clamber back into a kayak, one approach is to try to straddle the kayak from the bow, move along the shell of the boat to the cockpit and re-enter there. Otherwise the kayak can be stabilized with some help from another boat and the dunked paddler can climb back into the cockpit.

> **Safe Camping** CAUTION
>
> You may never have to right a capsized canoe or kayak if you practice a few common-sense rules. Never travel in bad weather, particularly in windy and wavy conditions. Stay close to shore, and never travel when there is a possibility of thunder and lightning. Keep in mind that practice makes perfect; try sinking and empty-ing canoes and kayaks in calm weather, remembering that less favorable conditions will prevail in real life.

Safe Camping
Don't use PFDs as a cushion to rest against or kneel on. Keep them out of direct sunlight, and once you've adjusted yours for size and fit, use an indelible marker to identify it. As an extra precaution, carry an extra paddle in case one breaks or inadvertently falls overboard and floats away.

The importance of wearing a Personal Flotation Device (PFD)—and knowing how to swim—can't be better illustrated than when you find yourself unexpectedly immersed in water. If you dunk when you're out alone, and you are far from shore, stay with the boat and wait for help. In bad weather, stay put at the campsite. It is foolish and stupid (and dare we say "idiotic?") to travel on the water in bad weather. If bad weather blows up, get to shore quickly and set up camp.

Slide the kayak over the top of a helper's kayak to empty the cockpit of water. Then rotate the boat so it's right-side-up and slide it back into the water.

Kayak-over-kayak rescue

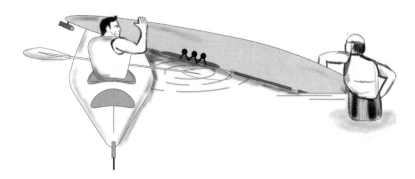

The Least You Need to Know

➤ Canoes and kayaks offer access to remote parts of the great outdoors. Kayaks are more stable than canoes, but offer less storage space.

➤ The two types of boats use different paddle designs and principles too: single-bladed paddles with canoes and double-bladed paddles with kayaks.

➤ Always wear a personal flotation device in canoes and kayaks. A Type III vest designed for paddlers offers freedom of movement and can be put on easily.

➤ Choose the right size paddle. Try out different lengths and styles before setting out. If you can, have an outfitter provide you with paddles of different lengths and blade sizes.

➤ Practice canoe and kayak rescue techniques before heading off on an excursion. Deliberately capsize boats in calm water, or practice in a swimming pool.

Chapter 19

Exploring the Outdoors on Two Wheels

In This Chapter

➤ Selecting the appropriate biking gear

➤ Determining what special equipment to travel with

➤ Defensive driving for the touring cyclist

➤ How to choose a bike for the trip

Besides canoes and kayaks, the other popular mode of muscle-powered transport is the bicycle. It's light, relatively inexpensive, versatile in its ability to carry both you and your stuff, and most people already know how to ride one. Bikes can be shipped on airplanes and popped on the roofs and backs of cars for easy transport. And they can also be ridden themselves to nearby campgrounds and outdoor vacation spots.

So why don't more outdoor adventurers and nature lovers use this wonderful form of transport? Perhaps they don't consider it, think that a biking vacation has to be like the Tour de France, or that a car is a better and more reliable way of getting to nature. None of these things could be farther from the truth, though any biking adventure *could* be done that way if the rider wants something more from an outdoor vacation.

I'LL TELL YA!...

Conventional Wisdom

Good bike stores will let you try before you buy. To determine the correct size frame, measure the distance between your crotch and the floor. This is your *inseam* length. Subtract 10 from this measurement to arrive at the approximate frame size for a proper fit. Make seat and handlebar adjustments to find the bike that's right for you.

There are also numerous pre-packaged and pre-planned bike vacations for people who want to tour Europe, ride through America's Southwest, or wend their way up and down steep coastal roads. These vacations can be bare-bones affairs where you ride with a group and provide everything yourself, from your bike to your food to your tent. They can also be deluxe getaways where everything is provided for you—where a bus carries all the amenities and joins up with the group at an inn every evening, just in time for a remarkable and fine dining experience.

Most bike campers will probably opt to organize and plan a two-wheeled vacation themselves by plotting their course on numerous road maps and cooking up their chow on a portable one-burner backpacking stove. If you're embarking on a more major camping expedition, remember to follow the same precautions and guidelines as you would for a backcountry trip: Carry a good first-aid kit and leave an itinerary with officials, friends, or family. If you're unsure of your abilities or don't have an idea of where to link up to convenient and safe bicycling routes, local bicycling clubs are good places to find itineraries and traveling companions. Cycling clubs can also provide equipment lists and recommended bicycles. Look for trip notices on bulletin boards at outfitters and outdoor equipment suppliers. For this chapter, I'll assume that you're planning a trip yourself, and want to know what kind of bike to ride and what special clothes and equipment you'll need.

Bikepacking—Mountain Bikes Rule!

Traveling by bike to camping locations via paved routes is one way of getting there. But traveling to your camping location by bike need not be limited to established roadways. By climbing aboard a mountain bike, which has thicker tires, a stronger frame, and is designed for more rugged conditions, you can share the wilds with backpackers. The trails you'll be traveling may have to be flatter and obstacle-free, but you can still go where backpackers have boldly gone before. Better yet, inquire at local bike clubs about bikepacking routes that traverse no-longer-used railway beds and logging routes. These are ideal corridors to less populated wilderness areas and locations.

You'll need approximately the same equipment to outfit your mountain bike as you would for a touring bicycle. Some jazzed up mountain bikes feature spring suspension systems, and these may hamper the easy addition of racks—an important and absolutely necessary feature for the bikepacker, since you'll have to carry between 30 and 40 pounds of gear and supplies with you on a typical three- or four-day expedition. Unlike the touring biker, you won't have the luxury of rolling to your roadside food supply every day, and that means you'll have to bring along adequate food for the duration of your trip.

Novices who are in the market for a new bike should consider purchasing a mountain bike over a model designed for touring. Mountain bikes may weigh considerably more because they are built for the rough stuff, and travel more slowly as a result, but they are certainly stronger and more durable, stable, and versatile in the long run (think of all those sidewalk curbs that a mountain bike can "hop" over).

Conventional Wisdom

When sharing trails with backpackers, bikepackers should look out for those *walking* on trails. Yield to hikers when you meet them—a fast-rolling bicycle packed up with you and your gear may be a fearsome sight and a danger to slower-moving traffic.

Seriously consider one for any kind of bike camping, whether you'll be packing up for a wilderness adventure, or rolling from one campground to another.

Shake, Shimmy, and Roll...

With the right attachments and modifications, your bike can become a close two-wheeled friend that will share the experiences of rolling down country roads and lanes past fields of flowers and rows of trees. The bike has a double role—it's both transportation and beast of burden for the camping gear that fits in a backpack. When you select gear, pay attention to the weight and the size of the equipment you take along. Similarly, the bike you end up using for a trip should be relatively lightweight and de-signed in some respects for the job at hand. Most bikes can be called into service as touring vehicles, but some are more appropriate for long-distance travel than others. Setting out to purchase a new bike for a trip is a bit like opening a can of worms; there are simply so many choices—frame materials, wheel diameters, even color. Choosing a new bike is no picnic for the novice, but the task can be conquered with little insight into how bikes are made and the features to look for.

Conventional Wisdom

For safety, choose the right size bike. You can roughly determine the right size for you by standing over the frame—there should be a 1- to 2-inch distance between it and your crotch.

Bike campers should be concerned with the type of metal used in the manufacture of the frame, which is in essence the body of the bike. Discussions of frames center around two factors: geometry and construction. Geometry defines the shape of the frame. The *diamond* frame is the standard—suited to all but the most demanding cyclists, or those

Safe Camping
Caveat emptor: Purchasing a bike from a discount store may be a mistake. You won't get expert advice and the bike may be poorly assembled, meaning that you're inviting future breakdowns, not to mention the on-road hazards that loose handlebars, brake slippage, and loose nuts pose. Buy from a reputable bike outfit.

who have bodies that don't match the offerings of most bike manufacturers. (Such cyclists may need to have their frames custom-made—a particularly expensive option for most people.) Women's frames, where the top crossbar is dropped, are weaker than standard men's frames. If there is any reason for riding such a bike, try out an alternative known as a *mixte* frame. Such a frame is built from two narrow tubes that run from diagonally from the top of the head tube to the to the back dropouts. A bike like this looks weird but works for people who aren't comfortable with a standard diamond frame.

Quality frames may be joined at tension points with *lugs* (fittings that join tubes together). Lately, lugless frames have become predominant, and these may be just as strong as designs that incorporate lugs. Cyclists should look for frames that are *brazed* rather than welded; the high heat needed to melt the metal in welding also weakens it. Slowly brazed metal doesn't suffer the same pitfall.

Other key criteria to consider in bike selection include:

➤ The frame should have eyelets for the attachment of air pumps, racks, and other accessories.

➤ The accessory parts should be standard, meaning that they're easy to fix with commonly found tools.

➤ The bike should be equipped with strong wheel frames made from metal alloys. Avoid steel frames, which are strong but heavy and don't encourage brakes to grab when wet.

➤ The bike should offer stability and ease of maneuvering at high speeds and when loaded with equipment. Load up for a test drive before you hand over your plastic.

➤ Sturdiness is a subjective criterion, based on the feel of the bike in the showroom. The bike should feel as though it will support you and a substantial amount of gear. Try before you buy and make sure your bike doesn't "shimmy" when you take sharp turns or lean into a turn.

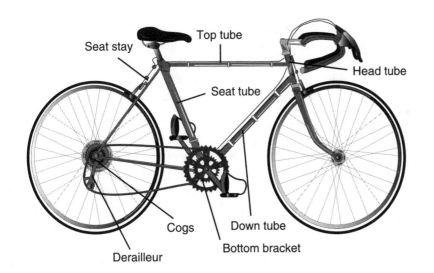

Key parts on a touring (road) bike

Mountain bike

Wheels...Tires and Tubes

Wheels begin with tires and tubes. If you look at the sidewall of a bike's tire you'll see two figures stamped into it, say 26×1.95, which is pretty wide and typical for a mountain bike. The first number refers to the wheel diameter, and the second number is the tire diameter. You can't change the wheel diameter, but you can alter the tire diameter based on the kind of performance characteristics you want from the tire. A skinny tire will allow

229

your bike to travel faster than a thicker, broader tire. When you're selecting tires, remember that skinny tires need to be inflated at a higher pressure, meaning you'll feel that the ride is harder than with a wider tire that requires less pressure. Wider tires are more resistant to punctures and that's why they're used on mountain bikes, which travel over rough ground.

When you look into tires you'll discover that there is a range of treads offered by a host of manufacturers. Wider mountain-bike tires have widely spaced lugs that stand high off the tire to encourage a good grip on muddy, uneven terrain. Tires designed for road bikes will have tightly spaced lugs, or have shallow rain grooves set into an otherwise smooth tire designed to travel over paved surfaces. If you really get into your tires there are front- and rear-specific tires designed for their particular roles in the biking equation. Front-specific tires feature lugs that are set up to cope with lateral action like steering action. Rear-specific tires have lug patterns that encourage straight-line traction and proper braking. A Kevlar tire is one that features a Kevlar bead instead of a wire one to grip the rim. Kevlar is stronger than wire, and for packability and portability, Kevlar also wins out: It is bendable, meaning that you can fold a spare up and take it with you.

Tubes

Tubes are rated according to tire size and the range in width they can be used for. A tube rated 26" × 1.95–2.5" will fit any 26-inch tire with widths between 1.95 inches and 2.5 inches.

A bike's wheels, along with its frame, are extremely important considerations. The wheels must be as light as possible and strong enough to support large loads on uneven roads. When looking at wheels, consider the rims, tires, hubs, and spokes. The rims and tires should be as light as possible; they are the components that your pedal power must set in motion. The heavier the wheels, the harder it will be to go from stop to start. Choose metal alloy rims over stainless-steel ones. Stainless-steel rims are much heavier and get slick when they get wet, making it harder to stop in rainy weather.

I'LL TELL YA!...

Conventional Wisdom
Make sure to carry the appropriate bicycle pump for your tires. Don't purchase a pump that features only the ability to pump up Presta valves if you typically use tires with Shraeder valves. If you use both, get a pump that accommodates adapters for both valve types.

CAUTION

Safe Camping
Carry an air pump that mounts to eyelets on the bike frame. A basic repair kit should include patches and rubber cement for punctured inner tubes. Carry an extra inner tube and tire in case of damage beyond repair.

Rules
Inflate tires to the recommended pressure indicated on the tire sidewall. If you are carrying a heavy load, you can inflate the rear tire to 10 pounds above the recommended pressure. On rough roads, dampen the bumps by letting some air out of the tires.

Rims should be designed for *wired-on* tires, as opposed to *tube tires*, which are generally thinner and harder to repair if you get a flat. Tire tubes will have one of two types of air valve: Shraeder or Presta. Shraeder valves are the most common and are the same as the ones on car tires. Presta valves are thinner-looking and can't be filled easily at gas station pumps.

The Hubbub on Hubs

Hubs are available in large- and small-flange versions (*flanges* are where the spokes attach to the wheels). Small-flange hubs provide a somewhat smoother ride. (A softer or harder ride may be academic until you've acquired greater cycling experience, but try discerning the difference between the two flanges when you're testing different makes and models in the store.) In addition to large and small flanges, hubs will be either *sealed* or *unsealed*. Sealed hubs hide the wheel bearings, keeping them cleaner and lubricated over the long haul, and thus making them more maintenance-free than unsealed versions.

Most wheels will have 36 spokes, a reasonable number for a reasonably heavy load. The more spokes, the stronger the wheel and the more weight it can support. Cyclists who carry extreme amounts of weight may opt for wheels with 40 spokes; for most people, this is overkill.

Have Bike, Will Travel

Most bikecampers and bikepackers don't step out of the door, don a helmet, and head off for their destinations. They use a faster and more capable way to get there: A car equipped with a racking system that supports several bicycles on the roof or at the back of the vehicle. Roof racks are usually multi-sport systems, meaning that they can be adapted to carry everything from bikes to canoes to kayaks. The heart of the system typically consists of two crossbars onto which sport-specific carrying adapters are fitted. If you engage in several kinds of activities, a multi-sport rack may be for you.

Rear racks attach to a vehicle by way of a series of straps, buckles, and hinges that use the trunk or back hatch for support. They are not as versatile as multi-sport systems, but if you'll only be hanging a few bikes out back from time to time, this system may be for you.

> **Conventional Wisdom**
>
> I'LL TELL YA!...
>
> If you are traveling by airplane, bus, or train to your cycling trip's departure point, phone ahead to see whether bikes can be accommodated. The bike will usually have to be boxed in a special carton provided by the carrier. If this is the case, be prepared to remove the pedals and loosen the handlebars so the bike can be packed in the carton.

Whichever system you use, make sure that your bikes and other sporting equipment are locked in place. For bikes, use a long cable lock snaked between bike wheels and frames and secured to the rack (if it is locked in place) or to the car's bumper (if you're using a rear-mounted system).

Gearing Up and Gearing Down

A bike is basically the equivalent of a car with standard transmission—but more so. Most bikes these days offer 21 speeds and a transmission system consisting of two handlebar-mounted shifters and a front-and-rear derailleur system that moves the chain from one sprocket to the next, up and down. Like a car equipped with a shift, you'll have to be riding the bike to get from one gear to the next. On older bikes, gear shifts were located where the head tube meets the handlebar tube—precariously close to the front wheel. The left-hand shifter controls the front derailleur, and the right-hand shifter the rear derailleur. Push forward on the right-hand shifter to go down a gear, and push backward toward you to go up. Use the left-hand shifter to change the gearing ratio more radically. You'll have to play around with the gears to get used to them and learn what they do. When going up hills, shift down. On flat terrain keep shifting up as you gain speed. On hills, shift into the highest gear if you want, or slow yourself down with your brakes.

There are many configurations of gears and derailleurs available—and a lot of mumbo-jumbo that goes with explaining how they work. On your quest for the perfect bike you'll encounter 10-, 12-, 15-, and 21-speed bikes. Ten-speed bikes are the most popular touring bikes, but you may want a heavier-duty mountain bike or "hybrid" (not as heavy as a mountain bike but not as light as a 10-speed touring bike). Mountain and hybrid bikes typically have 21 speeds.

How do you determine whether a bike is a 10-speed or a 21-speed?

Without going into too much detail, multiply the number of chain rings on the front by the number of cogs at the back. Ten-speeds will have two chain rings up front next to the right pedal and five cogs at the back above the rear derailleur on the freewheel. Twenty-one-speeds will have three chain rings and seven cogs. When gears are shifted, the rider is effectively changing the diameter of the rear wheel, which makes it easier or harder to climb hills or go faster over flat terrain, whichever is desired.

Putting Pedals to the Metal

Wide pedals are best for long-distance traveling. Pedals should also be fitted with toe straps and clips. They prevent feet from slipping off the pedals (especially in rainy weather), and help reduce wear and tear on the knees by holding the feet in place throughout pedaling revolutions. So-called "clipless" pedal systems are an ingenious alternative to traditional pedals with clips and straps. In this setup cleats in the sole of the cycling shoe "mates" with the pedal. Users claim that it is easier and faster to release your feet than in more traditional clip or strap systems. The cleats on these shoes are also recessed, making the shoes easier to walk in. Metal pedals—either stainless steel or alloys—should be selected over plastic pedals for the simple reason that they are more durable.

The Basic Bike-Camping Tool Kit

Tools are a biker's best friend when breakdowns occur on the road. Familiarize yourself with the following list and assemble a set of tools to match the sizes of hardware on your bike. And practice using any tool you purchase—the best tools are no good if you don't know how to use them.

➤ Screwdriver with 1/8-inch blade

➤ Allen wrenches (for various parts on bike)

➤ Adjustable wrenches (for bolts)

➤ A "Y" wrench with appropriate sockets (A triple-headed hex wrench with a plastic handle for ease of use. Sockets add versatility.)

➤ Spoke wrench (for trueing bent rims)

➤ Freewheel remover

➤ Oil or another lubricant (for chain, wheel, and other moving components)

➤ Needle-nose pliers (for gripping cables)

➤ Extra tube

➤ Patch kit (patches, sandpaper, rubber cement, tire-removal levers)

➤ Extra spokes and nipples

Safe Camping
No tool will be of any help if you don't know how to use it. Practice basic bike repairs *before* you set off on a trip; study up on how to fix the various component parts on your bike. Take a basic bike-maintenance course or consult some of the step-by-step books on the subject. At the very least, know how to repair a flat tire.

Packing Up and Moving Out

Racks you add on the fronts and backs of bikes make it possible to carry tents, sleeping bags, stoves, and the rest of the equipment that is otherwise crammed into a backpack or lashed inside the bowels of a canoe or kayak. Racks are sold as add-ons that are secured onto bikes, usually with screws that fit into eyelets on the bike's frame. Cordura carrying sacks (or *panniers*), are fitted to the frame and loaded with trip necessities. Because the rack is central to the bike's carrying system, it must be extremely strong and stable.

Panniers are sometimes referred to as "saddlebags" by novices and non-biking types. Saddlebags are designed to fit on a horse's back. What your metal steed requires are more properly called "panniers"—the equivalent of a backpack on two wheels.

Any good set of panniers will fit securely on the sides of a standard bike rack over the back wheel. Panniers attach with a system of hooks that fit over one of the top tubes on the top side of the rack. Hooks attached to the rear-wheel forks pull the panniers tight and hold them in position.

I'LL TELL YA!...

Conventional Wisdom

Why hassle with putting on your own bike rack when the shop where you purchased it will do it for a modest fee—usually $5? Before you walk away with your rack in hand, ask if the store can put it on your bike for you.

Like a backpack, panniers should be loaded properly. Heavy items should be packed on the bottom of each pannier to keep the load near the ground. Each pannier should be loaded with an equal amount of weight to help the riders stay balanced. Sleeping bags can be wrapped in a tarp and placed lengthwise along the flat part of the rack. The tent can be placed up front in an added handlebar bag or packed in the panniers.

Panniers leak, no matter how waterproof they seem; line them with plastic bags to keep everything dry. Be sure that panniers are "cut" at an angle near the pedals. This is important because this feature prevents turning feet from hitting the panniers. (Those with size 12 feet, take heed.)

Panniers are available in small, medium, and large sizes. Ideally, both panniers should offer between 1,500 and 2,000 cubic inches (by comparison an average backpack offers 4,000 cubic inches, and a set of small "commuter" panniers 1,000 cubic inches). You'll need to carry about 30 to 40 pounds of gear, supplies, and food for a three- to four-day excursion.

Why are bike campers expected to carry less than backpackers?

The answer is that bike campers don't have to carry as much food. Bikers can roll to food sources more easily, be they convenience stores, gas-station convenience stores, or roadside bakeries. Backpackers and bikepackers, by comparison, are farther from food, usually by days.

Panniers should be sturdy and backed with some sort of stiffener that will prevent bulges from getting nabbed by the rear-wheel spokes. When attached to the rack, they should also be secured firmly by whatever means you're using—usually by tightening the straps.

Panniers will have Velcro, zippers, or drawstrings as closures. External pockets should be filled with need-to-have items such as sunscreen, toilet paper, and lip balm.

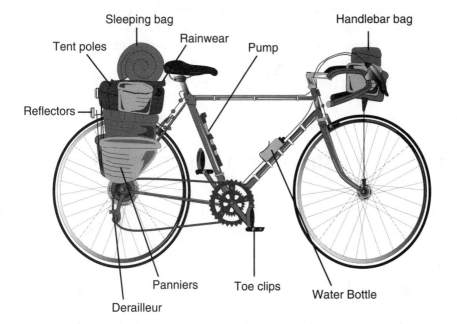

Sleeping bag

Tent poles

Rainwear

Pump

Handlebar bag

Reflectors

Panniers

Toe clips

Water Bottle

Derailleur

A fully loaded touring bike

Handlebar Bags

While panniers are designed to carry most of your camping supplies, handlebar bags can serve as extra storage for such items as your tool kit, keys, snacks, and maps. Most handlebar bags also feature a see-through plastic window in the top. Maps can be slipped under the window and may be consulted at a glance to keep track of trip progress. These smaller bags will offer an extra 500 cubic inches of storage space. Avoid handlebar bags that are too big: They can affect your steering and maneuverability for the worse.

Handlebar bags are mounted with a support system that consists of a shock cord and support rod that fastens to the front forks. This arrangement steadies the bag and holds it slightly off the handlebars, making the bars easier to grip.

Front Panniers

If you're a gear hog and willing to give up maneuverability and speed to carry more stuff, smaller panniers can be added to the front of the bike. A short front rack is attached to the bike and smaller panniers are strapped in place. For long trips, where campers want as many of the amenities as possible, front panniers can offer up to 1,000 cubic inches.

Rules

Drink plenty of water throughout the day during any bike trip to avoid dehydration. Water bottles may be secured to the bike frame with a special holder. Because you may be exert yourself more pedaling up hills, be sure to drink more after such bouts with gravity. To avoid dehydration, drink at least one gallon of water per day—before you become thirsty—and preferably more when you're exerting yourself for long periods.

In Praise of Tight Black Shorts and Other Gripping Matters

The well-dressed cyclist looks like a sleek flying insect with a colorful helmet, sunglasses, shirt, tight black shorts, and cycling shoes. Some may say that a cyclist's getup looks ridiculous, and most cyclists would have a hard time disagreeing. Looking buggy does not mean being crazy, however. In the cyclist's ongoing quest to be aerodynamic and sweat-resistant while optimizing pedal power, cyclists have come to adopt some funny-looking fashions.

Refer to the following clothing checklist for an idea of what to take along on your trip. Remember that your legs will bane the brunt of overzealous packing. To maintain optimum comfort, and reduce friction from bicycling shoes, wear synthetic socks and a silk sock liner to encourage the migration of foot moisture away from your skin. Specially designed cycling sunglasses protect your eyes from the sun—and from branches that bikepackers may encounter on wooded trails. Polyester cycling jerseys are designed to provide ventilation when needed; a zipper running from the neck to just above the stomach may be opened to allow fresh air in. Short sleeved versions are available for women, and long-sleeved jerseys may be used in colder weather. Long cycling tights may be substituted for bicycling shorts in colder conditions.

Bike camper's clothing list

	Packed ✔	Worn ✔
Cycling shoes	❑	❑
Cycling helmet	❑	❑
Cycling gloves	❑	❑
Camp shoes	❑	❑

	Packed ✔	Worn ✔
Bicycle shorts	❑	❑
Swimming trunks	❑	❑
Long-sleeved shirt (preferably wool or a wicking synthetic)	❑	❑
Cycling jersey or similar shirt (synthetic)	❑	❑
Sweater	❑	❑
Rain gear (Gore-Tex shell with hood)	❑	❑
Jogging pants (comfortable campwear)	❑	❑
Padded Cycling gloves	❑	❑
Socks (4 pairs and a silk sock liner)	❑	❑
Sunglasses	❑	❑
Bandana or sweat band	❑	❑

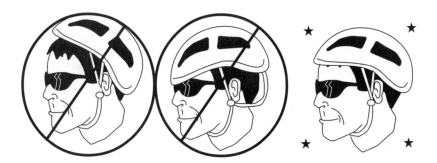

Correct adjustment of your helmet is critical to safety.

Helmets

Don't be a crash-test dummy. Throwing caution to the wind when it comes to helmets is foolish. Helmets protect cyclists from the most serious injuries—those to the brain. Improvements to helmets have made them lightweight, comfortable, and easy to take off and put on. Most have vents that channel air around the head, making them cooler to wear than their bulky predecessors. Look for helmets that are either *ASTME-* or *Snell-approved*, meaning that a model of the particular helmet has passed fairly rigorous tests for crash resistance. No helmet is effective if it isn't adjusted properly. Make sure it is properly positioned on your head, and that the straps are fastened tightly. Re-adjust your helmet periodically.

Bicycle Shorts

The girdle-like shorts that cyclists wear perhaps define them like no other piece of outdoor apparel. There is a method to the madness, however, for no self-respecting human being actually *likes* to reveal every flaw and feature of his or her body by wearing a tight pair of pants. Cycling shorts are made with as few seams as possible to prevent chafing, and are tight-gripping to resist the wind. Good quality shorts have a chamois lining in the crotch, which adds some softness and padding around a sensitive area of the anatomy. Most cyclists don't wear underwear under their shorts, leaving the chamois lining to soak up perspiration. The traditional black color disguises the dust and dirt kicked up during any bike trip (not to mention chain grease that goes along with fixing flat tires and carrying the bike).

Bike shorts should be tight-fitting but not so tight that they prevent movement. They should also ride up high enough on your back to keep you covered as you lean over the handlebars.

Shoes

For long trips, you'll need to pick up a pair of bicycling shoes—which experienced cyclists consider the most important part of the cycling outfit. The importance of shoes is the pivotal role they play in transferring power from the leg muscles to the bike's drivetrain—and their design bears this out. Cycling shoes have stiff soles that prevent the shoes from flexing, allowing the feet to transfer the most muscle power to the pedal. Cleated cycling shoes ensure an extra-good grip on the pedal, playing a role similar to that of the pedal's toe clips, except they help pull the pedal upward. To cut down on weight, the shoes have holes in them and are cut below the ankles. The best way to fit these shoes is to buy them so they fit tightly, assuming that they'll stretch. There are many makes and models of cycling shoe, including a more flexible sneaker type made by several of the leading athletic shoe manufacturers. The shoe selection also depends on the pedal system used on your bike. You'll need to be sure the shoes work with the system of the pedals.

Whatever brand and model of cycling shoes you end up getting, none will be completely acceptable as walking shoes. Around camp, you'll want to be wearing a pair of regular running shoes, sandals, or boots. Which means you'll have to remember to bring them along in your panniers.

Gloves

Cycling gloves are a breed unto themselves. These fingerless leather gloves are designed with the cyclist in mind. They have webbed netting on the outside and padded palms to cushion the hands against bumps in the road that are transferred to the handlebars.

The open-concept back keeps the hands cooler by allowing air to circulate. Gloves make cycling more comfortable, but aren't absolutely necessary items.

The Tour de France: Not!

Pacing and distance are two important concepts that relate to getting there. If you're starting out, take several day trips to get into shape and to assess your cycling abilities. Try to put your experiences into the context of a multi-day trip with some hills in between. Does a 50-mile trip really wear you out? Do your muscles feel sore the next day? How will you feel about setting up camp at the end of the day? The answers to all of these questions will be individual, but assessing your own endurance is important—not only for yourself, but in your cycling group (assuming you aren't going it alone).

Everyone in a group should 'fess up to their shortcomings in planning a trip. There is always the danger that everyone will overestimate their abilities and plan longer daily segments than can possibly be accomplished. The objective—as in all aspects of outdoor vacations—is to go slow, enjoy, and take time to smell the flowers (or at least enjoy the passing scenery). Local bike clubs can help with planning an appropriate vacation for every level of cyclist, from novices to the more experienced. Route maps with points of interest marked on them are often provided by clubs and can be invaluable trip resources. Of course, the type of terrain you're riding on will have a lot to do with how far and how fast you'll be able to travel. Always be realistic; allow time for repairs, flat tires, the recovery of sore muscles, rain, and days of rest.

> **Conventional Wisdom**
>
> It's better to ride in a lower gear where you can keep your cadence at about 60 to 90 spins per minute. When practicing your gearing, try and determine what this feels like so you can adjust your cadence on longer trips to the correct rate.

> **Rules**
>
> If backcountry biking is your game, stick to established bike routes and trails. *Hiking trails are no place for those traveling on two wheels.* Erosion caused by hikers' boot soles is already an environmental affront, and tire treads add insult to injury. A fast-moving mountain bike can bowl down unsuspecting hikers like pins in a bowling alley.

Safe Biking

Whether you're riding on established roadways or on a trail, follow the general guidelines below for safety and general riding etiquette.

> ➤ When sharing trails with hikers, make sure they know of your presence by yelling out a friendly greeting or sounding a bell.

> ➤ Do not create new trails with your bike.

> ➤ Learn and use hand signals for direction changes and other maneuvers.

> ➤ Cycle in a single file.

> ➤ Moderate your speed when approaching turns and hills.

> ➤ Avoid riding through streams.

> ➤ Pass others only when it is safe.

> ➤ Don't stray off a trail and avoid widening trails.

> ➤ Do not traverse closed-off trails or trespass on private property unless you have permission to do so.

> ➤ Practice low-impact cycling—ride only on designated trails, don't harass animals, and avoid skidding on natural surfaces.

Avoid traveling at night. Not only is it difficult to see road hazards, but it is difficult for cars and trucks to see you. If you must travel at night, be sure that you have adequate reflectors and lights. Many panniers come with reflecting panels, and racks feature a place where reflectors can be mounted. The best reflector, however, is a *slow-moving vehicle sign* (a reflective triangle). Collapsible triangles should be carried if there is any possibility of traveling at night. And because most headlamps won't light up the road far enough for riders to take evasive action when confronted with an upcoming hazard, ride slowly, especially when going downhill.

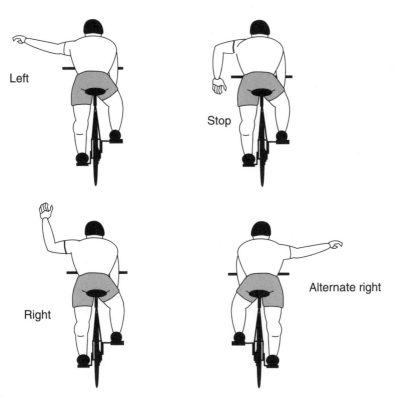

Hand signals

Left

Stop

Right

Alternate right

The Least You Need to Know

➤ If you have your heart set on a new bike, look for one that is sturdy and light. Assess the quality of the frame based on its construction method (it should be brazed, not welded together, for instance) and rigidity. But don't skip the most important criterion: The bike should be sized to you properly, be comfortable to drive, and easy to steer and maneuver.

➤ Choose a set of panniers (bike saddlebags) and a rack of good quality; pack them with the heaviest items in the bottom to keep the load close to the road.

➤ Panniers should be lined with plastic bags as double protection against wetness from the road.

➤ Carry a set of tools to handle roadside repairs, and know how to use them before you set out. For the not-so-mechanically inclined, courses taught by a local cycling club may be the answer if reference books on the subject leave you baffled.

➤ Practice makes perfect. Before setting out on a long trip, take several day-long trips with a fully loaded bicycle. If you are traveling in a group, be sure everyone is up to the trip before hand. Take short rides together if possible.

Part 5
The Big Trip

The trip looms in the not-too-distant future. Dreams of fresh air and encounters with nature dance in your head. Getting ready and taking off are weeks away; you're wondering whether you'll be able to handle an extended period in the outdoors. You realize that you haven't walked a mile in years, let alone strapped 40 or 50 pounds to your back and hiked on uneven terrain for hours on end. Come to think of it, you wonder how your pot belly will handle all the excitement—after all, you've been living Homer Simpson's lifestyle, sipping on Duff beer, stretched out on the couch, eating potato chips. Then a lightning bolt strikes—maybe it's time to get into shape for the big trip. But where to begin?

By shifting into gear and heading off to a gym—or simply walking for significant periods around the neighborhood—you can whip yourself into shape in a matter of weeks. I'm not talking washboard-flat abdominal muscles, but a reintroduction to exercise and the art of self-propelled motion. By leaving the car behind and preparing for the physical rigors of your upcoming trip (as described in this part of the book), you'll be able to transform yourself—in very little time—into an efficient walking machine, better able to hike up hills and take in the joys of nature in all her glory. On your way, you'll come across some wildlife, including a few pests like mosquitoes and black flies that are really there to remind us that we are alive. Follow the recommendations in the coming pages for shaping up and shipping out, and don't forget to take a pair of binoculars to look at the animals around you.

Limbering Up for the Big One

If you're like most people, you react to the very mention of the word "exercise" with a big groan. You've been bombarded with all the exercise propaganda you can take, and you've tried exercising time and time again—only to give up because of boredom, lack of time, or no visible payoff in weight loss or strength gain. And now you're thinking about loading up a backpack, throwing it over your shoulders and heading off into the wilderness without considering how you'll stand up to the rigors of the outdoors.

Take heart! Getting into shape before you start the outdoor adventure of a lifetime is really a pretty basic process, as you'll learn in this chapter. You really don't have to be an Arnold Schwarzenegger to get by. A basic general-fitness program will suffice to get you ready for the outdoors. If your vacation involves hiking, walk to work instead of driving or hopping on a bus. If distance prevents you from doing this, go for a long walk at lunchtime instead of eating out at restaurants or sitting at a desk with a sandwich. Take

Conventional Wisdom

If your conditional program includes cycling, make sure that you are road safe. While exercising, especially at night, use a powerful (preferably halogen) headlight and outfit your bike with rear reflectors. Glow-in-the-dark cycling vests offer additional safety.

Safe Camping

When you exercise at a gym or health club, make sure you know how to use the exercise equipment there properly. Ask trainers and fitness personnel how to correctly use equipment.

Safe Camping

Before embarking on any workout program or strenuous vacation, *consult a physician* who can help you evaluate what levels of activity are recommended for your state of physical fitness, age, and weight. If during any exercise you feel faint, suffer from shortness of breath, or feel chest pains, *stop immediately* and consult a physician.

the stairs instead of riding the elevator. Or join a nearby health club and use the running track to get in shape for the outdoors.

As we have seen, hiking isn't the only way to get to a destination. If you're planning a bike trip, try commuting to work on two wheels. Or jump aboard a stationary bicycle at a health club. If your outdoor vacation involves a good deal of canoeing, strengthen your arm muscles by lifting free weights or by using a Nautilis machine to build them up. Even simple pushups can greatly increase your ability to handle the extra physical stresses of an outdoor adventure.

If you aren't in top-notch physical condition, don't have any inclination toward shaping up, or simply want to embark on a trip without a nod to your overall physical condition, that's okay too. Any kind of outdoor activity involves some exercise—and hiking, biking, and canoeing are exercises unto themselves. Just be ready to suffer a few sore muscles at the end of every day, and don't try to outpace yourself by planning too much in the beginning. Ease your body into carrying the extra weight of a back-pack, paddling for long distances in a canoe or kayak, or pedaling for many miles on a bike. The shock of the extra exercise will wear off after a week, you'll feel better, and may be even lose those extra pounds you've been trying to take off. In other words, you'll feel better despite it all—and may even come to understand why exercise can contribute to your quality of life and overall well-being. To increase the enjoyment of a trip, however, try increasing your fitness level *before* heading off. You won't have to worry about your endurance, and you'll know what your limits are beforehand.

Even gardening can burn up to 300 calories per hour. If you're trying to shape up, consider working harder at the outdoor hobbies you already enjoy doing. But remember, to benefit from these activities, you need to do them at least three times a week.

Getting Fit for Your Trip

Whipping yourself into shape for an upcoming trip may be as simple as walking for an hour every day, or following a rigorous exercise program devised by an exercise specialist at your local health club. If you already exercise on a regular basis, try adopting a few more workouts designed around the type of trip and activities you'll be undertaking in the outdoors. Exercise those body parts that you'll be using on your trip. Swimming, for instance, can be added to weightlifting (or tacked on to a regimen of aerobic classes) for those planning a canoe trip. Swimming not only prepares you physically, but can strengthen your swimming abilities in the event that a canoe capsizes and you must remain afloat while righting the boat. The same goes for a bike vacation: Get leg muscles in shape by pedaling a stationary bike a couple of hours a week—or, better yet, get on a real bike instead of climbing into the car when you're doing errands. And of course, walk, walk, *walk* if you're heading off with a backpack.

Conventional Wisdom

I'LL TELL YA!...

Take care of your feet! When shopping for exercise footwear, be sure to buy only shoes that fit well and feel comfortable. Exercise shoes should not need a break-in period. Sprinkle foot powder in your shoes to help absorb perspiration and to discourage ailments such as athlete's foot and blisters.

Stomping Around the Neighborhood with a Pack Loaded with Books

To really get into the swing of things, pack your backpack with 30 to 40 pounds of books, old magazines, or gear and head off for a Sunday afternoon walk around town. You'll condition your back, hip, and leg muscles for the upcoming adventure, and at the same time be able to make necessary adjustments to your pack that will make it more comfortable to carry under real backpacking conditions. You may end up getting a reputation around town as a loon, but hey, it's better to be talked about funny than to not be talked about at all, right?

Conventional Wisdom

I'LL TELL YA!...

Choose the right footwear for the kind of exercise you'll be doing. Getting into shape is different from taking to hiking trails in a pair of stiff hiking boots. And exercise shoes designed for aerobics or walking are different from those meant for running and jogging. Running shoes have soles designed to absorb shocks, and are less flexible than walking shoes.

Designing Your Own Fitness Program

A fitness program should be based around three things: your current physical condition, your age, and flexibility. If you've been exercising regularly for years, then you probably have an idea of how you're doing in the grand scheme of things. If not, you'll have to put together your own fitness program yourself, or with the help of a personal trainer. In the quest for fitness, you'll be confronted with a number of terms and concepts that might not seem all that familiar—especially if you're just starting out.

The foundation for any fitness program starts with aerobic exercise. These kinds of exercises rely on large muscle groups moving in repeated rhythms that have the overall effect of strengthening your cardiovascular system (your heart and circulatory system). Essentially, by exercising aerobically you are trying to improve the oxygen consumption of your body. How powerfully your heart and lungs can deliver oxygen to the muscles determines your body's ability to endure stresses caused by exertion, and is an overall measure of your fitness. Swimming, bicycling, rollerblading, skating, and brisk walking are examples of aerobic exercises, and they illustrate that you don't necessarily need specialized equipment to carry out such exercises. If you don't do any kind of exercise other than aerobic, you're still well on your way to being in good shape.

I'LL TELL YA!...

Conventional Wisdom

Take your exercise program one day at a time, or rather every *other* day at a time. By designing your exercise program so you have one day on and one day off, you give your muscles a day to relax between workouts. Sore muscles are normal, but if your muscles get extremely sore, you've done too much.

The key to successful aerobic exercise lies in raising your heart rate so it remains within a certain "training zone" for periods of 20 minutes or more, at least three times a week. This is generally considered the minimum exercise requirement for healthy adults. Those embarking on an extensive hiking trip may benefit from maintaining higher heart rates for longer periods of time, four times a week.

Measuring Your Heart Rate

To determine if your cardiovascular system is benefitting from the level of exercise, you must first measure your pulse rate while exercising. To do this, take your pulse (by placing your fingers near the jugular vein in your neck or on one of your wrists) at some point during your workout; count the number of heartbeats you detect over a period of 10 seconds. Multiply this number by six to get your heart rate.

Determining Your Training Zone

After determining your heart rate, do this calculation: Subtract your age from 220, then multiply the result by 0.65 to determine the low end of your training zone. Determine the high end of your training zone by multiplying the result by 0.85. The following example illustrates the ideal training zone for a 33-year-old:

Low Range: 220 - <u>33</u> (age) = 187
$187 \times 0.65 = \mathbf{121.55}$

High Range: 220 - <u>33</u> (age) = 187
$187 \times 0.85 = \mathbf{158.95}$

To benefit from aerobic exercise, the subject's heart rate should be between 122 and 159 for 20 minutes or more in this example.

Warm-Up and Cool-Down Exercises to Increase Flexibility

Before you undertake any prolonged physical activity, physical fitness experts advise that you do warm-up exercises to increase flexibility and reduce muscle soreness, and aches, and pains. Before undertaking flexibility exercises, include a slow jog or run in your program to get your muscles working and primed for the stretching exercises that follow.

Try to hold stretches for 10 to 20 seconds. Stretch three times in each direction, or three times for arms and legs. Breathe in deeply before you stretch, and breathe out as you follow through. Avoid bouncing while you stretch, trying for slow, easy stretches. Avoid arching your back.

Here are 12 warm-up and cool-down exercises to get you going:

1. **Neck Stretch**

   With knees bent and feet shoulder-width apart, rotate your head to the right as you try to look over your right shoulder. Repeat this motion to the left, trying to look over your left shoulder.

2. **Side Stretch**

   With knees bent and feet placed shoulder-width apart, reach with one arm up and over your head to one side. Hold for 20 seconds. Repeat on the other side.

3. **Tricep Stretch**

   With knees bent, and feet positioned shoulder-width apart, place one hand between your shoulder blades. Then, with your other hand, pull your elbow behind your head and hold it there for 20 seconds. Repeat with the other arm.

4. Shoulder Stretch

With knees bent, and feet positioned shoulder-width apart, place your left hand on your right shoulder. With your left hand, push your right elbow across the front of your body to the left. Then repeat on the other side.

5. Calf Stretch

While facing a wall, place both hands on the wall at shoulder height with one foot placed ahead of the other. With the front knee bent and the back knee straight, lean forward until you feel the stretch in the rear leg. Repeat with feet in reverse positions.

6. Chest Stretch

Stand beside a wall with your feet roughly parallel to it and place the palm from one hand behind your back on the wall. Turn your shoulders away from the wall without moving your feet, and hold this position. Repeat with the other arm.

7. Bent-Over Shoulder Stretch

With your knees bent and your feet a shoulder-width apart, bend over and clasp both hands behind your back. Pull your arms up and hold them in place for two seconds while maintaining abdominal muscle contractions.

8. Side Groin Stretch

With your right leg extended to the side and your left leg straight, position your right hand on your right hip. Then bend your left knee while moving your body toward your left leg, and hold your position. Repeat with your left leg extended and your right leg straight.

9. Back Stretch

Lie on your back on an exercise mat and bring your bent knees toward your chest. Reach out and grasp your knees, pulling them closer to your chest until you feel the stretch affecting your lower back. Repeat three times, as directed.

10. Seated Hamstring Stretch

Seated on an exercise mat, straighten one leg out with your toes pointed upward. Bend the other leg with the foot toward the extended leg, then lean forward and reach with both hands for your toes. Hold this position for 20 seconds. Repeat with the other leg extended.

11. Groin Stretch

Join the soles of your feet together and grasp both ankles with your hands. Pull your ankles toward your body, with your elbows resting on your knees, and hold this position.

12. Pelvic Tilt

Lie on your back on an exercise mat and bend your knees. Tighten your abdominal muscles to press the arch of your back into the ground, and hold for 20 seconds.

Conventional Wisdom

Swimming is considered a very good cardiovascular exercise, meaning that it exercises the heart and lungs and thereby improves your overall well-being. Swimming is also a *low-impact* exercise (one that doesn't stress muscles but still improves them).

Strength-Building Exercises

Besides exercising aerobically, serious outdoor types will want to improve overall strength—that is, the ability to lift and handle heavy things. Although most outdoor activities don't require a great deal of strength, you might want to build up your arm muscles if you're going to be portaging a canoe (that is, carrying it over dry spots). Strength-building should be a part of a good overall exercise program, and you'll notice that bags and packs are easier to haul around if you follow some of the exercises outlined here.

There are a number of ways to develop strength in your muscles. The first involves *isotonic* exercises, in which the muscles move as they struggle against some form of resistance. Weightlifting is an example of an isotonic exercise. The second approach involves *isokinetic* exercises, which challenge the muscles with weight throughout an entire range of movement. Several types of weight-loaded exercise machines encourage isokinetic exercise. The third type of strength-building uses *isometrics*—the muscles are subjected to tension, but don't move during the exercise. Pushing against a wall without moving your muscles is an example of an isometric exercise.

Strength isn't all you want to build in muscles. You want to be able not only to lift heavy things for short periods, but also to be able to lift weight continuously for longer periods. When working with weights to build muscle strength and endurance, build yourself up slowly. Follow these guidelines:

➤ Undertake one to three sets at a time. A *set* is a series of repetitions that are followed by a short rest. A *repetition* is a complete cycle of an exercise. An example of a set would be 12 situps. When using Nautilius machines, undertake one to two sets at a time. When using free weights, undertake three sets.

➤ Do 8 to 12 repetitions in each set, starting out with a weight that you can lift comfortably eight times. Keep using this weight until you are able to carry out 12 repetitions with it. Increase this weight by 2 to 10 pounds in your next workout.

➤ Try to perform each repetition so that the exercised muscles are brought through a full range of motion. Exercise slowly, lifting the weight over a two- to three-second period, and take four seconds to lower it, exhaling on effort.

➤ Exercise large muscle groups first, then concentrate on the smaller muscle groups. Exercise all the muscle groups: upper body, trunk, and lower body.

Following are five weight-training exercises to carry you through:

1. **Military Press**

   Grip a barbell equipped with a weight you can lift without straining too much. Position your hands shoulder-width length apart. Rest the barbell on the front of your chest or on your shoulders behind you. Push upward until your arms are fully extended, then lower the barbell. Repeat.

2. **Lateral Raise**

   Grip two dumbbells of weights you can lift without straining too much. With your arms at your sides, raise and lower the weights away from the sides of your body to the height of your shoulders. Then lower slowly to the starting position and repeat.

3. **Crunches**

   Lie on your back and bend your knees while sitting up slowly and simultaneously raising your chest. Then slowly relax and lower yourself. Repeat.

4. **Half Squat**

   Grip a barbell equipped with a weight you can lift without straining too much. Position a barbell on your shoulder and bend slowly down at the knees, and then stand up straight again. As you complete the movement, push the weight up on your toes.

5. **Hamstring Curl**

   Set the weights at the end of a leg-curl bench to a weight you can lift without too much strain. Lying with your chest pressed against the bench (and with your hands gripping the edges or handles of the bench ahead of you), position the round pads just above the backs of your ankles. Pull your legs toward your buttocks as far as possible, pause, and slowly lower your legs. Repeat.

Conventional Wisdom

Exercise is only one part of training for a hiking trip. As in all successful "get-fit" programs, a good diet plays an important role in getting into shape. If you are overweight, consider cutting down on the number of calories you consume from food, and modify your diet to include more cereals and grains, less animal or saturated fats, and more fruit and vegetables. Consult your doctor or a dietitian to get you on your way to healthier eating habits.

Consider the Abilities of Those Going with You

Just because you've gotten into shape before heading off on an outdoor vacation, don't assume that the others going with you will be so fit. To encourage your camping and hiking partners to do the same as you, try planning your workouts together. Join a "Y" or health club together, go on walks in twos and threes, or organize official training sessions to get everyone to work together and into shape for the hike ahead. Getting together in groups like this is an excellent way to get motivated to limber up because it becomes a social activity as well.

One more benefit: Exercising together lets each member of the group evaluate the physical condition of the others, which can provide some insight into how far and long you'll be able to hike or travel on each day of the trip (which is also determined by the topography of the terrain) (Chapter 9). Consider whether you'll be hiking up hills or walking along flat stretches of land; try to simulate those conditions in some way. For instance, try climbing the stairs to your twentieth-floor office, or get on a stair machine at the gym. You'll soon get an idea of how fit you are—and what kind of trip to plan.

The Least You Need to Know

➤ Shape up before shipping out. A few hours' worth of exercise every week can pay off in big dividends on a trip. Getting into shape lets you concentrate more on the beauty of the outdoors than on your tired, sore muscles.

➤ Even if you haven't exercised for years, there's no reason not to start right now. You don't have to become an athlete to go on a hiking trip, but increasing the flexibility and strength in your muscles will certainly make your trip more fun.

➤ Exercise can be monotonous and boring; try exercising with others so a trip to the gym or health club becomes a social event—not just perceived as a session on the torture rack.

253

➤ Take exercise one step at a time. If you're out of shape or overweight, meet with your doctor to determine what exercises you can safely do. Trained personnel at a health club can help design a program that's right for you, whether it includes swimming, running, weight-training, or using some exercise equipment. Tell your doctor and exercise trainers of your plans for an outdoor vacation.

Chapter 21

Things That Fly, Slither, and Go Buzz in the Night

In This Chapter

➤ Fending off the onslaught of bugs with repellents

➤ Suiting up to prevent bug bites

➤ Dealing with itches and irritations caused by nature's smallest inhabitants

➤ Learning to be snake-savvy

We might as well face it: When taking to the woods, we're sharing the experience with a host of other creatures, both big and small. It is often the bigger creatures that scare us. But in practice, it's the smaller ones we'll be most concerned with.

I'm talking about bugs of course—those irritating pests that swoop down on you as you try to get from place to place, whether on foot or in a canoe. You're all familiar with the drill: These are the bugs that buzz in your ear and try to land on your head when you emerge from a refreshing dip in a lake. They're the devils that fling themselves at the tent walls and netting at night as you try to read a few pages before setting off for dreamland. They are often the most irritating aspects of spending any time outdoors, and they are the reasons why some campers throw in the towel and give up the hiking and camping game altogether. Don't let this be the case with you!

How Not to Go Buggy

Yes, you have to face up to the fact that no outdoor vacation will be without some form of irritation from insects, but you can avoid the onslaught by using a few modern inventions. They may not be as effective as napalm, but can do the trick in alleviating the pesky prevalence of insects in the wild. One of these preparations is known as DEET; this abbreviation for an unpronounceable, multi-syllable chemical formulation is contained in insect repellents of every description. DEET-based repellents come in different concentrations, expressed in percentages from 50 percent to 95 percent. The problem with DEET is that it has a "meltdown" effect on some plastics and can ruin cameras and some fabrics. Some photographers won't use repellents containing this substance for that very reason. A natural alternative is citronella oil, which will work to varying degrees of success. Other natural products are also available, usually in liquid form and applied from a small squirt bottle.

Conventional Wisdom

Don't apply insect repellents to broken skin, scrapes, and cuts. If the repellent used causes a rash or other reaction, discontinue use and see a physician.

Conventional Wisdom

Repellents with lower concentrations of the chemical DEET are just as effective as those with higher concentrations. Repellents with lower concentrations of DEET may need to be applied more often to remain effective, however.

Insects seem to be more attracted to some people than to others; if you're one of the succulent ones, look out. The good news is that the more time you spend in the woods, the less the bugs seem to like you. And bugs are definitely more attracted to some colors than others. Dark-colored clothing is an insect *attractant*, so avoid wearing it. Choose light-colored garments, and where insects are a real problem, don loose-fitting clothing that has tight-fitting cuffs. Hats are a must in the backwoods—as protection not only from the sun, but also from insects, which seem to really like getting tangled in your hair. In insect territory, a bandanna hung over the back of your neck and tucked in at your collar is another form of protection against the onslaught of biting insects. One more tip: Bugs are attracted to heat and CO_2 caused by exertion—so don't heat up by flailing your arms around to fend them off.

Look Like a Beekeeper—It's All the Rage

If you simply can't stand any contact with bugs and are still determined to venture into the woods for a vacation, you can make a fashion statement *and* protect yourself against the buzzing madness. Special bug wear, designed with the outdoors in mind, is available in the form of an impenetrable bug-net hat and jacket. The head net features a mesh veil that hangs over (and away from) your face and neck, while a matching jacket offers netting in the armpits to help keep you cool while allowing body moisture to escape.

Bug pants are also available. They have elastic around the ankle and loose, gaiter-like extensions that tuck into hiking boots. The overall effect looks like a beekeeper is roaming about the campsite with no honeycomb to tend.

Baseball caps with roll-down netting above the bill can also be purchased, and offer protection against insects at head level—though you'll have to work out a barrier system down below. If you're hiking in low-cut shoes, or are hanging around camp without the benefit of having your ankles covered by your hiking boots, be sure to wear heavy socks to protect you from nature's tiny bloodsuckers. Insects will always head for the most vulnerable part of your anatomy, and getting a bite on the ankle is no fun.

I'LL TELL YA!...

Conventional Wisdom

Early to bed, early to rise, makes campers less itchy and is much more wise. This variation on an old saying teaches us that bugs are more prevalent at night than during the day. This is especially true if the day is hot, sunny, and more windy than a cool, calm night. In buggy conditions, try going to bed early and getting up early to avoid the times when insects are most prevalent.

Discouraging Mosquitos and Other Flying Insects Naturally

There's nothing quite like a nice fire at the end of a long day of hiking. Roasting marshmallows and wieners on the end of sticks, and snuggling up in a sleeping bag conjure up visions of warmth and comfort. A fire is also good for keeping flying insects at bay; mosquitos and their nasty friends don't like the smoke given off by campfires. (Check to make sure that you can build a campfire in the area where you are camping.)

The key to controlling insects this way is to get close enough to the fire, but not so close that you burn yourself. You should be mostly downwind from the smoke, but a little in its path of travel to benefit from its insect-repelling qualities. If you are sitting next to a fire and using a sleeping bag as a makeshift throw, watch out for wayward embers from the fire. I have encountered many sleeping bags that bear the battle scars of a cozy session by the campfire. Given the price of a good sleeping bag, pay special attention to this advice.

Conventional Wisdom

I'LL TELL YA!...

Brightly-colored clothes, perfume, and sweet-smelling body lotions may attract stinging bees and yellow jackets. Avoid using these items in the outdoors as you may be mistaken by these insects for a bed of flowers.

Building Your Own Arsenal

In cases where fires aren't possible, as in the case of a fire ban, you'll have to resort to other tactics to discourage insects from taking a liking to you and sticking around.

Mosquito Coils

Commercially available *mosquito coils* are quite effective for keeping insects at bay. The only problem with these devices is that they take up room in your pack and need to be handled with some care because they can break. They are quite easy to use: Set up the coils on the stands provided and light the ends according to package instructions. The coils burn for a number of hours. Placed around a small perimeter, they can be your first line of defense. Don't burn these inside your tent.

Citronella Candles

If you don't like the idea of burning mosquito coils, take a hint from the garden-party crowd and burn *citronella* candles instead. The smoke given off by these candles is noxious to insects and can also create a comfort zone inside a small perimeter. The disadvantage of this method, as with mosquito coils, is their bulk and added weight inside a backpack. Their overall effectiveness, combined with their weight make them questionable for backpackers. If you're car camping or traveling by canoe, however, you may have the added luxury of including these bug-fighting options along with your gear. Don't burn these inside your tent, either.

Conventional Wisdom

Keep your tent's see-through insect netting in good shape. Even a small hole can be an opening for a determined bug intent on drinking your blood. Tent repair kits include net patches that can be cemented over holes. The same goes for holes in the tent fabric. Fix punctures and rips promptly to prevent an invasion from our multi-legged enemies on the ground.

Location, Location, Location

When windy conditions prevail, you are less likely to be bothered by flying insects; even though they are good at flying through the air, they are not built to be blown around in it. In bug season, if you have the luxury of choosing from a number of different sites, choose one that takes advantage of the wind and flying insects' inabilities to withstand it. If you're are canoeing, pitching your tent on an island instead of at an inland site will help tremendously with the bug situation.

Look at your maps and rule out any campsites that look like they could be situated near swampy or grassy locations. These are where bugs breed; camping close to one of these areas may drive you slowly mad as the night comes to sound like an insectarium.

Look around where you plan to pitch your tent, and be sure you're not setting up on an anthill. No matter how much you seal yourself inside a tent, insects always find ways of getting in when you tempt them with improperly closed zippers and panels. Make sure everything is battened down properly!

Lyme Disease: No Citrus Here

Just when you thought it was safe to go out in the woods, along comes Lyme Disease, a potentially fatal affliction brought on by the bite of the deer tick. Visitors to eastern woodlands are probably more at risk from being bitten by the deer tick than those visiting other locations. To avoid being bitten by ticks (which are usually no bigger than the head of a pin), make sure that your lower extremities are covered with pants. If you're hiking in shorts, frequent visual inspections of your lower legs by others in your group is a good idea. Also wear good socks and high-cut hiking boots (or pull your socks as far up your legs as possible). Apply insect repellent to your lower extremities.

Ticks are more prevalent in grassy areas and meadows, so avoid hiking in these kinds of places if you can. If you find a tick on your skin, encourage the insect to get off by applying some insect repellent to the bug. Or use a pair of tweezers to grasp the tick, and pull it off. Try to grasp the tick near its head, instead of at its body. If the tick's head remains embedded in skin, seek medical attention to have it removed.

Lyme Disease is no fun, and in its later stages can cause brain inflammation, heart problems, and arthritis. Fortunately, Lyme Disease can be treated if it is detected early enough. One of the main symptoms to look for is a reddish spot with a pale middle. Muscular pain, headaches, and a fever are other symptoms to watch for. If you return from a trip outdoors and suffer from any of these ailments, tell your doctor of your recent outdoor activities.

Here's How
Bees can leave their stingers in your skin; they should be removed. To remove a stinger, scrape it away with the edge of a credit card or knife blade. Avoid grasping the stinger, as more venom may be injected from the stinger's sac. Wash the sting and apply a bicarbonate-and-soda paste or calamine lotion.

Treating Insect Bites

Your mother always told you not to scratch at mosquito bites, because this would only make them itch more. If you were like most people, you scratched anyway and suffered the consequences. Commercial preparations now make the itch go away. These anti-itch formulations are available in tubes, and can provide instant relief. Hemorrhoid creams are effective for treating a more private condition, but they are also effective as bug-bite suppressors. If you have lots of fuel in your stove, heat some water and apply hot-water compresses to insect-bitten areas. Bicarbonate of soda (baking soda), mixed with water to make a paste, is also a good bug-bite salve, but you may not have included it in your backpack. Take it along; it can do double and triple duty as a toothpaste and boot freshener.

Little Miss Muffet Sat on Her Tuffet...

I'LL TELL YA!...

Conventional Wisdom

Ponds and muddy river and lake banks may be a breeding ground for leeches. If you swim in these places there is a chance that leeches will attach themselves to your body. Don't panic if you find one! And don't try to pull it off with your fingers. Instead, sprinkle salt on the leech to make it recoil and fall to the ground.

CAUTION

Safe Camping

If you are allergic to bee and wasp stings, be sure you carry medication to deal with a chance run-in with either one of these insects. Stings are usually more painful than dangerous for most people; a bicarbonate of soda paste made with water can greatly reduce the pain of a sting, and take the itch out of mosquito bites. Commercially available antihistamines for campers can be included in a basic first-aid kit.

Not many insects are more feared than spiders, even though spiders aren't part of the insect family at all. The very thought of eight creepy, hairy legs making their way across a web has inspired many a nightmare. And spiders have been featured in many movies, where they invariably do evil things.

Hikers and campers don't have much to fear; chance encounters with poisonous spiders are very rare. On the off chance that someone is bitten, the bite is often more painful than fatal (if this is any consolation).

There are only two types of poisonous spiders to be concerned about, if you insist on being concerned at all. They are the female black widow and brown recluse spiders. Black widows inflict a painful bite; symptoms will flare up within hours, when victims may suffer pain and cramping. Bites from a brown recluse may be painless and symptoms will crop up a few days or hours later. Symptoms include fever, and the wound can develop into gangrene. *A bite from a brown recluse is a medical emergency: Seek help immediately.* There is little you can do about a bite from a black widow but take some aspirins, Ibuprofen, or Acetaminophen to help diminish the discomfort.

How do you avoid being bitten in the first place? Spiders are probably more afraid of you than you are of them. But they do crawl into clothing and footwear from time to time, and they like wood piles. You probably won't see the culprit, but black widows have shiny black bodies that feature a telltale red hourglass underneath. Brown recluses are characterized by light brown bodies with a violin-shaped mark on the back.

Scorpions are related to spiders and inhabit more arid regions of the United States and some parts of western Canada. The sting from these devils is quite painful, but seldom life-threatening. Regional hiking and camping literature should advise you if poisonous spiders or scorpions are prevalent in the area where you are camping. Generally speaking, the larger the scorpion, the less toxic the poison. Some scorpion stings require immediate medical attention. Check the camping literature available in the area where you are camping to determine the danger of stings from scorpions. If you are camping in the backcountry and get stung, hike back to where you can get help. Take frequent rest stops along the way, and drink extra water. It's better to try and make it back than stay put. Scorpion stings are rarely fatal: Stay calm!

Snakes

If you're going to be hiking in snake country, you'll probably be advised by travel literature provided by state or park authorities. Most snakes are harmless, and the sight of a slither in your path shouldn't be more than a little shock. They are also more afraid you than you than you are of them. Of the many snakes in North America, you need only be concerned about four: the coral snake, copperhead, rattlesnake, and cottonmouth (or water moccasin). A bite from one of these snakes is seldom life-threatening for healthy individuals, but take some precautions.

Snakes strike at ankle level, and that's one good reason for covering your extremities with high-cut boots and socks. Snakes are nocturnal, meaning that they are creatures of the night. In snake country, avoid hiking after dark; walk carefully around the campsite. Snakes will seek warm places at night, and that's one good reason not to sleep under the stars without the protection of a tent's fabric between you and the outdoors.

One camping story recounts the luck of two campers who, in an arid national park, decided to forgo sleeping in a tent because the evening was clear and beautiful. They rolled out their sleeping bags and settled in for the night. In the morning they met several other campers who were shocked by the two campers' recollection of the night's sleeping arrangements. The two campers were equally shocked to find out how lucky they were not to have become the warm night's nest for a rattlesnake or two.

This story makes two points. The first is that the chances of being bitten by a snake are very few, even in snake country. The second is that campers should take extra care at night in snake country, even if the chances of being bitten are few and far between.

Treating Snake Bites

Although there is little likelihood that you will ever need to treat a snake bite, there is some question about what to do if you or someone else gets bitten. Snake-bite kits are available, but the consensus seems to be that they shouldn't be used except by those experienced in using them. Instead, calm the victim and move the bitten part of the body as little as possible. Firmly tie a bandage or piece of fabric above the bite, wind it down to cover the bite, and then tie it below the bite. Seek medical attention quickly.

The Least You Need to Know

➤ Dress to protect yourself from biting insects in the woods. A hat, combined with light-colored clothing are first steps in discouraging flying insects. A liberal application of an insect repellent is the second line of defense.

➤ DEET-based insect repellents work the best in the backwoods, but these formulations can damage plastic and fabric surfaces. A natural alternative is citronella oil, which is safe to use around most materials.

➤ Ticks may be carriers of disease. The best rule, of course, is avoidance, meaning that you should cover up extremities and avoid hiking through grassy meadows.

➤ Avoid setting up camp near a swamp or other bug breeding grounds. The best campsite is a windy one, and if you are canoe camping, choose an island rather than a mainland campsite, far from shore.

➤ Encounters with poisonous snakes are rare. Even so, prevent these scaly creatures from ruining a trip by wearing appropriate footwear and thick socks. In snake country, avoid hiking at night; sleep "indoors" in a tent, or off the ground on a platform.

Chapter 22

Critter Watching

In This Chapter

➤ Using binoculars to increase your power of observation

➤ Hints for capturing animals on film

➤ Learning to respect and watch animals in their habitats

➤ Looking for animal tracks

Getting away to the wilderness means you'll be sharing the outdoors with a host of larger creatures as well as the smaller ones you learned about in the last chapter. You may not see your fellow campers because they are either hiding or sleeping, but you can be sure they are there, either living in the shadows of the trees or nestled in their beds, even if that means a plot of grass or a dirt-filled knoll.

As you become familiar with the outdoors, you'll begin to notice some signs that the woods and trails are teeming with animal life. Without actually seeing them, you'll at least detect signs of their presence in the form of paw marks, claw marks on trees, and scats, either fresh or dried. And you'll certainly *hear* animals, whether it's the howling of wolves or the hooting of owls in the night. But the ultimate quest for nature-watchers is *seeing* animals, whether it is a majestic moose or a flat-tailed beaver waddling back into a lake just after it gets wind that something bigger—and maybe fiercer—is around.

Conventional Wisdom

In addition to using a case for your camera or binoculars, replace lens caps when you are through looking into your lenses. This will help prevent them from being scratched.

Conventional Wisdom

Use only lens cleaning tissue to wipe off fingerprints and other dirt from your lenses. Regular tissue can damage the coatings on lenses.

Opportunities for viewing animals in their natural habitats—instead of behind bars in zoos—are among the many reasons why countless campers and hikers take to the woods every year. Chance sightings of animals like rabbits and hedgehogs are delightful grist for stories and tales back in "civilization."

Of course there are animals that you want only to see or encounter from a distance. One of the most feared is the bear, which is no longer afraid of humans who have tempted and fed these potentially dangerous animals. Feeding animals in the woods is very poor form: Not only do animals begin to crave human offerings, they actually begin to depend on them for sustenance. Bears that return to campsites time and again for handouts usually end up being destroyed by authorities.

Don't stay away from the woods because you're afraid of wild animals—just have a healthy respect for the wildlife that surrounds you and follow a few common-sense rules explained in this chapter. Most animals will stay away from you unless they think there is a chance for a free meal, so don't condition them by providing one—even if they seem to ask for it.

Rules

Sharing the woods this way means leaving things as they were. You are a guest in the backwoods and should behave accordingly. Don't feed the animals; pack out or burn scraps in a fire. Also, don't harass wildlife by chasing it or moving close. If possible, allow an animal you encounter to continue what it was doing—eating, sleeping, resting, or traveling.

Animal Voyeurism 101

Hikers know that they don't need long raincoats worn without pants to get a thrill from looking at animals in the wild. What you will need is some idea of what animals to look for, however. Hiking literature often lists (with pictures) the types of wildlife living in the area where you'll be camping. Animals found in one place may not be found in another.

As with geography and landscape, animals vary from one place to another. In Wyoming's Grand Teton National Park, for instance, visitors may see bison, but the chance of seeing one of these massive creatures anywhere in Florida is nonexistent. Mountain lions inhabit Big Bend National Park in Texas, but aren't found in many other parks.

If you're serious about encountering wildlife on the trail, a number of good illustrated guidebooks can supplement the literature provided by parks and other camping facilities for the area where you are hiking. Appreciating wildlife also means taking certain precautions: Follow the advice given for dealing with potentially dangerous animals like bears and mountain lions. Most "dangerous" animals are more scared of you than you are of them, but there is a one-in-a-million chance that you will encounter an animal that has lost its fear of man. Keep your distance from wild animals (including deer, elk, moose, and so on), because they can charge when approached.

Hiking and camping literature tells visitors about the special kinds of wildlife that inhabit certain regions, as well as providing tips for viewing these animals.

Choosing Binoculars, Cameras, and Other Optics

Hunters enjoy aiming guns at animals. Hikers and campers, with true affection for wildlife and the outdoors, only aim binoculars and cameras at anything that moves in the wilderness. As glasses do for someone with poor vision, binoculars and telephoto camera lenses help nature watchers get closer without disturbing animals as they go about their business. Experienced birdwatchers know the value of good binoculars (and cameras equipped with the right kind of lenses), but most campers and hikers can learn a thing or two about selecting the right equipment for the trail, as described in the following sections.

Binoculars

Training your sights on wildlife means packing along a pair of binoculars designed for the rigors of the outdoors. There are many kinds available—from water-resistant models with camouflage-colored rubberized casings, to plain-Jane binoculars that look as though they belong on the bridge of a Navy destroyer. Backpackers will want to take along as little as possible in terms of weight and bulk; they should look for binoculars that are compact and lightweight. Unfortunately, these two attributes translate into higher prices compared to the bulkier models that may offer similar magnification and quality.

Price versus weight is only one of the compromises in selecting binoculars. Hikers and campers will want to look for shock-resistant models, and binoculars that are powerful enough to afford a closer look at animals in the wilderness without getting too close in person. A good pair of binoculars cost between $100 and $180.

Obviously, binoculars work by making things appear closer than they actually are. They accomplish this by taking the light reflected off objects and passing it through a series of magnifying lenses. The more distance between the lenses, and the longer the *optical path*, the more powerful the binoculars. Following this logic, a powerful pair of binoculars would be bigger and bulkier than a less powerful pair. Modern, more compact binoculars get around being bigger and bulkier by having prisms in the optical path that twist light around so it still travels a longer distance, but is contained in a smaller space.

When you're shopping for binoculars, you'll need to consider the factors listed next:

➤ Size/compactness

➤ Weight

➤ Durability

Conventional Wisdom

Binoculars, cameras, and other optics should be protected from moisture in the outdoors. Store them in rigid plastic containers like those used for food, or put them in sealable sandwich bags when storing them in a pack.

Conventional Wisdom

Weight-conscious hikers would almost prefer to be blind than to add something extra to their load. A lighter alternative to binoculars are *monoculars* (essentially binoculars with one lens tube removed). These mini-telescopes can be slung around the neck, positioned near the eye, and aimed at birds and other creatures quite handily.

➤ Water resistance

➤ Shock resistance

➤ Binoculars with at least a 6× magnification

➤ Fully coated optics

➤ Depending on price: Roof-prism binoculars or porro-prism binoculars

➤ Brightness determined by the size of the exit pupil

The Prism System

Binoculars suited to the outdoors are defined by the prism system used, and there are two main kinds to be concerned with: The *roof prism* and the *porro prism*. Binoculars with a roof-prism system are more compact and lighter; however, they are more expensive than binoculars employing a porro-prism system.

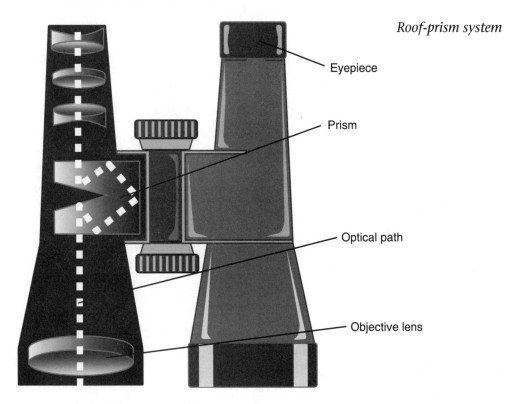

Roof-prism system

Eyepiece

Prism

Optical path

Objective lens

Porro-prism system

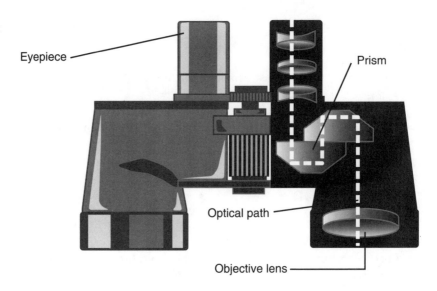

The Power of Light

Binoculars and other optics are rated according to the *power* of their magnification, and the size of the lens (in millimeters), at the front end of the binoculars. This lens is called the *objective* lens, and the larger it is, the more light it lets in. In low-light situations (as in wooded areas and at dusk and dawn), you'll want as large an objective lens as possible to spy on animals.

Binoculars are rated according to two numbers, such as 10 × 24. The first number identifies the *magnification power*, and the second number identifies the *size of the objective lens* in millimeters. Binoculars that make an object seem ten times closer than it is are rated with 10× number. Likewise, binoculars with an 8× rating will make objects appear eight times closer than they are.

Most nature watchers will want to carry a pair of binoculars that have a magnification between 6× and 10×. As discussed, the brightness of the magnified images seen in a binocular is determined by the size of the objective lens: The larger the lens, the brighter the image. This isn't absolutely accurate, however, because lens quality and magnification also have a bearing on how bright an image appears. The more powerful the lenses, the darker the image. As an overall measurement of brightness, however, the size of the objective lens will be a fair indicator.

> **CAUTION**
>
> **Safe Camping**
> Observe animals at a distance. View bears from a distance of at least 100 yards, and stay at least 25 yards away from tamer animals. If an animal detects your presence, you are too close. Retreat slowly and seek refuge in a safe place, if possible.

A Field with a View

Besides magnifying power, binoculars are rated for their field of view. In a nutshell, the field of view measurement for binoculars represents the spread of the viewing area in front of the objective lens. Binoculars should be rated between 260 and 375 feet, measured according to an object focused on at 1,000 yards in the distance. A wide field of view is good for watching animals, and other moving things. Binoculars with a wide field of view often yield fuzziness at the edges, so try before your buy to determine your level of acceptability.

One last way binoculars are rated is according to the size of their exit pupil, which relates to the brightness of the binoculars (as does the size of the objective lens, and how the lens is coated—as we'll see shortly). You can see the exit pupil on the binocular eyepiece lenses in the form of two white dots of light. The size of the exit pupil is arrived at by dividing the objective lens size by the power of magnification figure. A binocular rated 10×25 will have an exit pupil size of approximately 2.5mm ($25/10 = 2.5$). To compare the brightness between different binoculars, square the exit pupil size. In the example given, the binocular would have a brightness of 6.25 ($2.5 \times 2.5 = 6.25$). A binocular with an exit pupil of 2.9 would have a brightness of 8.41 ($2.9 \times 2.9 = 8.41$). The larger the squared result, the brighter the images viewed with the binocular.

Coatings

A certain amount of light hitting a lens is lost before it enters the lens, limiting the brightness and clarity of the viewed scene. Coating a lens with chemicals prevents light from being lost, and brightens and sharpens the scene. Binoculars may feature *coated optics*, and *fully coated optics*. With fully coated optics, the lenses and prisms are coated several times and are better than lenses that are coated only once.

Smile, You're on Candid Camera

Binoculars are great for observing wildlife, but not so great for capturing it. Hikers and campers will often want to bring back photographic testimonials of their encounters with nature. Modern, lightweight cameras encourage this, and the quality of the photography you bring out of the woods doesn't have to resemble an old Daguerreotype, even if you have only modest skills. For capturing wildlife on film, you'll need a decent camera fitted with a decent lens. Smaller, pocket-size automatics may be all-around good choices for backpacker who doesn't want to contend with the weight of a full-fledged 35-millimeter camera and its accompanying lenses. Remember that fully automatic cameras rely entirely on batteries to make them work, so be sure you pack extra batteries.

Lenses

For nature watching, you should use a 35mm camera of one kind or another to capture wildlife on film. Large, *single-lens-reflex* cameras (SLRs) may be fitted with a variety of lenses that simulate what you would see normally. *Telephoto* lenses magnify far-away images; *wide-angle* lenses exaggerate the width of a scene. For photographing nature, cameras are typically equipped with "normal" lenses, rated at 50mm, and telephoto lenses, rated between 80mm and 150mm. Wide-angle lenses, typically rated at 28mm, are used for photographing scenics and landscapes.

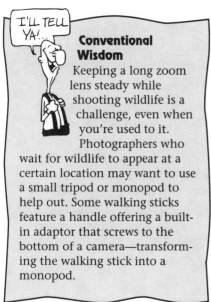

Conventional Wisdom

Keeping a long zoom lens steady while shooting wildlife is a challenge, even when you're used to it. Photographers who wait for wildlife to appear at a certain location may want to use a small tripod or monopod to help out. Some walking sticks feature a handle offering a built-in adaptor that screws to the bottom of a camera—transforming the walking stick into a monopod.

Professional wildlife photographers often shoot with powerful telephoto lenses, but use tripods to stabilize their cameras (due to the added length of this kind of lens). The upper limit for amateur photographers will be a camera with a 200mm lens. Anything longer can't be held with any degree of steadiness. *Zoom* lenses offer a range of lenses that go from 50mm or so to 200mm, and are probably the most versatile lens for shooting wildlife in all its forms. A zoom lens is good because it is a number of lenses all in one, and lets photographers focus on animals in their various environments.

Exposure and Film Speed

F-stop also refers to the *aperture size* of the lens (that is, the size of the adjustable hole that admits light to expose the film). The f-stop is adjusted by twisting a ring behind the focusing rings, and controls the amount of light permitted to land on the film inside the camera. The higher the f-stop, the smaller the opening in the lens. Shutter speed is important for correct exposure too; most photographers can't hold a camera steady enough to shoot below 1/60 of a second. Fast-moving subjects need to be photographed at 1/125 of a second or more. The higher the shutter speed, the faster the camera's shutter opens and closes. Film speed also pays a part: 100 and 200 ASA film is a good choice for well-lighted conditions, whereas 400 ASA film is used in dimmer, less well-lighted environments. The higher the film speed, the more light sensitive it is. Correctly exposing a picture is a balance of lens aperture size, shutter speed, and the speed

Conventional Wisdom

Taking pictures of large animals from the side of the road from a car window may sound obnoxious, but in truth, animals are less afraid or spooked by a car than by the sight of a person.

of the film used. In bright conditions, such as deserts, photographers may want to use less light-sensitive film, high shutter speeds, or small aperture sizes to get a proper exposure. In wooded, cloudy, or darker conditions, successfully capturing pictures of wildlife may depend on using "faster" (more light-sensitive) film, slower shutter speeds, and wider aperture sizes. Use the charts that come with the film you buy to determine the correct settings for your camera, and the kinds of conditions you are taking pictures in.

Table 22.1   Film sensitivity by ASA rating

ASA	Sensitivity to Light
25	Low
64	Low
80	Low
100	Medium
125	Medium
200	Medium
400	High
1,000	High

If all this sounds complicated, don't despair. With a little practice and experimentation, you'll come to understand the interplay between shutter speed, aperture size, and film speed. And if you're baffled by the technicalities of taking pictures—and your intention is simply to capture the wildlife you see in the field, without becoming an expert in exposure and photographic theory—most modern cameras will set everything automatically.

Rules

If you are traveling through a wilderness area and see a moose or bear mulling about at the side of the road, slow down, pull in, and stop. Slowly roll down your window and use the window as a support for your camera. Don't pull up too close to animals; they are sometimes unpredictable and may charge the car or run away if they feel threatened.

Exposure chart for different photo situations

Load/unload in subdued light. Set camera or meter to ISO 400/27°.
Existing light exposures: Flash: Electronic-see camera instructions.

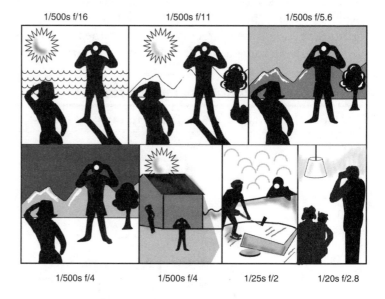

In Praise of Automatic Cameras

Small, automatic cameras will typically offer a lens that goes from normal to telephoto, and is adjusted by simply using the buttons on the camera to control the lens's focal length. A lens like this typically goes from 35mm to 80mm or more, effectively offering a variety of lenses in between. Water-resistant cameras are good for canoeists and kayakers who want to capture creatures living in water conditions. On some of our sea kayaking trips along the California's Monterey Coast, a water-resistant camera let us concentrate on taking pictures rather than worrying about protecting the camera from water splashes. We were able to take pictures of sea otters curled in kelp fronds, as well as pelicans that had set down near the shore, all thanks to a camera that had a rubberized casing around it. In Maine, we took pictures of curious seals that popped up in the water around our kayak after they had jumped into the water off a rock island because we had scared them.

Swinging Single-Use Cameras

Are you afraid that your $900 Nikon won't make it back from your trip unscathed—especially when you consider it will be raining most of the time during your trek? Or maybe you don't have a camera and don't feel like shelling out big bucks to purchase one? The answer to your picture problems may lie in widely available single-use cameras made by the big film companies.

These inexpensive cameras are automatic cameras that contain a roll of 35mm film and are sent back whole, lens and all, for processing. Although you are limited somewhat by the non-interchangeability of the lens, these cameras more than make up for this shortcoming by being available in different models (panoramic, waterproof, and all-purpose) for versatility. Also, you don't have to worry about them getting stolen, lost, of damaged. For about $10 this is an elegant solution to most picture-taking problems.

Tips for Seeing and Photographing Wildlife

Refer to the general guidelines below for taking better pictures in the outdoors. If you're serious about photography, you can probably find courses to take at local camera clubs.

➤ Learn about the wildlife in the area where you are traveling.

➤ Be patient and prepared to wait for the kind of animals you want to see.

➤ When photographing birds, use a fast shutter speed and be prepared to anticipate the bird's flight path.

➤ Set a camera's exposure for the subject, not its surroundings.

➤ Select the appropriate film for the conditions in which you are taking pictures; decide whether you want to use slide film or have color prints made.

➤ Use tree stumps and bushes to disguise yourself from animals you want to photograph, especially those that might be spooked by your presence.

➤ Use a zoom or telephoto lens to bring wildlife up close.

➤ When waiting for an animal to appear in the wild, keep checking exposure and focusing adjustments—you may only have split-second to snap a picture.

➤ Photograph large, potentially dangerous animals at a safe distance.

Identifying Animal Scats and Tracks

Finding animals in the wild to look at or take pictures of may be a bit of a chore in itself, because most of them have been conditioned to run from things that are bigger than they are. Look for clues in the natural environment that tell you of an animal's presence. Scats and tracks will tell you that animals are in the area. Like humans, animals are creatures of habit; if you find droppings (scats) or animal tracks, chances are an animal will be passing that way again. If you're in a wildlife preserve, your chances of encountering animals indigenous to the area increase tremendously—and your opportunities to see and photograph wildlife will be good.

Here's How

You may want to take pictures of animal tracks for future reference. To get the best results, use a *macro* lens, or the close-up setting on a zoom lens. Frame the track in your view finder so that it takes up the whole image area. If the track is in the sun, shade it so that you get the most definition.

Brochures describing the animals found in your neck of the woods will have pictures of the animals in the area where you are traveling, and they should have pictures of animal tracks and their scats—or droppings.

Playing detective in the woods is a great pastime, and you may well come to be an expert at identifying animals. Look for tracks in the mud on trails; try to put a name to the animal track you see.

Animals, because they are creatures of habit, also create paths and trails as they go back and forth between their food sources and sleeping places. An obvious rift in a swatch of grass or meadow is probably the trail for some animal. Animals will also use the trails of humans to get from place to place—why create a new path if you don't have to?

Animal tracks to look for

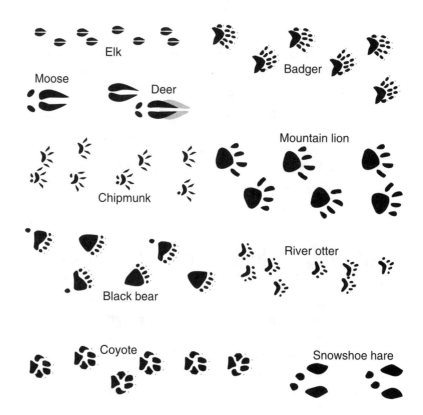

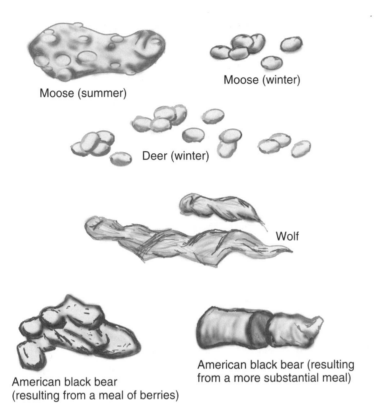

Scats to look for

Moose (summer)

Moose (winter)

Deer (winter)

Wolf

American black bear
(resulting from a meal of berries)

American black bear (resulting
from a more substantial meal)

The Least You Need to Know

➤ Consult brochures and guide books to find out what animals you're likely to encounter in the area where you are traveling.

➤ If you are taking pictures or observing large and potentially dangerous animals, take
care not to get too close. View bears from a distance of at least 100 yards, and stay at
least 25 yards away from tamer animals.

➤ Binoculars help you get close to animals without disturbing them or risking your
safety if the animal is large and potentially dangerous.

➤ Binoculars are rated in several ways, but nature watchers should choose a pair that
offers a magnification of at least 6×, and preferably 10×. Small, lightweight binoculars employ a roof-prism system—more expensive than those with porro-prism
systems (which take up more room when packed).

➤ Large, bulky camera gear is a backpacker's enemy. But lighter, all-in-one cameras with zoom lenses made especially for use in the outdoors are good choices for those who want to limit weight and bulk. Single-use cameras are good choices too; you don't have to worry about them getting lost, damaged, or stolen.

➤ Animal tracks and droppings provide clues that animals can be spotted in particular locations. Learn to identify the tracks of animals where you're hiking and you'll be able to wait at that location for them to return.

Part 6
Outward Bound and Beyond

By leaving civilization and trekking into the deep woods, you leave behind many conveniences but get to rub shoulders with trees and other greenery. Sometimes, however, rubbing yourself against green things (particularly poison ivy or poison oak) isn't much fun. By acquainting yourself with what poisonous plants look like, you can avoid them and minimize unpleasant encounters with the nastier members of the vegetable kingdom.

Minor scratches, cuts, and bruises are par for the course—as are tired feet and the exhilaration that goes with knowing you've reached your destination. But bad things happen to good people, and they happen to good campers, too. Being armed against the vagaries of the outdoors with a good first-aid kit and some specialized training can mean the difference between a successful trip and a spoiled one. If your adventures take you far from medical care, pursue a course in cardiopulmonary resuscitation and emergency medical treatment. In the unlikely event of a serious mishap, you'll know what steps to take.

If you hanker for a backpacking trip overseas, research your trip carefully and determine whether you'll need shots to keep yourself safe and healthy. The world's your oyster, and your feet can take you there with the right preparation and planning, as detailed in this part of the book.

Chapter 23

Safety and First Aid for Idiots—Dealing with Major and Minor Bummers

In This Chapter

➤ Handling emergencies

➤ Assembling a first-aid kit

➤ Treating minor problems

➤ Dealing with major problems

A medical emergency at any time, under any conditions, is a downer. In the backcountry, it may result in the whole trip being ruined because a large amount of time may be spent getting help, then bringing it to an injured person in the hiking party. But don't let fear of a mishap discourage you from reaping the rewards of a vacation in the outdoors.

You should face facts, however: Any backpacking trip—and any outdoor activity, for that matter—involves a certain amount of risk, no matter how cautious or careful you are. Slips and falls are par for the course, as is the occasional sunburn, scrape, scratch, and bruise. Most first aid in the backcountry

Safe Camping
Many hikers may want to carry a cellular phone with them on their hiking expeditions. Help can be summoned at the touch of a button if something goes wrong. Just remember, the range of your phone may not be adequate if you are deep into the backwoods, or cellular service may be unavailable where you're camping.

CAUTION

will revolve around minor mishaps such as these, and not around the horrors of broken limbs, heart attacks, and fractured skulls. These things can happen, however, and you should be prepared to handle more serious emergencies. This chapter teaches you the basics, and points out areas where you may want to gain more emergency training.

Checkups before Checkout

Conventional Wisdom
Before heading off on a trip, go for a checkup at the dentist. Have any loose fillings repaired, and have the dentist check for any potential problems, such as cracked teeth, that may cause discomfort on the trail.

Any trip where you'll be exerting yourself more than you normally would goes hand-in-hand with a checkup from the doctor. If you're in prime condition in your 20s, you *may* not need a checkup, especially if you exercise regularly and eat well. If it's your first time out on a long trip or you're overweight and older, get a checkup before you set out. (That's assuming you've ignored everyone's advice in the past about getting regular checkups in the first place). While you're at the doctor's, check to make sure your tetanus shots are up-to-date. Your friends may want you silenced, but a case of lockjaw would be no picnic for you.

Take a Course in First Aid, CPR, or Emergency Medical Treatment

If you're passionate about hiking and camping and will be doing most of your traveling in the backcountry, take a first-aid course offered by the American Red Cross or a similar organization. Local fire departments and the police may offer training in emergency or "first-responder" first aid. Knowing how to revive someone using cardiopulmonary resuscitation (CPR) is a valuable skill—both on and off the trail. The object of CPR is to get the heart and lungs working by combining rescue breathing and chest compressions.

Conventional Wisdom
Don't drink alcohol to warm up, and don't feed alcohol to an injured person. Alcohol impairs judgment and there is no room for it in pressing medical situations.

Proper training in this procedure is highly recommended, and only those who have been certified in this procedure should attempt it. If you take and pass a CPR course, you'll get a diploma or badge that tells everyone that you can save their lives.

First aid in the age of AIDS requires some care. You will have to use your judgment when administering CPR or rescue breathing: Wipe the mouth of the victim with a piece of clothing or a cloth before proceeding. Never touch blood. Either have the victim control his/her own bleeding or use gloves. Wash hands after helping a bleeding victim.

Control any bleeding by applying pressure to the injured area with bandages or bunched up clothing. Elevate injured body parts so they are above the heart, but make sure that limbs aren't broken. You can use the patient's own body to immobilize an injured limb. A broken arm (especially the upper arm) can be positioned across the chest and tied with strips of cloth that encircle the torso. Similarly, tie a broken leg to its uninjured partner at several locations. Look around for a stick, or use a paddle to immobilize the injured limb.

Those who will be traveling on or around water should be sure that at the very least they know how to do mouth-to-mouth resuscitation in case someone drowns and needs to be revived.

Assembling a Basic First-Aid Kit—the Virtual Pharmacy

Besides CPR and emergency resuscitation courses, no one taking a backpacking excursion should be without a basic first-aid kit. Pre-assembled kits can be purchased cheaply from outdoor suppliers, and typically include a manual that describes the proper use of the supplies provided in the kit. Depending on the length and distance of the trip, you may want to spring for a "deluxe" kit, containing the requisite medical ingredients to make up a virtual pharmacy. More modest kits will likely do the trick, however.

Most backpackers prefer to assemble their own kits, keeping supplies in a small pouch or hard-plastic container. Whatever you choose, your kit should include most of the items listed next. But also remember to include any special medications that you or your hiking partners take regularly. If any among you is asthmatic, don't forget inhalers and other medications: You will be exerting yourselves, and this may increase the chances of an attack. Consult guides and books on first aid; acquaint yourself with the basic procedures for dealing with broken bones, dislocated knees and shoulders, and head injuries. Most injuries will be minor, but on the off-chance that a more serious emergency arises, it's nice to be familiar with some more advanced first-aid procedures.

> **I'LL TELL YA!...**
>
> **Conventional Wisdom**
> In addition to a good first-aid kit, commercially available emergency dental kits complete with emergency dental fillings and pain killers are available from outdoor supply stores. Add oil of cloves to your first-aid kit as an effective temporary treatment for toothaches.

> **I'LL TELL YA!...**
>
> **Conventional Wisdom**
> Be on the lookout for hives and nests. When traveling in yellow jacket season, avoid the temptation to flail your arms and brush away these pesky buzzing insects: They are more likely to sting you if they feel threatened.

The Basic First-Aid Kit

General Supplies

- ❏ Cotton-tipped swabs
- ❏ Vaseline
- ❏ Band-Aids
- ❏ Medical tape (1-inch and 2-inch width)
- ❏ Elastic (Ace) bandage and fasteners
- ❏ Triangle cravat—a large bandage that can be used as a sling and for holding dressings in place
- ❏ Wound-closure strips
- ❏ Gauze (4 × 4, 2 × 2)
- ❏ Abdominal pads
- ❏ Tongue depressor
- ❏ Iodine
- ❏ Scissors and tweezers
- ❏ Soap
- ❏ Moleskins (for blisters)
- ❏ Needle
- ❏ Matches
- ❏ Latex medical examination gloves
- ❏ Disinfectant (rubbing alcohol/iodine)
- ❏ Calamine lotion (for insect bites and poison plants)
- ❏ Antibiotic cream

Basic Medications

- ❏ Acetaminophen (Tylenol) or Ibuprofen (Advil)
- ❏ Antacid tablets
- ❏ Antihistamine (for insect bites and mild allergic reactions)
- ❏ Bismuth subsalicylate (Pepto-Bismol)
- ❏ Zinc oxide (heavy duty sun block)
- ❏ Medication for chronic conditions
- ❏ Corticosteroid cream anti-inflammatory (by prescription)

To Evacuate or Not?

When faced with any form of emergency in the backwoods, you'll have to evaluate whether you'll need to evacuate. You may be faced with a situation where there are only two of you, and one of you is unable to walk. In this circumstance, there is little choice but for one of you to go get help and bring it back. If you've registered with authorities in the area where you're hiking and have provided some sort of itinerary, someone will eventually come to find you when you don't return after several days. In this case, staying with a victim of a mishap is probably the best plan of action. The relative urgency of the illness or injury will guide your decision. Someone suffering from a scorpion sting or snakebite doesn't necessarily need to be left behind while someone goes for help. If you are only three or four hours from assistance it's better to try and make it back, even if injured. If someone is incapacitated and can't make it back, stay with the injured party until help arrives.

If there are at least two able bodies in your group, sending one person back for help may be a good plan, but only if that person can retrace the trail and is good enough at back-woods orienteering that you are assured of success (one injured, one lost, and one wandering equals one hell of a situation). If you choose this plan of action, be sure that the returning person has positively determined—and marked on a map—where the camp is located before he or she sets off.

There are wilderness survival guides that explain how to make a stretcher from branches ripped from trees, but transporting a victim to help—usually over a course of days—is generally thought unwise, even if you have the skills to put an emergency stretcher together. You may end up doing the injured person more damage than they'd sustain by staying put.

In any scenario, try to stay calm and weigh the alternatives. By staying calm yourself, you also prevent the injured party from panicking—he or she already has enough to worry about.

Treating Poison Ivy, Poison Oak, and Poison Sumac Rashes

Not all plants are our friends—poison ivy, poison oak, and poison sumac are relegated to the outdoor adventurers' Hall of Shame. Most hikers and campers who come into contact with one of these plants will suffer from a severe skin irritation—an itchy red rash filled with blisters. This ugly mess is caused by the chemical urushiol on the plants' leaves and stems. The lucky few who don't develop a rash when they come into contact with these plants aren't necessarily safe from a reaction in the future. Most who come into contact with the leaves and other parts of these plants will develop a rash within 24 to 48 hours of contact.

You can best prevent encounters with these plants by knowing what they look like. Poison ivy and poison oak have three shiny toothed or lobed leaves, and grow as vines or shrubs. The plant may have berries that are white or slightly green. Poison sumac grows as a small shrub and has a grouping of seven to eleven leaves on each stem. It grows in sandy, coastal conditions around the Great Lakes and other coastal areas, but also thrives in wet, swampy conditions. Poison ivy and poison oak grow across the country in various locations. Signs at popular campgrounds and camping literature will alert you to these plants. Avoid touching any plant that looks vaguely like it may be poisonous.

*Irritating plants
to avoid*

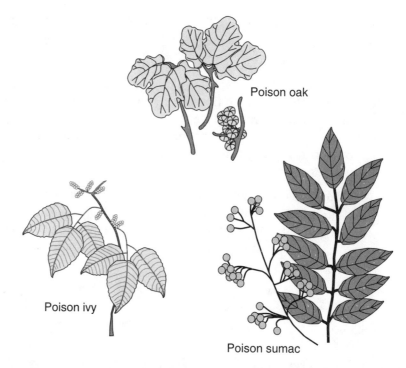

Poison oak

Poison ivy

Poison sumac

If you do come into contact with poison ivy, poison oak, or poison sumac, follow these guidelines for minimizing irritation and treating the affected area (hopefully you won't have used any of these plants as a cushion):

➤ Remove any of the plant's oil as soon as possible by washing the affected area with soap and water.

➤ Swab the affected skin area with alcohol. An alcohol-soaked towelette is useful for this purpose.

➤ Once a rash has developed, apply a corticosteroid cream.

➤ Take antihistamines to lessen itching.

➤ Apply calamine lotion to the affected skin area.

➤ Do *not* apply benzocaine-based pain relievers such as those used to treat sunburn. Spraying on such a pain reliever may further irritate the affected skin and discourage the irritant from being removed.

➤ Avoid touching any article of clothing that has come into contact with any of these plants.

What to Do when Faced with a Major Bummer

A brush with a poisonous plant, minor scratches, and small cuts and bruises aren't really a big concern. But if a major emergency arises, will you know what to do?

In all likelihood, you won't—and that's why courses in emergency medical treatment are highly recommended. If you're reading this book on your way out the door to a great outdoor adventure, it's too late for that. But you *can* understand some of the main principles that will help you keep a severely injured person comfortable and alive until help arrives—which is probably the best you can do without specialized training. Emergency evacuation of an injured person can do more harm than good, so the best course of action is to be able to respond correctly to a number of emergency situations, follow your instincts, and cope as best you can until help arrives.

Monitoring Life Signs

After a serious fall, cardiac arrest, or other traumatic injury, the first thing helpers should do is assess the condition of the injured person. If the victim is unconscious and doesn't respond to your questions, check for a pulse and look for signs that the person is breathing. A pulse may be detected near the Adam's apple in the neck; check breathing by looking carefully at the victim's chest to see if it rises and falls, as it would if the victim were asleep. Also listen for signs of breathing near the mouth. If there is no pulse, administer CPR if you are trained to do so. If the victim has a pulse but is not breathing, administer mouth-to-mouth resuscitation. Note: An injured person's tongue may be obstructing the throat, preventing the victim from breathing. Clear any obstructions in the victim's throat with your fingers.

Conventional Wisdom

First aid in the age of AIDS requires some care. Your first-aid kit should contain a pair of medical examination gloves. Wear these when helping victims who are bleeding. You will have to use your judgment when administering CPR or rescue breathing: Wipe the mouth of the victim with a cloth before beginning these procedures. Wash hands, if possible, after helping a bleeding victim.

I'LL TELL YA!...

Safe Camping

Stay away from swift-running streams and rivers. The rocks, trees, and ground beside them may be slippery and dangerous. If you must travel beside a swift-flowing stream or river, watch your footing and concentrate on keeping your balance. A heavy backpack is no friend in these circumstances. Wading and fording fast-flowing streams is a big no-no, especially if the water is extremely cold. Loosen the hip-belt of your backpack before crossing a stream. That way if you fall in, your pack can be ditched so it won't drag you down.

CAUTION

285

Control any bleeding by applying pressure to the injured area as explained later in this chapter.

Heart Attacks

Heart attacks in the backwoods are a big problem, and may be mistaken, as many are, for indigestion or heartburn. The victim should be told to sit down, and then be made as comfortable as possible by loosening tight, constricting clothing. Victims typically experience chest pain that is often described as crushing or squeezing pressure. The pain may radiate to the shoulders, arms, neck, jaw, or back. Sweating, nausea, and shortness of breath may accompany the pain. Someone should get help immediately. Victims should not attempt to return to the trailhead, but should stay put until help arrives. Arrange for an emergency evacuation as soon as possible.

A heart attack can lead to cardiac arrest, where the heart stops completely and the victim falls unconscious. If this happens, administer CPR if you are qualified to do so.

Controlling Bleeding and Immobilizing Breaks

If a victim is bleeding as a result of a fall or other traumatic event, the flow of blood can be controlled by applying pressure directly to the wound. Use gauze bandages or spare clothing to apply pressure and to soak up blood. If bandages become soaked with blood, don't remove them; apply more over them. Once bleeding has been stopped, tightly wrap medical tape over the bandages. Elevate injured body parts so they are above the heart, but make sure that limbs aren't broken.

If you suspect that a limb is broken or fractured, splint it using a branch, walking stick, or tent pole to stabilize it. One of the best ways to immobilize is to use the patient's own body.

For example, for a broken arm (especially the upper arm), place the bent arm on the chest and tie it to the body with strips of cloth that encircle the torso. Similarly, tie a broken leg to its uninjured partner at several locations.

Victims who have fallen and who complain of numbness or tingling in their legs or arms *should not be moved!* In these cases, suspect a spinal cord injury; *any* movement could worsen the victim's condition. If the victim is unconscious and liquid is running from the ears, this could be a sign that the spinal cord has been injured. Do not move the victim, but treat bleeding accordingly. Arrange for an emergency evacuation as soon as possible.

I'LL TELL YA!..

Conventional Wisdom

Know how to operate your camp stove properly! Pressurized gas can flare up and cause a severe burn. Test your stove out in the backyard before going on a trip, and read the instructions that come with your stove for information on correctly operating it.

Shock

Shock is caused by the failure of the cardiovascular system to deliver adequate amounts of blood to the body's organs, depriving them of oxygen and leading to their ultimate failure. Shock may be brought on by a severe open wound, a spinal cord injury, profuse bleeding, or a severe burn. Signs of shock include:

➤ Profuse sweating

➤ Rapid breathing

➤ Bluish-colored lips

➤ Labored breathing

➤ Gasping

➤ A fast pulse

➤ Thirst

➤ Nausea, vomiting

Treat victims of shock by laying the victim on a flat surface and propping up the victim's feet so they are eight to twelve inches above the head. Cover the victim with a blanket and control bleeding, if necessary. *Do not* feed shock victims water or alcohol. Arrange for an emergency evacuation as soon as possible.

Heat Exposure

Too much sun, physical exertion, and failure to drink enough water is a recipe for disaster. Heat cramps, heat exhaustion, and heatstroke can strike outdoor adventurers in hot, humid weather. Cramps in the abdominal area and legs during hot weather are signs that victims should sit down and rest in shady conditions. Those suffering from heat cramps should drink water and abstain from further physical activities.

Symptoms of heat exhaustion include reddish skin, headache, nausea, and dizziness. In more severe cases, victims will vomit. Move the victim out of the sun and give him or her water. If the condition worsens, seek medical help immediately.

Both heat cramps and heat exhaustion may signal the onset of heatstroke, an extremely serious condition. Body temperature may climb to a dangerous 106° F and is accompanied by reddish, hot skin on the victim. The object here is to cool the victim down by applying water-soaked cloths to exposed skin, and by fanning the victim. Give the person water—if he or she is still conscious—and treat him or her for shock (discussed above). Check for a weak pulse. If the victim's heart stops, administer CPR if you are qualified to do so. Arrange for an emergency evacuation as soon as possible.

Take the following steps to minimize heat-related sickness:

➤ Drink plenty of water—frequently, and *before* you feel thirsty.

➤ Wear a hat or bandana.

➤ Take breaks when you are exerting yourself.

➤ Wear clothing that allows the air to naturally cool the body.

Preventing and Treating the Big "H"

Hypothermia results when the body can't generate enough heat to maintain normal body temperature. Hypothermia is brought on by exposure to cold, wet conditions over time, and *can* occur at above-zero temperatures. People who are in poor physical shape or are tired are more at risk than others. Condition yourself for an adventure outdoors (see Chapter 20) and stop hiking if you get tired.

Almost anyone, however, can suffer from hypothermia if cold weather blows up, or a pelting rainstorm emerges. In these circumstances, seek shelter and take the necessary steps (outlined below) to prevent it. Warning signs include shivering, slow or slurred speech, disorientation, lack of coordination (immobile or fumbling hands, stumbling), drowsiness, and exhaustion. *Hypothermia is a life-threatening condition;* seek medical help and follow these steps:

Conventional Wisdom

The main thing to avoid on the trail is getting cold and wet. This could lead to hypothermia. Dressing in layers, having a good outer shell, and wearing wool, which insulates even when wet, helps prevent hypothermia. If you're hiking in cold weather, also be sure to keep your extremities covered. Always wear good socks, a warm hat, and gloves or mittens.

➤ Seek shelter from bad weather under a tent or natural barrier.

➤ Get the victim into dry clothes.

➤ If the victim is conscious, administer warm, non-alcoholic drinks such as tea or bouillon.

➤ Make a fire to warm the victim up.

➤ Keep the victim awake.

➤ If hypothermia is serious or the victim has lost consciousness, remove both your clothes and the victim's and climb into a sleeping bag together. Encourage skin-to-skin heat transfer between you and the victim.

➤ Do not continue on a hike, even if the victim seems to have recovered.

Prevent hypothermia by following these recommendations:

➤ Wear waterproof clothing.

➤ Dress in layers, and in clothing that wicks moisture away from the body.

➤ If clothes become wet, take them off and put on dry ones.

➤ Take cover in cold, windy conditions.

➤ Pack warm clothing (made of wool or pile) on all hikes.

Conventional Wisdom
Keep hands warm by wearing mittens instead of gloves. In extremely cold weather, mittens are a must despite the decrease in dexterity compared with gloves.

I'LL TELL YA!...

Dealing with Frostbite and Preventing It

In extremely cold conditions, exposed skin can freeze. When this happens, the affected skin whitens or appears grayish in color. This condition is known as frostbite, and can be quite serious if the affected area is not treated accordingly. Victims may feel numbness or pricking in the affected area.

Frostbitten skin should be thawed out slowly. If the frostbitten area is on the face, slowly warm the affected skin by covering it with your or someone's hands; warm extremities in an armpit. Avoid rubbing the affected area and never apply direct heat to the area. If there is a chance that the skin can be refrozen, do not attempt to treat frostbite. There is an increased chance of scarring if you do this. Seek medical attention for severe cases of frostbite.

Dressing for Prevention

The best way to prevent injuries is to dress properly. In cold weather make sure that you have adequate thermal protection, particularly for your extremities (hands and feet), and for your head. That means a balaclava in extremely cold conditions where there is a chance of frostbite, or at the very least a good wool hat or synthetic equivalent. Mittens are warmer than gloves, though you lose a bit of dexterity in wearing them. Whatever you do, make sure to purchase the best cold-weather clothing you can.

Dealing with Animal Bites

Animal bites are a serious matter. If you have cornered an animal in the wild—or gotten too close through some fault of your own—then you deserve to be bitten. Animals that attack even though they haven't been provoked may have rabies. If someone in your hiking party gets bitten by an animal, encourage the wound to bleed and wash it under a stream of water with soap. Disinfect the wound and cover it with a bandage. Get medical attention promptly.

The Least You Need to Know

➤ Knowing how to administer cardiopulmonary resuscitation (CPR) and artificial respiration (AR) are important skills for the backcountry hiker. Courses offered by the American Red Cross and others outline the correct procedures for administering CPR and AR.

➤ CPR should only be administered by those who have been trained to do it properly.

➤ Assemble a basic first-aid kit and carry it with you on any outdoor trip. Pre-packaged kits are available at outdoor equipment suppliers, but you may want to include your own supplies.

➤ Dress for the weather you'll be encountering. In wet, rainy weather, dress in layers so you can add clothing as it gets cold, or take it off as you get warm.

➤ Consult recognized first-aid guides for procedures on the correct treatment of medical problems in the outdoors.

Chapter 24

Not-So-Advanced Boy and Girl Scout Skills

In This Chapter

➤ How to build and select wood for a campfire (where permitted)

➤ Some knot-tying skills

➤ Building makeshift shelters

My first flirtation with the concept of the outdoors began when I begged my mother to buy me a pair of Buster Brown shoes that had a compass built into the insole and a variety of miniature animal tracks for treads. The idea was that any five- or six-year-old could remove one of the shoes and use the compass under the flap inside to navigate his or her way out of trouble. The small animal tracks provided clues about the animals using the woods with you. For a kid, the idea of the outdoors was romantic, even if the shoes were impractical dress shoes and more of a conspiracy by adults to get kids to wear something tonier than a pair of worn-out sneakers.

Still, the idea of an adventure in the outdoors, even if it remained an idea, was neat—and a pair of shoes that could transport you there with a few bells and whistles was, in retrospect, worth the discomfort of wearing the things.

In adulthood, to rely on a pair of dress shoes with a compass inside to get you out of trouble would be ridiculous. In the real outdoors, some skills are nice to have—especially if your plans include packing everything you need into the woods for an adventure lasting a week or so. Most advanced camping skills are acquired after many years of improvising and experimentation. You'll discover some things that work, and other things that don't. In life, as in the woods, experience is the best teacher, but there are some skills you should take with you. These are covered in this chapter; and they include building a campfire, learning a few knots, and building a makeshift shelter—just in case your tent is destroyed or gets lost five miles back on the trail.

> ### Rules
>
> Carry a good pocketknife, such as a Swiss Army brand. These knives feature a range of tools and blades that can be extracted from the handle and used for various purposes. Among the assortment of hard-working features to look for are scissors, a serrated-edged blade, screwdriver, magnifying glass, awl, corkscrew, and can opener. (Remember, dull tools are dangerous. Always keep them sharpened.)

Surefire Bets for Building a Fire

Check fire regulations in the area where you are camping to make sure fires are permitted. If they are, make sure that it is okay to forage for firewood from the forest floor: You may have to pack in your own firewood if foraging is prohibited.

The importance of carrying a ready supply of wooden matches—or better yet, a butane lighter—can't be overstated. Unless you *really know* how to make fire by rubbing two sticks together, don't go out in the woods without some means of lighting a fire. In a pinch, you can use a magnifying glass (or the lenses of your glasses) to start a fire, but the tinder you use must be dry enough to ignite quickly, and it must be sunny out. This rules out using this method at night, but if you get stranded and need to wait it out a few days, it may be the only way to go. Fires may be difficult to start with a lighter or match in damp, rainy, and windy conditions. One safety accessory to consider is a magnesium fire starter. Pieces of magnesium are whittled off next to twigs and cinder: The magnesium flakes are ignited by scraping the magnesium starter edge with a knife to create sparks.

> **I'LL TELL YA!...**
>
> **Conventional Wisdom**
>
> In wet, rainy conditions, a fire is harder to start. Lay a crisscrossing bed of twigs over wet ground and place tinder on top of them. Try to use a good amount of tree bark as kindling, and shield the fire from large breezes and wind, which could blow the fire out.

Whatever method you choose, follow these general rules for lighting a fire:

➤ Check local fire regulations to make sure you can legally build a fire or pick up wood from the wilderness floor. Many areas prohibit fires, but in an emergency—to keep an injured person comfortable until help arrives, for instance—you may opt to break the rules.

➤ Locate a source of highly combustible *tinder* you can use to light larger pieces of wood for the fire. Dried tree bark, pine cones, evergreen needles, and smaller pieces of wood on the forest floor work as starter fuel. Pitch, or the gooey, sticky substance that oozes from the base of conifers (evergreens), can also be collected for tinder. Gather a good amount of the material you use, and build a small mound over which you can lay bigger pieces of wood, or "kindling."

➤ Collect a good amount of *kindling*—dried twigs and other pieces of dead wood no more than an inch thick—to lay over the tinder in a pyramidal or cross-hatch fashion. Build the kindling up, making sure it's stacked loosely enough to allow an adequate amount of air to fuel the (eventual) flames.

➤ Once the tinder and kindling are in place, lay larger pieces of dry wood over the top in a pyramidal formation, making sure there's enough air space between the pieces of wood. Don't get overzealous: Start with wood that is *slightly* larger than the kindling; as it gets consumed by the flames beneath it, add bigger pieces until you have a good, hot fire going.

> **Conventional Wisdom**
> Look for truly dry wood to burn in a campfire. Dead pieces of wood on the forest floor may have absorbed water and are effectively useless for getting a fire going. Once a fire has started and is burning well, one or two pieces of this wood can be added if other suitable wood can't be found.
>
> I'LL TELL YA!...

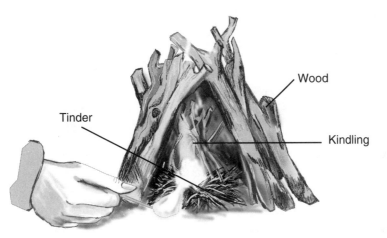

Building the perfect campfire, where it's allowed

Tinder

Wood

Kindling

The Unconfusing Guide to Knot Tying

Whole books are available on the art of knot tying. In the backwoods, you *really* need to know only three knots—and these will serve you well in a range of situations: the standard *square knot*, the *bowline*, and *the taut-line hitch*. They are good for securing a range of things in place—hanging your food and supplies out of the reach of bears, setting up a clothesline between two trees where wet clothing can be hung to dry, or securing tarps while making lean-tos and emergency shelters.

The square knot can be used for joining two similar, but shorter, pieces of rope. Follow the accompanying figures to learn how to tie these knots.

You can never have too much synthetic rope, and you'll need at least 50 feet to animal-proof your campsite. Some campers recommend using nylon parachute cord. Avoid using standard clothesline, which stretches and is affected by moisture.

I'LL TELL YA!...

Conventional Wisdom

You'll need rope to hang your food high out of reach of bears and other wildlife, and to dry out clothes. Nylon line and parachute cord are the best materials for camping.

Knot #1: The Taut-Line Hitch

Knot #2: The Bowline

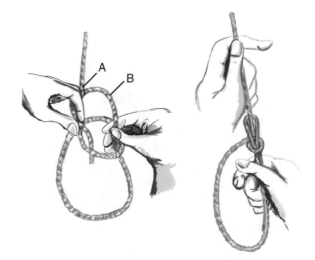

Knot #3: The Square Knot

Erecting and Building Alternative Structures

As discussed in earlier chapters, the tent is not the only form of shelter available to the outdoor adventurer. In many respects, a tarpaulin is more useful because it can be rigged to allow many people to stand under it; a stove placed at the edge of the shelter can be operated with relative safety. (Bringing a stove inside a tent is dangerous.)

Use the taut-line hitch to secure the various *rigging points* to branches, tree trunks, and other natural anchor points. Camping tarpaulins feature a number of eyelets that are evenly spaced around the edges, designed to be secured with rope (and the knots described earlier).

Stronger structures can be manufactured in an emergency by draping the tarpaulin over a jerry-rigged frame made from crisscrossing branches and securing the whole affair between two trees. Never strip branches from living trees unless it is to build an emergency shelter. You can also use the tarpaulin to make an A-frame shelter. All these options are shown next.

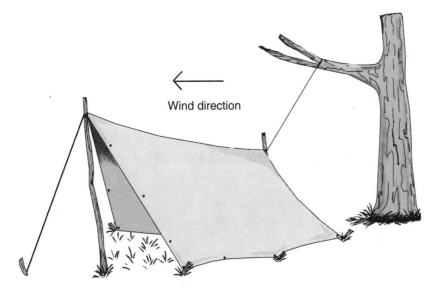

Wind direction

A tarpaulin called into action and secured at key anchor points

A tarpaulin can be draped over a jerry-rigged frame

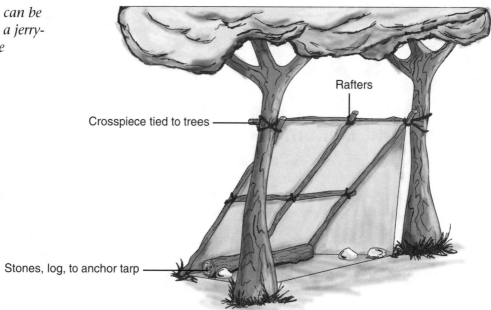

Rafters

Crosspiece tied to trees ———

Stones, log, to anchor tarp ———

A tarpaulin suspended by a center rope strung between two 5- to 6-foot branches, and then staked into the ground

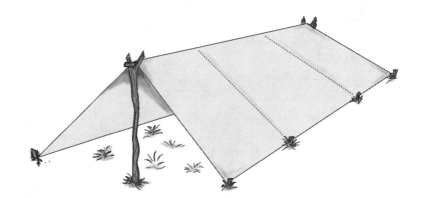

Building a Structure from Branches and Leaves

In an emergency—when your tent has been ripped to shreds by a gust of wind or has been carried down the rapids and over a waterfall, never to be seen again—you can build a makeshift structure in which to sleep. A *lean-to* is a basic structure over which branches, sticks, leaves, evergreen boughs, and so on can be interleaved to create a barrier to wind and rain.

The chances of ever having to create a structure like this are remote, but the concept is pretty straightforward if you ever get into a situation where you have to make one.

Depending on what you have to work with, a knife with a serrated blade can be used to saw pieces of wood to size—two 4-foot lengths for the front and a 5 ½- to 6-foot length for the spine. Join the three framing members at the top by binding them together with rope (or wet, fibrous branches pulled from bushes or trees at the front). Then create the walls with whatever materials are available.

A frame for a lean-to

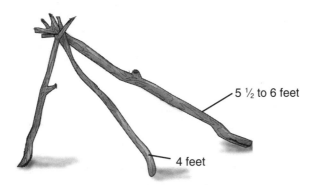

5 ½ to 6 feet

4 feet

Signaling for Help

Camping, hiking, and all outdoor sports all involve some level of risk. But knowing this doesn't necessarily mean you'd know what to do in case of an extreme emergency, if you or someone in your group could not hike out of the woods for some reason, or got hurt along the way. If you couldn't return to civilization how would you signal for help?

If you've left an itinerary with wilderness area authorities, friends, or relatives, you could count on someone sending help. But if help is days away and you or someone in your group is injured you may need to call for help with smoke and mirrors, and we're not talking magic here.

Whenever there is a chance of being disconnected from civilization for days on end, put together an emergency signaling kit consisting of a fire starter, a whistle, and fluorescent surveyor's tape. A magnesium fire starter can be used to start fires in miserable, wet weather. A whistle can be used to signal in fog, or at night. And fluorescent surveyor's tape can be strung around a treed perimeter to indicate your presence. Portable flares may also be fired high in the sky to call for help.

Remember the internationally recognized "signal of threes" when summoning help. Three fires built in a

> **Conventional Wisdom**
> Practice using your map and compass. Knowing how to use these items is a big step toward "being found." If you get lost, don't panic. Try and determine where you are with your map and compass.
>
> I'LL TELL YA!...

triangle 50 feet apart seen overhead by a plane means "help"; three blasts from a whistle means "help"; three flashes of light from a flashlight means "help." If you're trying to signal to an overflying airplane, you can also use clothing laid out in a clearing to create ground-to-air symbols that mean something to pilots.

Ground to air symbols

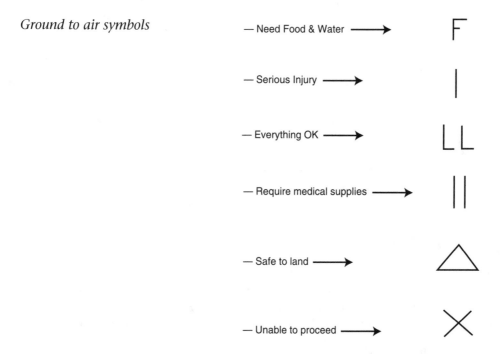

As an alternative to signaling for help with symbols and flares, small signal mirrors can be aimed at airplanes in bright, sunny conditions to signal for help. These mirrors have cross-hairs for aiming the mirror at aircraft overhead, or at boats across a large body of water.

Use the sun's reflection in a mirror to signal for help.

The Least You Need to Know

➤ Fire-building skills are among the most important. Being able to build a fire in bad weather conditions, and with less-than-perfect wood, is the true test of a seasoned outdoor adventurer. Developing your fire-building skills is a good safety measure too.

➤ Learn how to tie a bowline, taut-line hitch, and square knot and you're well on your way to becoming a Girl or Boy Scout. These knots are the basics, and all you'll likely ever need to learn.

➤ A tarpaulin is an important piece of equipment. It can be adapted as emergency shelter, and makes life on the trail more sociable by providing a large shelter under which several people can congregate.

➤ Practice making a lean-to from scratch. As an emergency shelter, a lean-to can be called into service should your tent and tarpaulin get mashed, mangled, or lost.

Chapter 25

Going Farther Afield

In This Chapter

➤ Traveling in faraway places

➤ Checking travel requirements

➤ Staying healthy in foreign lands

For many, the allure of camping and backpacking lies not with traveling into the domestic woods, but venturing off into foreign lands. These destinations may be as close as Mexico and South America, or as far-flung as Asia and the Middle East. Planning for, and learning about, any place you are traveling is important, but if you're going overseas, extra diligence in learning about a place can pay off big—especially if you're planning to carry everything (including your "house") on your back. This chapter takes a look at such issues.

Do your research and learn about the places where you'll be traveling. The "rainy season" in some countries means torrential downpours and near-impossible camping conditions. And don't forget about your clothing—tropical conditions mean lightweight clothing that can be dried easily when it gets drenched with sweat. Learn about the customs of places where you'll be going; be sure that they accommodate backpackers. Make sure that pitching a tent is okay where you travel, and that you get permission before breaking camp in an unestablished campground. Look in your local library for books on hiking and backpacking, and the places you'll be traveling.

Matters of Passports and Visas

Far-flung countries may require special visas, so don't wait until the last minute to apply. This goes for passports too: Make sure yours is up to date and not about to expire. You don't want to be booked on a flight leaving tomorrow and find, on your arrival at the airport, that your paperwork isn't in order or your passport will expire in the middle of your trip. If you run into trouble, an embassy or consulate may be miles away; the inconvenience of getting there, lining up, and filling out forms may eat up a good part of your trip. This brings up a recommendation: that you determine, in advance, the whereabouts of your home country's consulate or embassy in the regions where you'll be traveling. Taking their addresses and phone numbers will help you locate them quickly if you need help during your trip.

Seasoned travelers rely on an around-the-neck hanging wallet that can be concealed under your shirt or blouse. Carry traveler's checks and your passport in this type of traveler's wallet.

Conventional Wisdom
Take along some familiar foods when embarking on a trip to a foreign country. Freeze-dried and dehydrated foodstuffs won't add that much weight, and they'll be welcome fare when you are faced with unfamiliar foods at your destination.

Tips for the World-Wide Wanderer

Wherever you're going, make sure to follow a few simple, commonsense rules for a pleasant, well-planned excursion. Before you get to your destination, do the following to ease into your trip effortlessly.

Conventional Wisdom
Get route and trail maps before you depart. English-language maps may not be available where you land, or they may not be available at all—in any language. Read as much as you can, and try to talk with other travelers who have visited distant places before you.

➤ Research your destination carefully to determine availability of campsites.

➤ Have a hiking partner keep a photocopy of your travel documentation in case your passport or visa is lost. Having the document numbers handy will speed up the replacement process if this becomes necessary.

➤ Check travel advisories issued by the Department of State for the places you'll be visiting. Take heed of any warnings that are issued. Get advisories by calling 1-202-647-5225. If you're online, fact sheets for countries can be accessed at http:/www.stolaf.edu/network/travel-advisories.html

➤ Get a small amount of local currency *before* your departure. When you arrive at your destination, you'll be acquainted with the local currency and won't have to submit to the first place that exchanges dollars for rupees.

Rules

Many countries do not have the same sanitation standards as those in North America. Drink only water that you know is safe; always use a water filter, boil the water, or add purification tablets to water you suspect is unsafe. Avoid eating unpeeled fruits and uncooked vegetables in areas where Montezuma's Revenge (diarrhea) is known to be prevalent.

Get the Right Immunizations and Shots

Some especially nasty diseases run amok in distant lands. Travelers to distant lands are often required to get the right immunizations and booster shots before visas are issued. (In some places, for instance, you might want to be sure you bring along anti-malaria pills.) Don't forget your own medications for chronic or recurring problems. Even with the right shots, you should arm yourself against the usual mishaps that can occur; and a well-stocked first-aid kit will go a long way to handling small emergencies.

Safe Camping

When you go for your pre-trip medical exam, ask your doctor for some sterile, disposable syringes and needles, along with a note explaining the presence in your first-aid kit. If you become sick and need an injection in a country with questionable hygienic standards, produce your own syringe to avoid the possibility of contracting infectious diseases from unsterilized needles. Some countries may consider syringes drug paraphernalia. Bone up on the antidrug policies of your destination country.

Get boosters well in advance of long trips to countries such as Africa, Asia, and South America. Check with your doctor about immunization boosters needed to protect yourself against diphtheria, polio, tetanus, measles, rubella, and mumps. You may also need inoculations to combat yellow fever and cholera, depending on the region in which you are traveling.

When you're at the doctor's getting your vaccinations, ask if you can obtain some general antibiotics for your trip. Most doctors will accommodate your request and fill out a prescription for penicillin or some other antibiotic, making sure that you understand the conditions under which the medication should be administered. A bottle of pills is no replacement for a doctor, however—and if a serious, prolonged medical problem arises, you should make every attempt to get to a qualified doctor for help. Listings of qualified and certified doctors in foreign countries are available for the asking. On returning home, tell your doctor of your travels if you come down with even the mildest ailment.

Finding Fuel: Camp Stoves and Cooking

Airline regulations worldwide don't permit the carriage of any flammable materials or liquids. This means that you'll have to leave your camp stove's fuel behind and hope for the best when you touch down. If your sights are set on traveling the world, purchase a camp stove that can burn a range of fuels (see Chapter 6). Stoves that burn white gas are good in North America, but white gas isn't readily available in other parts of the world. So-called *multi-fuel* stoves can use everything from gasoline to kerosene to boil water and cook dinner; the extra expense of one of these stoves is well worth it if you'll be traveling farther afield.

Along with a multi-fuel stove, make sure to carry a stove repair kit in case something breaks down. Clean your stove regularly when using dirty fuels such as gasoline and kerosene.

The Least You Need to Know

➤ Have a physical examination before you go on a long trip in a foreign country. Make sure you are up to date on your immunizations.

➤ Decontaminate untreated water with purification tablets, by boiling it, or using a portable water filter. Eat only peelable fruits and cooked vegetables in areas where travelers get "turista" or Montezuma's Revenge. Also, carry a treatment for diarrhea.

➤ Carry photocopies of travel documents in case your originals get lost and replacement is necessary. Having your passport number and visa number handy will speed the replacement of important travel documents.

➤ Also have a record of serial numbers for traveler's checks: If they are ever lost or stolen...well, you know the drill.

WHERE'D YOU SAY YOU GOT THIS?

Sources and Resources

The National Parks of the United States

Many spectacular trips can be planned in America's most valuable public outdoor recreation areas. Call or write for brochures.

Acadia National Park
Established 1919
41,933 acres
P.O. Box 177
Bar Harbor, ME 04609
(207) 288-3338

National Park of American Samoa
Established 1993
9,000 acres
National Park of American Samoa
Pago Pago, American Samoa 96799
(808) 541-2693

Arches National Park
Established 1971
73,379 acres
P.O. Box 907
Moab, UT 84532
(801) 259-8161

Badlands National Park
Established 1978
242,756 acres
P.O. Box 6
Interior, SD 57750
(605) 433-5361

Big Bend National Park
Established 1944
801,163 acres
P.O. Box 129
Big Bend National Park, TX 79834
(915) 477-2251

Biscayne National Park
Established 1980
181,500 acres
P.O. Box 1369
Homestead, FL 33090
(305) 247-7275

Bryce Canyon National Park
Established 1928
35,835 acres
Bryce Canyon, UT 84717
(801) 834-5322

Canyonlands National Park
Established 1964
337,570 acres
125 West 200 South
Moab, UT 84532
(801) 259-7164

Capitol Reef National Park
Established 1971
241,904 acres
H.C. 70, Box 15
Torrey, UT 84775
(801) 425-3791

Carlsbad Caverns National Park
Established 1930
46,766 acres
3225 National Parks Highway
Carlsbad, NM 88220
(505) 785-2232

Channel Islands National Park
Established 1980
249,354 acres
1901 Spinnaker Drive
Ventura, CA 93001
(805) 658-5700

Crater Lake National Park
Established 1902
183,224 acres
P.O. Box 7
Crater Lake, OR 97604
(503) 594-2211

Death Valley National Park
Established 1994
2,067,628 acres
P.O. Box 579
Death Valley, CA 92328
(Also in Nevada)
(619) 786-2331

Denali National Park and Preserve
Established 1917
National Park: 5,000,000 acres
National Preserve: 1,500,000 acres
P.O. Box 9
McKinley Park, AK 99755
(907) 683-2294

Dry Tortugas National Park
Established 1992
64,700 acres
P.O. Box 6208
Key West, FL 33041
(305) 242-7700

Everglades National Park
Established 1947
1,506,499 acres
P.O. Box 279
Homestead, FL 33030
(305) 242-7700

Gates of the Arctic National Park
and Preserve
Established 1980
National Park: 7,523,888 acres
National Preserve: 948,629 acres
P.O. Box 74680
Fairbanks, AK 99707
(907) 456-0281

National Park Glacier Bay and
Preserve
Established 1980
National Park: 3,225,284 acres
National Preserve: 57,884 acres
P.O. Box 140
Gustavus, AK 99826
(907) 697-2232

Grand Canyon National Park
Established 1919
1,217,158 acres
P.O. Box 129
Grand Canyon, AZ 86023
(602) 638-7888

Grand Teton National Park
Established 1929
309,994 acres
P.O. Box Drawer 170
Moose, WY 83012
(307) 733-2880

Great Basin National Park
Established 1986
77,100 acres
Baker, NV 89311
(702) 234-7270

Great Smoky Mountains
National Park
Established 1934
520,269 acres
Gatlinburg, TN 37738
(Also in North Carolina)
(615) 436-1200

Guadalupe Mountains
National Park
Established 1972
86,416 acres
H.C. 60, Box 400
Salt Flat, TX 79847
(915) 828-3251

Haleakala National Park
Authorized 1916
28,099 Acres
P.O. Box 369
Makawao, HI 96768
(808) 572-9306

Hawaii Volcanoes National Park
Established 1916
229,177 acres
Hawaii National Park, HI 96718
(808) 967-7311

Hot Springs
Established 1921
5,839 acres
P.O. Box 1860
Hot Springs, AR 71902
(501) 623-1433

Isle Royale National Park
Authorized 1931
571,790 acres
800 East Lakeshore Drive
Houghton, MI 49931
(906) 482-0984

Joshua Tree National Park
Established 1994
794,000 acres
74485 National Monument Dr.
Twentynine Palms, CA 92277
(619) 367-7511

Katmai National Park and
Preserve
Established 1980
National Park: 3,716,000 acres
National Preserve: 374,000 acres
P.O. Box 7
King Salmon, AK 99613
(907) 246-3305

Kenai Fjords National Park
Established 1980
580,000 acres
P.O. Box 1727
Seward, AK 99664
(907) 224-3175

Kings Canyon
Established 1940
461,901 acres
Sequoia and Kings Canyon
National Parks
Three Rivers, CA 93271
(209) 565-3134

Kobuk Valley National Park
Established 1980
1,750,421 acres
P.O. Box 1029
Kotzebue, AK 99752
(907) 442-3760

Lake Clark National Park and
Preserve
Established 1980
National Park: 2,636,839 acres
National Preserve: 1,407,293 acres
4230 University Drive, Suite 311
Anchorage, AK 99508
(907) 781-2218

Lassen Volcanic National Park
Established 1916
106,372 acres
Mineral, CA 96063
(916) 595-4444

Mammoth Cave National Park
Established 1941
52,708 acres
Mammoth Cave, KY 42259
(502) 758-2328

Mesa Verde National Park
Established 1906
52,122 acres
Mesa Verde National Park, CO
81321
(303) 529-4461

Mount Rainier National Park
Established 1899
235,612 acres
Tahoma Woods, Star Route
Ashford, WA 98304
(206) 569-2211

North Cascades National Park
Established 1968
504,781 acres
2105 Highway 20
Sedro Woolley, WA 98284
(206) 856-5700

Olympic National Park
Established 1938
922,651 acres
600 East Park Avenue
Port Angeles, WA 98362
(206) 452-0330

Petrified Forest National Park
Established 1962
93,533 acres
P.O. Box 2217
Petrified Forest National Park, AZ
86028
(602) 524-6228

Redwood National Park
Established 1968
110,232 acres
1111 Second Street
Crescent City, CA 95531
(707) 464-6101

Rocky Mountain National Park
Established 1915
265,727 acres
Estes Park, CO 80517
(303) 586-2371

Saguaro National Park
Established 1994
19,061 acres
3693 South Old Spanish Trail
Tucson, AZ 85730
(602) 296-8576

Sequoia National Park
Established 1890
402,482 acres
Sequoia and Kings Canyon
National Parks
Three Rivers, CA 93271
(209) 565-3134

Shenandoah National Park
Established 1935
196,466 acres
Route 3, Box 348
Luray, VA 22835
(703) 999-2266 (recording) or
(703) 999-2299

Theodore Roosevelt National Park
Established 1978
70,447 acres
P.O. Box 7
Medora, ND 58645
(701) 623-4466

Virgin Islands National Park
Authorized 1956
14,689 acres
6310 Estate Nazareth
Charlotte Amalie, VI 00802
(809) 776-6450

Voyageurs National Park
Established 1975
218,035 acres
3131 Highway 53
International Falls, MN 56649
(218) 283-9821

Waterton-Glacier National Park
(Waterton-Glacier International
Peace Park)
Established 1910
Glacier (Montana): 1,013,572
acres
Waterton Lakes (Alberta,
Canada): 73,800 acres
West Glacier, MT 59936
(406) 888-5441

Wind Cave National Park
Established 1903
28,292 acres
R.R. 1, Box 190
Hot Springs, SD 57747
(605) 745-4600

Wrangell–St. Elias National Park
and Preserve
Established 1980
National Park: 8,331,604 acres
National Preserve: 4,856,721 acres
P.O. Box 29
Glennallen, AK 99588
(907) 822-5235

Yellowstone National Park
Established 1872
2,219,791 acres
P.O. Box 168
Yellowstone National Park, WY
82190
(Also in Montana and Idaho)
(307) 344-7381

Yosemite National Park
Established 1890
761,236 acres
P.O. Box 577
Yosemite National Park, CA 95389
(209) 372-0200

Zion National Park
Established 1919
146,598 acres
Springdale, UT 84767
(801) 772-3256

State Tourism Offices

State tourist offices can point you toward campgrounds, hiking areas, and state parks across the country. Phone or write for information.

Alabama Bureau of Tourism
532 South Perry Street
Montgomery, AL 36130
(205) 261-4169

Alaska Division of Tourism
Box E
Juneau, AK 99811
(907) 465-2010

Arizona Office of Tourism
1480 East Bethany Home Road
Phoenix, AZ 85014
(602) 255-3618

Arkansas Department of Parks
and Tourism
One Capitol Mall
Little Rock, AR 72201
(501) 682-7777

California Tourism Office
1121 L Street
Sacramento, CA 95814
(916) 322-1396

Colorado Tourism Board
1625 Broadway
Suite 1700
Box 38700
Denver, CO 80202
(303) 592-5410

Connecticut Department of
Economic Development
210 Washington Street
Hartford, CT 06106
(203) 566-3977

D.C. Convention and Visitors
Association
1575 I Street, NW
Suite 250
Washington, DC 20005
(202) 789-7000

Delaware Tourism Office
99 King Highway
Box 1401
Dover, DE 19903
(302) 736-4271

Florida Division of Tourism
126 Van Buren Street
Tallahassee, FL 32301
(904) 487-1462

Georgia Department of Industry
and Trade
Box 1776
Atlanta, GA 30301
(404) 656-3590

Hawaii Visitors Bureau
2270 Kala Kaua Avenue
Honolulu, HI 96800
(808) 923-1811

Idaho Travel Council
State Capitol Building
Boise, ID 83720
(208) 334-2470

Illinois Travel Information Center
c/o Department of Commerce
and Community Affairs
310 South Michigan Avenue
Chicago, IL 60604
(312) 793-2094

Indiana Department of Commerce, Tourist Development
Division
1 North Capital Street
Suite 700
Indianapolis, IN 46204
(317) 232-8860

Iowa Development Commission,
Tourist Travel Division
600 East Court Avenue
Des Moines, IA 50309
(515) 281-3100

Kansas Department of Travel and
Tourism
400 West 8th Street
5th Floor
Topeka, KS 66603
(913) 296-2009

Kentucky Department of Travel
Development
Capitol Plaza Tower
Frankfort, KY 40601
(502) 564-4930

Louisiana Office of Tourism
Box 94291
Baton Rouge, LA 70804
(504) 925-3860

Maine Publicity Bureau
97 Winthrop Streep
Hallowell, ME 04347
(207) 289-2423

Maryland Office of Tourist
Development
45 Calvert Street
Annapolis, MD 21401
(301) 269-3517

Massachusetts Department of
Commerce and Development,
Division of Tourism
100 Cambridge Street
Boston, MA 02202
(617) 727-3201

Michigan Department of
Commerce, Travel Bureau
Box 30226
Lansing, MI 48909
(517) 373-0670

Minnesota Office of Tourism
375 Jackson Street
250 Skyway Level
St. Paul, MN 55101
(612) 348-4313

Mississippi Department of
Economic Development, Division
of Tourism
1301 Walter Sillers Building
Box 849
Jackson, MS 39205
(601) 359-3414

Missouri Division of Tourism
Truman State Office Building
Box 1055
Jefferson City, MO 65102
(314) 751-4133

Montana Travel Promotion
Division
1424 9th Avenue
Helena, MT 59620
(406) 444-2654

Nebraska Department of
Economic Development, Division
of Travel and Tourism
301 Centennial Mall South
Box 94666
Lincoln, NE 68509
(402) 471-3796

Nevada Commission on Tourism
Capitol Complex
Carson City, NV 89710
(702) 733-2323

New Hampshire Office of
Vacation Travel
Box 856
Concord, NH 03301
(603) 271-2343

New Jersey Office of Travel and
Tourism
CN-826
Trenton, NJ 08625
(609) 292-2470

New Mexico Tourism and Travel
Joseph Montoya Building
1100 St. Francis Drive
Santa Fe, NM 87503
(505) 827-0291

New York Division of Tourism
One Commerce Plaza
Albany, NY 12245
(518) 474-4116

North Carolina Travel and
Tourism Division
430 Salisbury Street
Box 25249
Raleigh, NC 27611
(919) 733-4171

North Dakota Tourism Division
Liberty Memorial Building
Capitol Grounds
Bismarck, ND 58505
(701) 224-2525

Ohio Department of Develop-
ment, Division of Travel and
Tourism
Box 1001
Columbus, OH 43266
(614) 466-8844

Oklahoma Tourism and
Recreation Department
505 Will Rogers Building
Oklahoma City, OK 73105
(405) 521-2406

Oregon Economic Development,
Division of Tourism
595 Cottage Street, NE
Salem, OR 97310
(503) 378-3451

Pennsylvania Bureau of Travel
Development
416 Forum Building
Harrisburg, PA 17120
(717) 787-5453

Rhode Island Tourism Division
7 Jackson Walkway
Providence, RI 02903
(401) 277-2601

South Carolina Department of
Parks, Recreation, and Tourism
Box 71
Columbia, SC 29202
(803) 734-0127

South Dakota Division of Tourism
Capitol Lake Plaza
711 Wells Avenue
Pierre, SD 57501
(605) 773-3301

Tennessee Department of
Tourism
Box 23170
Nashville, TN 37202
(615) 741-2158

Texas Travel and Information
Division
Box 5064
Austin, TX 78763
(512) 463-8971

Utah Travel Council
Council Hall
Capitol Hill
Salt Lake City, UT 84114
(801) 533-5681

Vermont Travel Division
134 State Street
Montpelier, VT 05602
(802) 828-3236

Virginia Division of Tourism
202 West 9th Street
Suite 500
Richmond, VA 23219
(804) 786-4484

Washington Tourism
Development
101 General Administration
Building
Olympia, WA 98504
(206) 753-5600

West Virginia Tourism
Information Office
State Capitol Complex
Charleston, WV 25305
(304) 348-2286

Wisconsin Division of Tourism
123 West Washington Avenue
Box 7606
Madison, WI 53707
(608) 266-2161

Wyoming Travel Commission
Frank Norris Jr. Travel Center
Cheyenne, WY 82202
(307) 777-7777

The National Parks of Canada

Canada's pristine public wilderness areas promise adventure and wonderful opportunities for outdoor recreation. Phone or write for information on rules, regulations, and availability of campsites before you take off.

Aulavik National Park
Agreement in principle 1992
4,710 square miles
Western Arctic District
Parks Canada
Box 1840
Inuvik, Northwest Territories
X0E 0T0
(403) 979-3248

Auyuittuq National Park Reserve
Established 1976
8,588 square miles
Box 353
Pangnirtung, Northwest
Territories
X0A 0R0
(819) 473-8828

Banff National Park
Established 1885
2,656 square miles
Box 900
Banff, Alberta
T0L 0C0
(403) 762-1500

Bruce Peninsula National Park
Agreement in principle 1987
Approximately 32 square miles of
the proposed 59 square miles has
been acquired from willing
sellers.
Box 189
Tobermory, Ontario
N0H 2R0
(519) 596-2233

Cape Breton Highlands National
Park
Established 1936
366 square miles
Ingonish Beach
Cape Breton, Nova Scotia
B0C 1L0
(902) 285-2270

Elk Island National Park
Established 1913
75 square miles
R.R. 1, Site 4
Fort Saskatchewan, Alberta
T8L 2N7
(403) 992-6380

Ellesmere Island National Park
Reserve
Established 1988
14,586 square miles
Parks Canada
Box 353
Pangnirtung, Northwest
Territories
X0A 0R0
(819) 473-8828

Forillon National Park
Established 1974
94 square miles
Box 1220
Gaspe, Quebec
G0C 1R0
(418) 368-5505

Fundy National Park
Established 1948
80 square miles
P.O. Box 40
Alma, New Brunswick
E0A 1B0
(506) 887-2000

Georgian Bay Islands National
Park
Established 1929
10 square miles
Box 28
Honey Harbour, Ontario
P0E 1E0
(705) 756-2415

Glacier National Park
Established 1886
520 square miles
Box 350
Revelstoke, British Columbia
V0E 2S0
(604) 837-5155

Grasslands National Park
Agreement in principle 1975
Currently 162 square miles; target
is 350 square miles
Box 150
Val Marie, Saskatchewan
S0N 2T0
(306) 298-2257

Gros Morne National Park
Agreement in principle 1970
722 square miles
Box 130
Rocky Harbour, Newfoundland
A0K 4N0
(709) 458-2417

Gwaii Haanas National Park
Reserve
Agreement in principle 1987
577 square miles
P.O. Box 37
Queen Charlotte City, British
Columbia
V0T 1S0
(604) 559-8818

Ivvavik National Park
Established 1984
3,926 square miles
Western Arctic District
Parks Canada
P.O. Box 1840
Inuvik, Northwest Territories
X0E 0T0
(403) 979-3248

Jasper National Park
Established 1907
4,200 square miles
Box 10
Jasper, Alberta
T0E 1E0
(403) 852-6161

Kejimkujik National Park
Established 1974
155 square miles
Box 236, Maitland Bridge
Annapolis County, Nova Scotia
B0T 1B0
(902) 682-2772

Kluane National Park Reserve
Established 1976
8,500 square miles
P.O. Box 5495
Haines Junction, Yukon Territory
Y0B 1L0
(403) 634-2251

Kootenay National Park
Established 1920
543 square miles
Box 220
Radium Hot Springs, British
Columbia
V0A 1M0
(604) 347-9615

Kouchibouguac National Park
Established 1979
92 square miles
Kouchibouguac, New Brunswick
E0A 2A0
(506) 876-2443

La Mauricie National Park
Established 1977
207 square miles
C.P. 758, 465, 5th Street
Shawinigan, Quebec
G9N 6V9
(819) 536-2638

Mingan Archipelago National
Park Reserve
Established 1984
58 square miles
P.O. Box 1180
1303 Digue Street
Havre-Saint-Pierre, Quebec
G0G 1P0
(418) 538-3331

Mount Revelstoke National Park
Established 1914
100 square miles
Box 350
Revelstoke, British Columbia
V0E 2S0
(604) 837-5155

Nahanni National Park Reserve
Established 1976
1,840 square miles
Bag 300
Fort Simpson, Northwest
Territories
X0E 0N0
(403) 695-3151

North Baffin Island National Park
Lands withdrawn for park pur-
poses in 1992
8,592 square miles
Eastern Arctic
Parks Canada
P.O. Box 1720
Iqaluit, Northwest Territories
X0A 0H0
(819) 979-6277

Pacific Rim National Park Reserve
Agreement in principle 1970
110 square miles
Box 280
Ucluelet, British Columbia
V0R 3A0
(604) 726-7721

Pelee Point National Park
Established 1918
6 square miles
R.R. 1
Leamington, Ontario
N8H 3V4
(519) 322-2365

Prince Albert National Park
Established 1927
1,496 square miles
Box 100
Waskesiu, Saskatchewan
S0J 2Y0
(306) 663-5322

Prince Edward Island National Park
Established 1937
8.5 square miles
2 Palmers Lane
Charlottetown, Prince Edward Island
C1A 5V6
(902) 566-7050

Pukaskwa National Park
Agreement in principle 1971
725 square miles
Highway 627
Hattie Cove, Box 39
Heron Bay, Ontario
P0T 1R0
(807) 229-0801

Riding Mountain National Park
Established 1929
1,148 square miles
Wasagaming, Manitoba
R0J 2H0
(204) 848-2811

St. Lawrence Islands National Park
Established 1914
3.5 square miles
2 County Road 5, R.R. 3
Mallorytown Landing, Ontario
K0E 1R0
(613) 923-5261

Terra Nova National Park
Established 1957
154 square miles
Glovertown, Newfoundland
A0G 2L0
(709) 533-2801

Vuntut National Park
Agreement in principle 1993
1,678 square miles
Parks Canada
P.O. Box 390
Dawson City, Yukon
Y0B 1G0
(403) 993-5462

Waterton Lakes National Park
Established 1895
195 square miles
Waterton Park, Alberta
T0K 2M0
(403) 859-2224

Wood Buffalo National Park
Established 1922
17, 299 square miles
Box 750
Fort Smith, Northwest Territories
X0E 0P0
(403) 872-2349

Yoho National Park
A small reserve was created in
1886, and later enlarged in 1901
and named Yoho Park Reserve.
507 square miles
Box 99
Field, British Columbia
V0A 1G0
(604) 343-6324

Bibliography

Allan, Melinda. *Canoeing Basics*. New York: Hearst Marine Books, 1994.

Angier, Bradford. *How to Stay Alive in the Woods*. New York: Collier-Macmillan Ltd., 1970.

Armstrong, Diana. *Bicycle Camping*. New York: The Dial Press, 1981.

Berger, Karen. *Hiking & Backpacking*. New York: W.W. Norton & Co., 1995.

Bigon, Mario and Guido Regazzoni. *The Morrow Guide to Knots*. New York: Quill, 1982.

Brown, R.W., M.J. Lawrence, and J. Pope. *The Larousse Guide To Animal Tracks: Trails and Signs*. New York: Larousse & Co., 1984.

Fletcher, Colin. *The Complete Walker III*. New York: Knopf, 1994.

Getchell, Annie. *The Essential Outdoor Gear Manual*. Camden, ME: Rugged Mountain Press, 1995.

Golad, Frank (ed.). *Sports Afield Outdoor Skills*. New York: Hearst Books, 1991.

Harrison, David. *Sea Kayaking Basics*. New York: Hearst Marine Books, 1993.

———. *Kayak Camping*. New York: Hearst Marine Books, 1995.

Jacobson, Cliff. *Camping Secrets: A Lexicon of Camping Tips Only the Experts Know*. Merriville, Indiana: ICS Books, Inc., 1987.

Mason, Bill. *Song of the Paddle: An Illustrated Guide to the Art of Canoeing*. Toronto: Key Porter Books, 1995.

———. *Path of the Paddle: An Illustrated Guide to Wilderness Camping*. Toronto: Key Porter Books, 1988.

Rezendes, Paul. *Tracking & the Art of Seeing: How to Read Animal Tracks & Signs*. Charlotte, VT: Camden House Publishing, 1992.

Riviere, Bill. *The L.L. Bean Guide to the Outdoors*. New York: Random House, 1981.

Runtz, Michael, W.P. *The Explorer's Guide to Algonquin Park*. Toronto: Stoddart Publishing, 1993.

Seidman, David. *The Essential Sea Kayaker: A Complete Course for the Open Water Traveler*. Camden, ME: International Marine Publishing, 1992.

Townsend, Chris. *The Backpacker's Handbook*. Camden, ME: Ragged Mountain Press, 1993.

University of California, Berkeley. *The Wellness Encyclopedia*. Boston: Houghton Mifflin CO, 1991.

Wilkerson, James, A. (ed), Cameron C. Bangs, M.D., and John S. Hayward, Ph.D. *Hypothermia, Frostbite, and Other Cold Injuries: Prevention, Recognition, and Prehospital Treatment*. Seattle: The Mountaineers, 1986.

———. *An Illustrated Guide to Attracting Birds*. Menlo Park, CA: Sunset Books, 1990.

———. *Restoring the Body: Treating Aches and Injuries*. Alexandria, VA: Time-Life Books, 1987.

Glossary

A-frame   An older-style tent featuring a mid-support that runs the length of the tent.

Anorak   A one-piece outer shell that slips over the head and has no front zipper from which body heat can escape.

Backcountry   Where no man has gone before—or at least it seems that way.

Backpack   Cargo-carrier that attaches to your back with shoulder straps.

Bait   Something—worms, small fish, etc.—used to lure prey.

Bearing   A direction taken by reading a compass.

Bivouac   A type of tent that accommodates only one person. Sometimes referred to as "body bags" or "bivvys."

BLM   Bureau of Land Management.

BLM map   Official map published by the BLM.

Bowline knot   A knot used to form a loop that neither slips nor jams.

Breathable/Waterproof fabric   A special fabric that allows body moisture to escape while keeping rain or other external moisture from getting in. Gore-Tex is one such fabric.

Cambrelle   A quick-drying synthetic lining often used in hiking boots.

Camp stove   An absolute necessity for camping. Choose from models that burn white gas, kerosene, and propane/butane. Multi-fuel models burn a range of fuels.

Canoe   An open-hulled boat that is paddled.

Car camping   A method of camping where the vehicle is parked in an established campsite and camper use the vehicle to carry and hold supplies.

Chickee   An elevated, sheltered wooden platform built along interior rivers and bays where no dry land exists.

Cirrus clouds   A cloud formation that is typified by looking wispy and having arched "tails."

Citronella candles   Candles made with citronella that when lighted repel insects.

Compass   A direction-finding device that is used with a map to plot a hiking route.

Contour lines   The lines on a map indicating the elevation of terrain.

Cumulus clouds   Large, puffy white clouds seen high in the sky in good weather.

Declination   The measurement describing the difference between true north and magnetic north.

DEET   The chemical diethyl-meta-tolamide in insect repellents.

Dome tent   A wind-resistant tent, shaped like a geodesic dome and supported by a system of crisscrossing support poles.

Down   Insulation made from either goose or duck feathers (goose feathers are considered superior). Down is considered better than any synthetic choices available.

Draft tube   The tube running the length of the zipper in a sleeping bag that blocks the transfer of cold air through the zipper into the sleeping bag.

Duluth pack   A large bag used by canoeists to hold supplies and equipment.

Exposure   The direction something—your tent or campsite—is facing.

External-frame backpack   A backpack where the framing members are exposed.

F-stop   The aperture size of a camera lens. The higher the number, the smaller the lens opening.

Film speed   A measurement of photographic film's light sensitivity. The higher the number (ranging from 60 to 400 in most cases), the more light sensitive the film.

Fly   The water-resistant "roof" of tents. They are often secured to the tent's framing members and staked out, away from the tent.

Fly fishing   A method of fishing using small, fake flying insects to snare fish.

Foam sleeping mat   A backcountry mattress made from either closed-cell or open-cell foam.

Forest Service   A public land management agency that is part of the Department of Agriculture.

Forest Service map   Maps created and provided by the U.S. National Forest Service.

Giardia   The organism found in untreated water, responsible for causing giardiasis.

Gore-Tex   A breathable, waterproof fabric favored by outdoorspeople.

Groundsheet   A 10-mil thick polyester sheet that is laid under a tent to protect the floor.

Heat exposure   A condition resulting from a combination of too much sun, physical exertion, and heat.

Heavyweight hiking boots   Hiking boots that weigh in at more than four pounds—for experts only!

Hip belt   A belt on a backpack that straps around the body close to the hips and makes carrying a backpack easier.

Hollofil II   A synthetic fill commonly used in sleeping bags and made by Dupont. Hollofil II fibers are hollow, and therefore offer more warmth for equivalent weights than fills made from solid-filament fibers.

Hoop tent   A lightweight tent design incorporating one or two.

Hypothermia   A life-threatening condition in which body temperature drops to dangerously low levels.

Internal-frame backpack   The most popular kind of backpack. The frames of the backpack are concealed.

Kayak   A portable boat with a single hole in its deck for its passenger, who propels the boat using a two-bladed paddle.

Kindling   Small, dry pieces of wood that are the basis for building a good fire.

Layering   A principle that applies to "dressing for success" in the outdoors: Dressing in at least three layers of clothes permits travelers to add a layer when it gets cold and remove a layer when it gets hot.

License (for backcountry camping)   Official permission to hike and camp on backcountry trails usually attached to some nominal fee.

Lightweight hiking boot   Hiking boots that weigh under three pounds.

Line (fishing)   Rated according to how much weight it can withstand before breaking. Ultralight line is rated as four-pound test and under.

Lite Loft   A synthetic sleeping bag fill made by 3M and designed for backpackers who insist on cutting weight down at almost any cost.

Loft   The thickness of insulation when it is uncompressed in a sleeping bag.

Low-impact backpacking and camping   A camping ethic that treats nature with respect.

Lures (fishing)   Colored tackle placed on the end of a fishing line to attract and snare fish.

Lyme disease   A potentially fatal disease spread by ticks, usually in eastern woodlands.

Magnetic north   Maps are based on true north readings, as opposed to magnetic north readings, which are approximately 1,300 miles from true north. See *True north*.

Midweight hiking boots   Hiking boots that weigh 2-3/4 to 4 pounds a pair.

Moleskin   A special bandage applied over a blister to reduce the friction between a hiking boot and skin.

National Park Service   The U.S. land management agency responsible for national parks and a variety of other public recreational offerings.

National Park Service map   A map describing the various features of a National Park or other area.

North Star   Also known as *Stella Polaris* is a good direction finding indicator because it is never more than two degrees from true north.

Nubuk   A brushed-top leather with a suede-like appearance; very durable and water-proof.

Orienteering   A competitive sport where you find your way across country using a map and compass.

Pack out   Part of the low-impact camping ethic "pack-in, pack out."

Panniers   The "saddlebags" that fit over a bicycle carrier to hold equipment and supplies for a trip.

Pile   A soft polyester material that is a substitute for wool in cold conditions.

Poison ivy, oak, and sumac   Plants that produce an oil that acts as an irritant to skin, causing an intensely itching rash.

Polarguard HV   A hollow-fiber synthetic fill that is an upgrade of its predecessor, Polarguard.

Polartec   Polyester fleece fabrics that are available in different weights.

Poncho   A one-piece covering that protects wearers from rain. It should be big enough to cover a person wearing a backpack.

PVC   Polyvinyl chloride. A rigid, durable plastic.

Reels   The part of the fishing rod that holds the line.

Rip-stop nylon   A nylon fabric that features heavy, crisscrossing threads that make it tear-resistant.

Rods   Part of the fishing apparatus to which the reel is attached.

Seam sealer   A coating applied to the rain fly and seams of a tent for waterproofing.

Shell   The top layer, a rain- and wind-resistant garment that covers the other layers of clothing.

Sleeping bags   An insulated sleeping sack for use outdoors.

Space blanket   A waterproof emergency blanket that is made with Mylar. Space blankets are waterproof and conserve warmth by reflecting body heat back to the person it covers.

Square knot   A basic knot used to join two pieces of line together.

Stratus clouds   Cloud formations that appear layered.

Stuff sack   The Nylon bags where equipment and clothing are placed inside a backpack.

Taut-line hitch   A knot that enables you to tighten its hitch.

Thinsulate   A good insulation made by 3M that is commonly used in outerwear.

Tinder   Fine combustible material used to start fire.

Topographical map   A map that reveals the contour of the terrain with contour lines.

Travel pack   A backpack that converts into a suitcase (or vice versa) for multiple use.

True north   The point used by mapmakers in indicating direction. See *Magnetic north*.

Upper   The top part of a hiking boot, made of leather, split suede, or a combination of leather and synthetics.

Vestibule   An add-on to the front of a tent that affords covered storage space.

Water filter   A portable device for removing contaminants—particularly giardia—from drinking water. Filters are most effective when their screen mesh measures between 0.2 and 1.0 microns.

Index

G

331